WRITING FOR MULTIMEDIA

Entertainment, Education, Training, Advertising, and the World Wide Web

Timothy Garrand

Focal Press

Boston Oxford Johannesburg Melbourne
New Delhi Singapore

Focal Press is an imprint of Butterworth–Heinemann.

A member of the Reed Elsevier group

Recognizing the importance of preserving what has been written, Butterworth–Heinemann prints its books on acid-free paper whenever possible.

Library of Congress Cataloging-in-Publication Data
Garrand, Timothy Paul.
Writing for multimedia: entertainment, education, training, advertising, and the world wide web / Timothy Garrand.
p. cm.
Includes index.
ISBN 0-240-80247-0
1. Interactive multimedia. 2. Writing. I. Title.
QA76.76.I59G37 1997
808'.066006—dc20 96-23700
CIP

British Library Cataloguing-in-Publication Data
A catalogue record for this book is available from the British Library.

The publisher offers special discounts on bulk orders of this book.
For information, please contact:

Manager of Special Sales
Butterworth–Heinemann
313 Washington Street
Newton, MA 02158–1626
Tel: 617-928-2500
Fax: 617-928-2620

For information on all Focal Press publications available, contact our World Wide Web home page at: http://www.bh.com/fp

10 9 8 7 6 5 4 3 2 1

Printed in the United States of America

Writing for Multimedia
The Book at a Glance

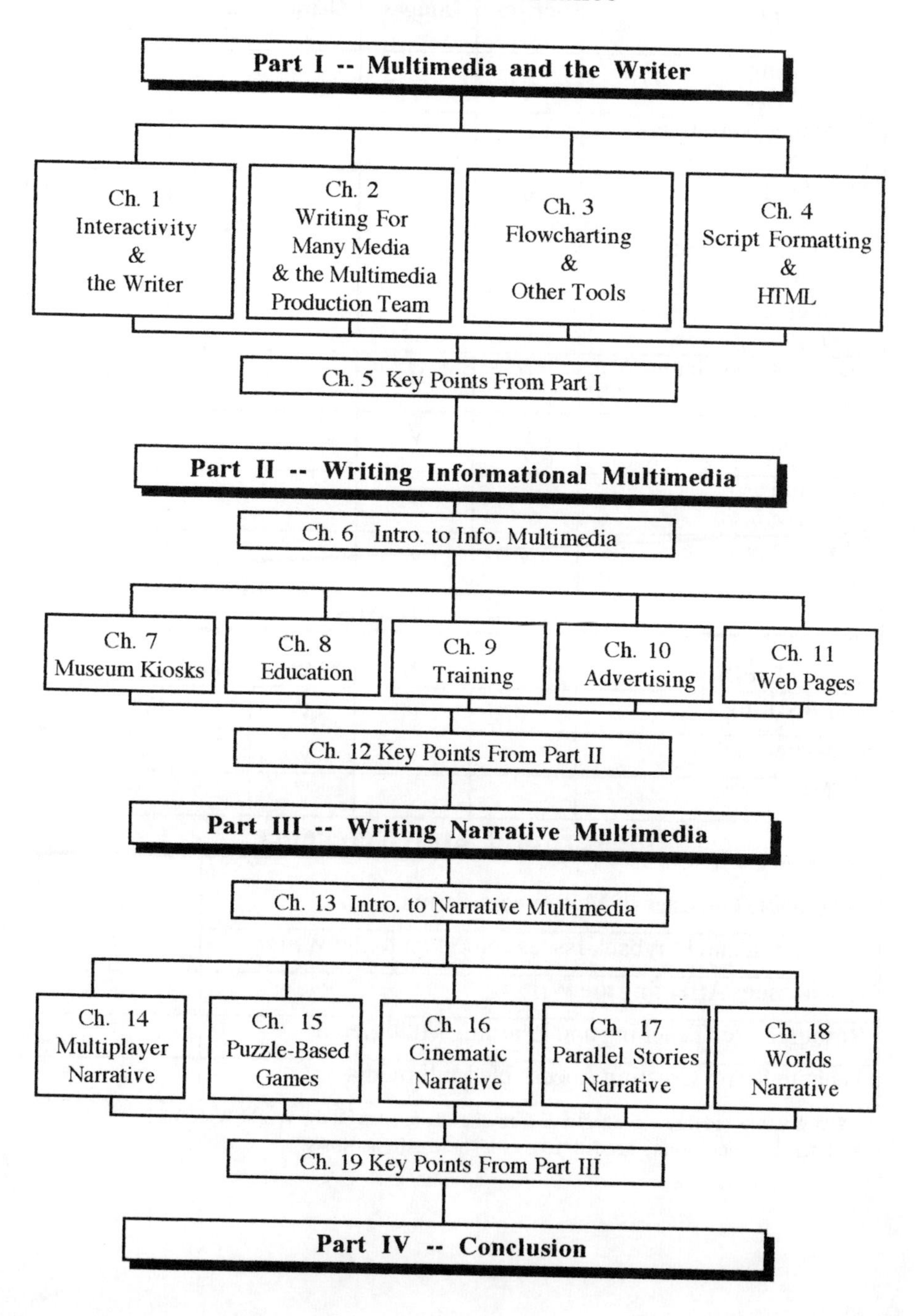

Writing for Multimedia

The CD-ROM at a Glance

Additional Multimedia Program Material				
Genre and Title	**Scripts**	**Images**	**Demos/Video**	**WWW Links***
Advertising *Personal View*		√		√
Cinematic Narrative *Voyeur*	√	√		√
Museum Kiosks *Nauticus*	√	√		√
Multiplayer Narrative *Patrol Theater*	√	√		√
Parallel Stories Narrative *The Pandora Directive*	√	√	√	√
Puzzle-Based Games *The 11th Hour*	√	√	√	√
Training *Vital Signs*	√	√		√
Web Sites *T. Rowe Price*		√		√
Worlds Narrative *Dust*	√	√	√	√

Software Demos				
Types of Software	**DOS**	**WIN**	**MAC**	**WWW Links***
Scriptwriting	√	√	√	√
Flowcharting		√	√	√
HTML		√	√	√

Background and Reference	
Searchable Glossary of Multimedia Terms	√
Production and Playback Issues Important to the Writer	√
Legal Issues Affecting the Writer	√
Resources for Teaching and Learning Multimedia	√
Techniques for Creating Accessible Multimedia	√

* WWW Links are direct connections from the CD to sites on the World Wide Web. An Internet connection is needed to access these external links.

BOOK CONTENTS

CD-ROM CONTENTS

N.B. All sections of the CD-ROM will include links to pertinent sites on the World Wide Web that can be accessed if the reader has an Internet connection.

ACKNOWLEDGMENTS

I'd first like to thank the editors and staff at Focal Press for their help and support writing and producing this book and CD-ROM. I also want to thank the readers of the first draft: Annette Barbier and Glorianna Davenport.

This book could not have been written without the generous donation of script samples and images by the copyright holders. Many thanks to CyberFlix Inc., Trilobyte Inc., Chedd-Angier Production Company, T. Rowe Price Associates, Access Software Inc., National Scouting Museum of the Boy Scouts of America, Ziff-Davis Interactive, D.C. Heath and Company, Harvard Community Health Plan, and Philips Media.

Equally crucial was the time generously donated by the many writers and designers interviewed for this project. In the informational programs, they include: Kevin Oakes, Deborah Astudillo, Steve Barney, John Cosner, Fred Bauer, Matt Lindley, and Peter Adams. The storytellers are: Madeleine Butler, Jane Jensen, Shannon Gilligan, Tony Sherman, Matt Costello, Dave Riordan, Lena Marie Pousette, Aaron Conners, and Andrew Nelson. A full list of all who contributed is at the back of the book.

I owe a special debt to writer Maria O'Meara, who contributed interviews and material for two case studies and critiqued the first draft of the manuscript.

Of course, none of this would have been possible without the patience and support of my wife, Anne Fenn, and my daughter, Danielle. It is to them that I dedicate this book.

ACKNOWLEDGMENTS

INTRODUCTION

This is a book on writing for multimedia . . . and much more.

This book is a detailed explanation of the process for creating interactive multimedia that both the multimedia newcomer and the experienced multimedia professional will find invaluable. A wide variety of programs (education, training, games, interactive movies, advertising, etc.) are discussed. These programs include examples of all the major multimedia formats, including CD-ROM, CD-I, video disc, and the World Wide Web.

Part I, "Multimedia and the Writer," examines the particular demands that multimedia makes on the writer, including interactivity, writing for many media, organizational tools, and script formatting.

Parts II and III, "Writing Informational Multimedia" and "Writing Narrative Multimedia," are devoted to in-depth case studies of a wide variety of multimedia programs, ranging from training, to the interactive movie, to advertising on the World Wide Web. Some of the top writers and designers in multimedia reveal their secrets for creating powerful multimedia programs. Their ideas are documented with extensive script samples, flow-charts, and other writing material.

The attached CD-ROM includes script samples, screen shots, program demos, multimedia production information, scriptwriting software, and much more.

Read this book and CD-ROM interactively; choose what is valuable to you.

If you are a *MULTIMEDIA NEWCOMER*, start at the beginning of the book and browse through the background material on the CD-ROM.

If you are an experienced *MULTIMEDIA PROFESSIONAL*, focus on the later chapters and the case studies to see how some of the top professionals in the field work their magic.

If you are or want to become a *WORLD WIDE WEB WRITER-DESIGNER*, you will benefit from the chapters about online programs and from the other multimedia case studies as well, because many of the techniques used in the disc-based programs can now be applied to Web-based multimedia.

If you are a *GAMER*, read the last part of the book to learn how some of the classic games were created.

If you are a *MEDIA SCHOLAR*, study the entire book for a solid grounding in the principles and practices of multimedia.

So turn the page or pop in the CD-ROM, browse the Contents, and choose the material that suits your needs.

Tim Garrand
tpg@interwrit.mv.com

PART I

MULTIMEDIA AND THE WRITER

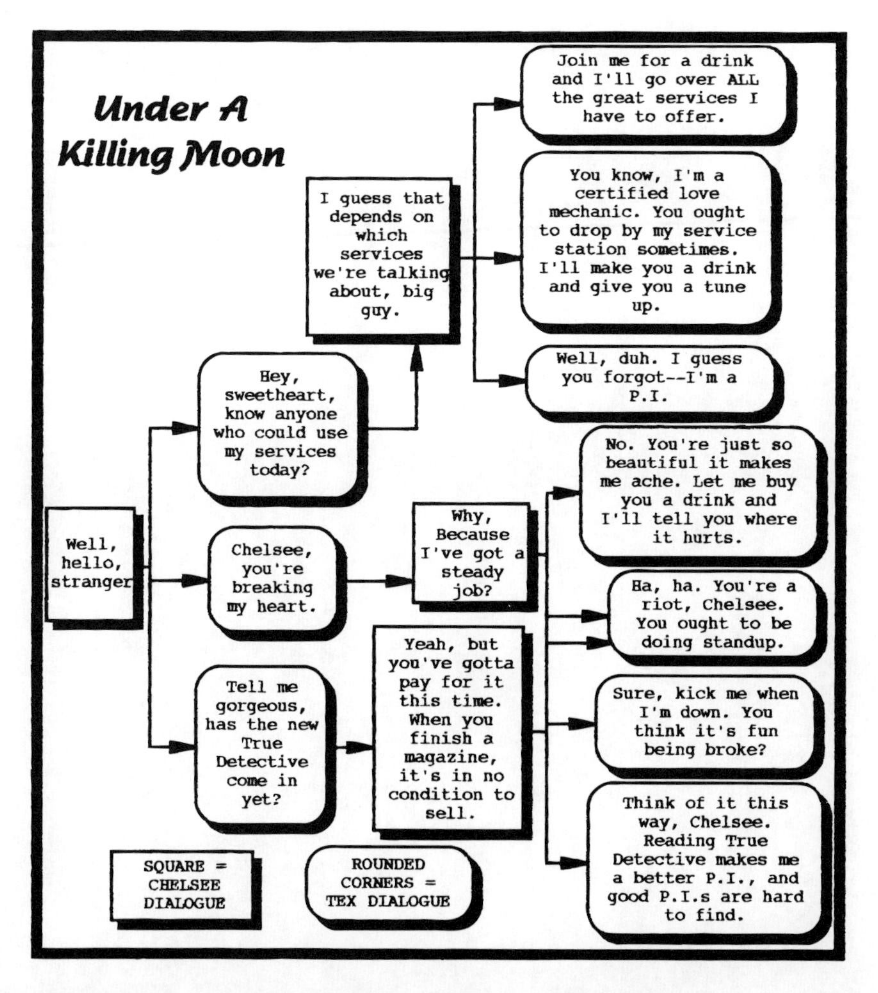

A portion of the writer's flowchart for an interactive dialogue scene in *Under a Killing Moon*. Courtesy of Access Software, Inc. © 1994 Access Software, Inc.

1

INTERACTIVITY AND THE WRITER

MULTIMEDIA AND THE WRITER

Interactive multimedia is:

- A viewer choosing which door to open in *Myst* to find the secret of the island.
- A biology student using *ADAM: The Essentials,* who clicks on an icon that turns the medical drawing on the screen from male to female.
- A trainee bank teller answering a question on the computer screen and being told that it is incorrect and immediately linking to review material.
- A government student surfing the White House Web site and listening to Socks meow.

Interactive multimedia is a communication medium that uses any combination of sound, pictures, video and text to communicate to the user interactively.

Multimedia can be presented on disc (e.g., CD-ROM, laser disc, floppy) or online (e.g., World Wide Web, America Online, Local Network). Interactive multimedia has dozens of uses, with the most common being video games, educational programs, corporate training, advertising, reference material, the interactive movie, and Web pages.

The multimedia writer creates proposals, treatments, walkthroughs, scripts, design documents, and all the other written material that describe the content of a multimedia production. This can include developing overall structure, dialogue, characters, on-screen text blocks, narration, and much more. The key difference between writing for linear media, such as television and movies, and writing for multimedia is the interactivity, which allows the user of the program control over the flow of the information or story material.

INTERACTIVITY VERSUS CONTROL

Potential Interactivity

Interactivity means that the user interacts with the information or story material on the computer in myriad ways, such as those described in the opening paragraph of this chapter. The potential interactivity of multimedia is awesome. It is possible to interact not merely by scene or shot, but by altering individual objects within a shot, or a single character's actions in a scene, or even the facial expressions or the appearances of characters.

Limits to Interactivity

There are practical limits to the potential interactivity. The viewer's equipment has to be powerful enough to support the level of interactivity.* And even if the viewer has the best system in the world, if the source material is a CD-ROM, a floppy disk, or some other closed system, the player is working with a finite number of options. He or she can access only what the makers place on the disc.

This limitation disappears when multimedia is delivered online through the World Wide Web or other online services, which allow users to link instantly to thousands or perhaps millions of other multimedia sources throughout the world. At present, however, because most Web surfers use a modem, the slow speed of nontext links can make the online multimedia experience frustrating.

If it were technically possible for the user, is unlimited interactivity the most effective way to communicate with multimedia? It depends to a great degree on what your goals are. If you are trying to tell a story, such as the interactive narrative *Voyeur* (profiled in Chapter 16), the degree of interactivity you can allow and still create believable characters, intriguing plot, and suspense will be far less than if you are simply creating a world for viewers to explore, such as *SimCity 2000*. *Voyeur* designer David Riordan echoes the feeling of many multimedia developers when he says, "Infinite choice equals a database. Just because you can make a choice doesn't mean it's an interesting one." (Riordan) He says that the creators of multimedia must maintain some control for the experience to be effective.

THINKING INTERACTIVELY

Thinking of All the Possibilities

The stumbling block for most new interactive writers is not limiting interactivity and maintaining control over the multimedia experience. Most new

*See the Background Section of the CD-ROM for a detailed discussion of the effect of playback and delivery systems on the presentation of a multimedia program.

writers have the opposite problem of overly restricting interactivity and failing to give users adequate control over the flow of information. This is because limiting options is what most linear writers have been trained to do. In a linear video, film, or book, it is essential to find just the right shot, scene, or sentence to express your meaning.

In writing for interactive, "the hardest challenge for the writer is the interactivity—having a feel for all the options in a scene or story," says Jane Jensen, writer-designer of the Gabriel Knight series (Jensen). Tony Sherman, writer-designer of *Dracula Unleashed* and *Club Dead* agrees. Unlike a linear piece in which it is crucial to pare away non-essentials, in interactive the writer must "think of all the possibilities." (Sherman)

Viewer Input

It is difficult to predict how the viewer will interact with all the possibilities in a piece. Jane Jensen warns that this can sometimes make multimedia "a frustrating and difficult medium. . . . You have this great scene, but you have to write five times that much around it . . . to provide options. When your focus is on telling the story, that can feel like busy work and a waste of time." (Jensen)

For example, you have a telephone in one scene that your player must dial to call his uncle and find out who the murderer is. This is near the end of the game, and getting the telephone number itself has been one of the game's goals. The writer needs to anticipate all the things players might try to do with that telephone. What if players get the telephone number from playing the game earlier, and they jump ahead to the telephone scene? What should happen when they dial? Should they get a busy signal? What if they dial the number after they have gotten it legally in the game, but they don't have all the information they need, such as knowing the caller is their uncle? Should the writer give them different information in the message? What if they dial the operator? What if they try dialing random numbers?

This can be equally complex in an informational multimedia piece where you must anticipate the related information that the viewers will want to access and all the different ways they may want to relate to the key information. *Compton's Interactive Encyclopedia*, for example, allows users to explore a particular piece of information through text, pictures, audio, videos, maps, definitions, a time line, and a topic tree. The design of the program allows all of these different approaches to be linked together if the viewer desires. This means students studying Richard Nixon can mouse-click their way from an article about Nixon to his picture, to an audio of his "I am not a crook speech," to a video about Watergate and Nixon's resignation, and finally to a time line showing other events happening during his presidency.

Knowing the User

A key way to anticipate users' input is to know as much about them as possible. This is also important in linear media, but it is even more crucial in interactive multimedia because the interactive relationship is more intimate than the more passive linear one. Knowing the audience is absolutely essential. Knowing what the user considers appealing will affect every element of a production, from types of links to interactive design.

LINKING

Links are the connections from one section of a multimedia program to another section of the same program or (if online) to a totally different program. The simplest link is a text menu choice that the user clicks to bring up new information. When writers develop links, they must make a number of decisions:

- What information or scenes will connect with other information or scenes?
- How many choices will the user have?
- What will be the result of those choices?
- Will the links be direct, indirect, or delayed?

Immediate or Direct Links: An Action

In an immediate or direct link, the viewer makes a choice, and that choice produces a direct and immediate response that the viewer expects. For example, in the script sample that follows from the training program *Vital Signs*, the student can click the words "systolic" or "diastolic" in an on-screen diagram of an artery. Once the student makes a selection, he or she is immediately given additional information on this subject, as listed at the bottom of the script page. This is an example of a direct link. (The direct link words "systolic" and "diastolic" and the information that the links connect to are in boldface type or underlined for purposes of illustration.)

VITAL SIGNS—BLOOD PRESSURE LESSON

(GRAPHIC/VIDEO: Animated diagram of artery with red dots flowing left to right, and vein, with blue dots flowing right to left.)

TEXT:

Blood Pressure Measurements:
Systolic and Diastolic

Artery

(Muscle)

Vein

(Valves)

(AUDIO: NARRATOR (VO): Blood flows from the heart in arteries, which have muscles to help keep it moving. Blood returns to the heart through veins, which don't have muscles, but do contain valves that prevent blood from flowing backwards. Blood pressure consists of two measurements—systolic and diastolic.

SELECT each to learn more. (When you've finished, SELECT "GO AHEAD" to continue.)

Feedback:(AUDIO + TEXT) Highlight term when chosen

Systolic = NARRATOR (VO): (ARTERY AND VEIN FREEZE AT HEIGHT OF FLOW) Systolic values measure the pressure at the height of the pulse wave.

Diastolic = NARRATOR (VO): (ARTERY AND VEIN FREEZE DURING PAUSE) Diastolic readings measure the pressure during the relaxation period between beats.

Indirect Links: A Reaction

Indirect links, also called "if-then" links, are more complex. Users do not directly choose an item, as in the example above. Instead, they take a certain action that elicits a reaction they did not specifically select.

The following example is taken from the walkthrough for the interactive movie *The Pandora Directive*. The walkthrough describes the program's story and the main interactive options for the user. At this point in the story, you/the user are trying to escape with the woman Regan, but you have been cornered by the villains, Fitzpatrick and Cross.

> You get the choice of shooting Fitzpatrick, shooting Cross, or dropping the gun. If you try to shoot Fitzpatrick, you get trapped alongside Regan and Cross; then everybody dies, safely away from Earth. If you try to shoot Cross, he kills you before you ever get into the ship. If you drop the gun, you get to the spaceship.

An example of an indirect link in an informational piece is a student who fails a test in a certain subject area and is automatically routed to easier review material, instead of being advanced to the next level. The student did not make this direct choice. It is a consequence of his or her actions. Figure 1–1 shows how a student who could not answer an arithmetic question in a math tutorial might be sent back to an arithmetic review module as opposed to being advanced to the more difficult algebra material.

Intelligent Links or Delayed Links: A Delayed Reaction

Intelligent links remember what choices the user made earlier in the program or on previous plays of the program and alter future responses accordingly. These links can be considered delayed "if-then" links. Intelligent links in a story create a realistic response to the character's action; in a training piece, they provide the most effective presentation of the material based on a student's earlier performance.

In *The Pandora Directive*, for example, you as the player are a detective who is trying to get in touch with Emily, a nightclub singer. You meet Emily's boss, Leach, well before you meet her. If you are rude to him, he mistrusts you. Later in the script when you try to rescue Emily, he will block your entrance to her room, and she will be strangled. If, however, you are nice when you first meet him, he lets you in, and you save her.

INTERACTIVE DEVICES

The designer and writer must develop interactive devices that will make players aware of the interactive possibilities they have created. These devices include on-screen menus, help screens, icons, props, other characters, and cues imbedded in the story itself.

Icons

Various types of icons are used for interactive devices. In *Voyeur* they are used to inspire viewers to look into the rooms of the mansion that are visible from

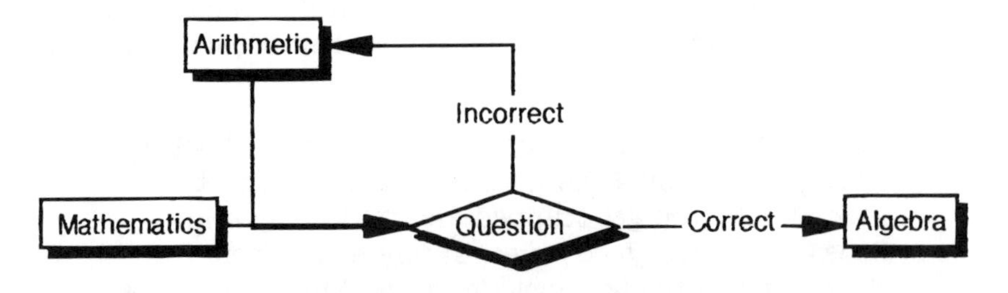

Figure 1–1 Indirect links: A reaction to user input.

the voyeur's apartment. If the voyeur moves the camera over a room in which there is action to view, an eye icon appears. If there's something to hear, an ear appears. If there is evidence to examine, such as a letter, a magnifying glass appears. Clicking on the icons causes the material to be presented.

A different type of icon is used in the MIT Media Lab video *Train of Thought*. This interface shows a large image of the current action but includes three smaller windows containing still frames of other action that users can click on and view. The smaller windows are consistent in their placement and type of content. Interview sequences appear in a small window within the main image. The characters' thoughts and dreams appear to the right of the main image, and another clip is below. (Halliday 81) One of the difficulties of this type of icon is presenting enough image in the still frame to motivate the player to interact.

Laura Teodosio and Walter Bender at the MIT Media Lab are trying to address this problem by developing something they call "salient video stills." Rather than just a random frame taken from a scene, a salient still incorporates all of the key elements of the scene in a sort of collage. A salient still essentially "tries to translate a narrative told in the language of the cinematographer into the language of the photographer." (Teodosio and Bender 7)

Menus and Other Text

Although the text menu is a traditional way to access material in informational multimedia, it can disrupt the flow of a narrative. With current technology, however, a menu appears to be the only option if a story designer wants a high degree of interactivity. In *Under a Killing Moon*, written by Aaron Conners, the player has control of character actions extending to the shot level. One of the ways the player achieves this control is through menus, which offer a wide variety of options, including: look, get, move, open, and talk. The player can even choose the tone of the lead character's dialogue by picking menu choices such as "Rugged Banter," "Indignant," and "Reeking of Confidence." (See *The Pandora Directive* case study in Chapter 17 for a more detailed discussion of response attitudes.)

Sometimes words on the screen are optional. In *Under a Killing Moon*, players can pull down an optional hints window. This helps orient them in the game and tells them their interactive options. Sometimes written material is integrated into the story itself. Shannon Gilligan's *Who Killed Sam Rupert*? includes an investigator's notebook that keeps track of what the detective-player has done so far in the game.

Props

Props are a popular interactive device. In *Under a Killing Moon*, the character can click on objects in the room to get information. Depending on the object, a player might hear a voice-over wisecrack about a painting or even see a full-motion video flashback, showing the detective's relationship with the object. In the educational CD-ROM *Sky High*, users can click on various props in a scene such as toy helicopters and birds to bring up additional information related to that aspect of flight.

Props that a character can actually use as he or she might in real life are particularly effective. The player in *Voyeur* has a camera with a zoom lens to use for exploring and recording evidence of the crime. Telephones are also used to give clues in this game and others. *Sky High* has a camera that students can use to take shots of the information on the screen.

Characters

Characters are another way to guide interactions. Sometimes this is the primary function of the character. The investigators in *Who Killed Sam Rupert* and *Gabriel Knight* both have assistants who remind them of appointments, give them telephone messages, or suggest people to talk to. Other characters, who are not primarily information givers, might say things that suggest a location to visit or a person to interview. This technique is frequently used in *Dracula Unleashed*.

A character can also be used as a guide to lead the viewer through the material. This can be successful in both narrative and nonnarrative pieces. In the video game *Astronomica*, the daughter of the doctor who disappeared approaches you/the user directly by banging on your bedroom window and asking you to help find her father. She leads you to her father's lab, where she works on the main computer, and sends you into the exploratorium to solve the problems there. She also appears now and again on a small communications monitor in the exploratorium to give you tips and encouragement.

Structure as an Interactive Device

The overall structure of a piece is one of the main ways interaction can be motivated in a narrative. In *Voyeur*, the player is a voyeur in an apartment building across from a mansion. The character's only reason for existing is to peer into the mansion's windows.

In the narrative informational *A la rencontre de Philippe*, the player is motivated to learn about Paris through the role of helping Parisian friends find an apartment.

Conclusion—Challenge of the Interactive Device

The challenge of the interactive device is to design something that will motivate interaction without radically disrupting the flow of information or story material. A well-designed interactive device will not pull us out of the dream state of storytelling or disrupt our train of thought as we pursue information. In short, interactive devices must be well integrated into the material.

INTERFACE DESIGN

Another way to help users find their way through the complex structure of an interactive multimedia production is through good interface design. The amount of input the writer is allowed into the interface design depends on the designer and the project, but the writer must consider interface design when developing the script. Interface design is crucial in deciding how multimedia content will be organized. It determines the structure of the script for the writer and dictates how the viewer will interact with that content.

An interface can be as simple as a list of words in a clickable menu that organizes the information into content categories. The interface can also be much more complex such as the interface for the interactive narrative *Voyeur,* which allows the user to interact with the story material in a variety of ways using items in the voyeur's apartment (Figure 1–2). The camera can be used to spy on the mansion across the street, the TV can be watched for background information, the FedEx envelope can be clicked on to mail evidence, and the telephone can receive calls.

Figure 1–2 Interface for *Voyeur*. Courtesy of Philips Media. © 1993 Philips Interactive Media.

The interface also affects the navigation of the piece—how the viewer can travel through the information or story and the order in which the information will be presented. This is often demonstrated through flowcharts and diagrams. (See page 83 for examples.) *Clinton: Portrait of Victory* uses a simple hierarchical menu for navigation in which users can first choose one of the following: "The Assignment," "The Candidate," or "The Campaign." "The Campaign" choice yields further options: "The Primaries," "The Convention," "On the Road," "The Debates," and "A Bold Finale."

A key technical element that affects interface design is the authoring program or story engine that the particular production is using. Authoring programs and story engines are software that allow the elements of a multimedia program to be assembled into a coherent informational program or story. Before writers think about interface design, they should be aware of what the authoring programs or story engines being used are capable of. With an off-the-shelf authoring program, such as Macromedia Director, the writer can read about it or even try it out. If a story engine is proprietary to a specific company, however, the writer may have to rely on the company's designers and programmers for information.

The Map

A good interface design represents the interface in a concrete manner that the user can easily grasp. This representation is often called a map. It illustrates how the player should interact with the interface and navigate through the program. It can be as simple as a text menu or a complex image like the one used in *Voyeur*. Sometimes it is literally a map, as in *Dust: A Tale of the Wired West* in which the player can consult a map of Diamondback, New Mexico, to orient himself and decide where to go next. (The actual interface of the game is a 3-D animation of the town buildings and citizens whom the viewer can interact with.)

Sometimes the map is a flowchart of the entire production, as in the Oakes Interactive training piece for Fidelity Investments retirement counselors. In this program, a student can bring up the flowchart of the whole program and access any area of it by clicking on one of the labeled boxes.

Metaphors

The maps of Diamondback, the voyeur's telephone and TV, and the training program flowchart are types of metaphors that help the audience understand the organization of an interactive piece. For software developers, the metaphor is a concrete image or other element that represents an abstract concept, making it clear and comfortable to the user. Perhaps one of the best-known software metaphors is the desktop. Windows PCs and Macs present the abstract concepts of computer files, directories, and software as file folders and documents that users can arrange and work with on the desktop.

Metaphors are also used to design individual screens and navigational aids. According to designer Aaron Marcus, "Consistency and clarity are two of the most important concerns in developing metaphors." (Marcus 98) Familiarity to the viewer is a third item that could be added.

Consistency means that users should not have to use buttons as the main navigational tool on one screen and then suddenly switch to a different approach, such as clicking on pictures in the next screen. Both of these are valid metaphors for linked information but are confusing when mixed. Consistent placement of the same types of information in the same place on the screen is also important. For example, navigation buttons are often located at the bottom.

Creating familiar metaphors ties into knowing your audience. A valid metaphor for the structure of an elementary school education CD-ROM might be a street in a town. This is something students are familiar with. It makes sense for them to click on a library to get information or a movie theater to see a film. On a micro-level, a common metaphor is a book that opens. Click a dog ear to turn a page. Click the table of contents to go to a chapter.

Familiar metaphors help orient viewers with the main interface and map, but this certainly doesn't mean they have to be cliché or boring. Certainly a designer who can push the envelope without losing the audience should by all means go for it. There is lots of room to be creative. It is important to make even the minor elements of a production work well. For example, one of the frustrating things in multimedia is the "wait-state" image. Many programs are content to give the standard clock or hour glass, but there is no rule that the wait-state image cannot be fun. *A.D.A.M. The Inside Story*, an anatomy program, shows a skeleton with a cup of coffee. Some children's programs have scurrying animals.

Another area that could use some thought is the on-screen frame for text blocks or partial screen video. Movie screens and TVs have become tired metaphors and should be avoided. Integrate your text and videos into the piece with metaphors that are meaningful to the subject matter.

Input Devices

Writers might also give some thought as to how the users will input their responses to the program. Standard choices include the keyboard, mouse, and touchscreen, but sometimes the input device can be integrated into the material. Instead of a mouse, *Welcome to West Feedback*, a music game, uses a toy guitar plugged into the computer as the input.

CONCLUSION

Although design elements are not always under the control of the writer, it clearly makes sense for the writer who develops the concepts that a program is based on to suggest key ways these concepts will be delivered to the audience.

REFERENCES

Davenport, Glorianna. "Bridging Across Content and Tools." *Computer Graphics* 28 (February 1994): 31–32.

Halliday, Mark. "Digital Cinema: An Environment for Multi-threaded Stories." Master's thesis, Massachusetts Institute of Technology, 1993.

Jensen, Jane. Telephone interview with the author, July 1994.

Marcus, Aaron. "Making Multimedia Usable: User Interface Design." *New Media* 5 (February 1995): 98–100.

Riordan, David. Telephone interview with the author, June 1994.

Sherman, Tony. Telephone interview with the author, July 1994.

Teodosio, Laura, and Walter Bender. "Salient Video Stills: Content and Context Preserved." Paper presented at the ACM Multimedia '93 Conference, Anaheim, CA, August 1993.

2

WRITING FOR MANY MEDIA AND THE MULTIMEDIA PRODUCTION TEAM

WRITING FOR MANY MEDIA

The necessity of writing for many media in the same production is as demanding on the multimedia writer as is dealing with interactivity. Unlike a print writer who can focus on honing skills with the written word, or the screenwriter who can specialize in communicating with images, the writer of multimedia must be expert in a variety of techniques: writing to be read (journalism, poetry, copywriting), writing to be heard (radio, narration), and writing to be seen (presentations, film/video). This is because multimedia can easily incorporate many types of media in a single production or even a single screen, and multimedia can manipulate these media in ways not before possible.

Depending on the project, a multimedia writer will write print proposals; text blocks that will be read from the computer screen; narration or other audio that will play over simple illustrations; video scripts; and dramatic action, dialogue, and character development. Often writers also write ancillary material, such as hints files and help screens. (One major game includes a comic book).

There are some basic style differences in each of these types of writing. Following are a few guidelines, but if there is an area where you feel you are particularly weak, consult some of the references listed in the references section of the CD-ROM.

Print

Print in multimedia is primarily seen in text boxes read from the computer or other viewing screen. Text on the screen is most common in multimedia informational, educational, and training pieces. Because readers can go back and read material again, the text can contain complex ideas or statistics.

A multimedia writer writing text blocks for an information piece can take a few tips from print journalists:

- Be accurate, check your facts, and be sure you understand what you are writing.
- Keep sentences short, and use simple sentence construction.
- Use the lead or first sentences to tell simply and clearly what the following text is about.
- Use the active voice (for example, "The dog bit the man," not, "The man was bitten by the dog").
- Use descriptive nouns and verbs; avoid adjectives and adverbs.
- Choose each word carefully, and avoid jargon or technical terms unless you are writing for a specialized audience.
- Write to fill the allotted space. Often pieces must fit a specific on-screen format.

If you are using text blocks to help tell a story, they provide a number of advantages over video alone. Perhaps the most significant is that the writer can easily tell the reader certain things, such as background on a character—"George was the saddest person in town,"or issues dealing with time—"George gradually grew happier during the twenty years of his marriage." This type of material is very difficult to show in film or video.

Audio

Writing where the audio carries the bulk of the meaning, as it does in radio, occurs fairly often in multimedia for a very practical reason: Audio takes less disc space and memory than video. Because of this, it is not unusual for multimedia productions to have sections that are essentially radio scenes.

This type of writing demands the skills of the radio writer, or the ability to write to be heard as opposed to being read. In addition to the print writer's skills of being accurate, simple, and clear, the radio writer must:

- Write conversationally, the way people talk. Radio is the most intimate medium. When most radio announcers talk through the mike to thousands of people, they imagine they are talking to just one person, because that is how most people experience radio: one person and a radio. This is the same intimate way most multimedia is experienced: one person and a computer.
- Write visually. A well-written audio-only piece can stimulate vivid images in the audience's minds. A famous radio ad once convincingly portrayed a ten-story-high hot fudge sundae being created in the middle of Lake Michigan. Create such pictures in the audience's mind by using:

- Concrete visual words
- Metaphors and other comparisons to images the viewer already knows
- Sound effects
- Different quality of voices (sexy, accents, etc.)
- Music
- Words and phrases that appeal to other senses, such as touch, smell, and taste

- Write material to be understood on the first play. Unless an instant replay is designed into the program, audio is more difficult to replay than text is to reread.
- Keep it simple. Be aware that the writing will be heard and not read. Avoid abbreviations, lots of numbers, unfamiliar names, and anything else that cannot be easily understood just by hearing it.
- Read all your work out loud when you are rewriting, or better yet, have someone read it out loud to you. You'll be amazed at how much of your perfectly acceptable written prose is unspeakable as dialogoue or incomprehensible as narration.

Examples of Audio-Only Scene

Examples of audio scenes include informational programs in which narration carries the bulk of the meaning, narrative pieces where voice-over is heavily used, and dramatic scenes in which audio dominates and the images are limited, such as the following example from the interactive narrative *Voyeur*. In this scene the player is looking at closed window blinds and listening in. Notice the use of visual writing, sound effects, and different voices to create images in the audience's mind. (These items are in boldface type.)

CHLOE'S ROOM, LARA AND CHLOE. **SLIGHT KNOCK** ON DOOR.

LARA
(knock on door)
Chloe?

CHLOE
Yeah Come on in Lara . . .

LARA
(embarrassed)
Oh, I'm sorry I didn't know you weren't **dressed** . . .

CHLOE
No, no, no don't worry about it, man, don't worry about it.

LARA
(nervous **laughter**)
Maybe if I had a **tattoo** there, Zack would take a closer look . . .

CHLOE
Yeah? You like that? I'm not sure what hurt more, the tattoo or the hangover . . .

LARA
What am I doing wrong with him?

CHLOE
Oh, Lara would you stop it right now! Don't buy into Zack's bullshit. You're a babe. You're gorgeous. You've got a **terrific body**. You just don't know how to package it. . . . I have got the most terrific outfit for you. It's going to look killer on you. I swear to God.

RIIING! She's interrupted by phone call.

CHLOE
Look, . . . Hold on a minute.
(**into phone**)
Yeah? . . . Oh, hi. . . . Well, not exactly . . . Hey man I'm working on it. . . . will you give me a fucking break . . . Hold a sec.
(**to Lara**)
Lara, could you . . . come back here tonight. . . .

LARA
I don't want to be a pest . . .

CHLOE
Oh, come on, come on, it'll be fun . . . please, come on, come by around eight.

LARA
OK. . . . see you then . . . (**door closes**)

CHLOE
(**back to phone**)
Like I told you, give me a couple a more days . . . I'll get you the damn money. . . . . Fine.

Film and TV

Writing for film and TV is an important skill for the multimedia writer because multimedia is moving increasingly in the direction of full-motion, full-screen video and animation. Here the viewer is seeing the results of the writing, not just reading or hearing them as in print and radio.

Writing for film and TV is a complex subject, about which many books have been written. Further complicating this topic are the very different demands on the scriptwriter of documentary and fiction.

It is difficult to reduce the specifics of scriptwriting to a few rules, but the scriptwriter's concerns include:

- Show, don't tell. Discover dramatic action to present the information. Don't have long-winded interviews about poverty in the ghetto; show scenes of poverty in the ghetto. Don't have your character tell us about how sad they are; develop dramatic action that shows this.
- Structure. Have a clear grasp of how to structure a film or video. Academy Award-winning screenwriter Sheridan Gibney claimed that scriptwriting has more in common with architecture than with writing. He said that screenplays are built, not written. Shots build scenes, scenes develop sequences, and sequences create plots and subplots. Much of film and TV follows established structures that writers should be familiar with. (These structures are discussed in Part III of this book.)
- Setup. Exposition is one of the hardest elements to portray in film and TV, and without proper exposition, characters are shallow, themes are undefined, and the setting is unclear. Exposition includes background information on the characters, setting, and the back story (events in the story that happened before the beginning of the current narrative). An example of important back story occurs in the classic film *Casablanca*. This film begins in Casablanca but essential back story includes the lead characters' romance that occurred in Paris a year earlier. Unlike print, where it is fairly easy to "tell" the reader about background information, in film and TV this material needs to be shown. In multimedia, novice film/TV writers often either have the characters talking incessantly about things that happened years ago or dump the entire back story into a separate background file and assume everyone has read it. Such a background file might be accessible from a program's help or hints menu.
- Characterization. Several critics have stated that there are a limited number of stories but an unlimited number of unique characters. Finding and developing unique characters is essential in most fiction films and many documentaries.
- Conflict. Conflicts must be clearly defined. Most film and video focuses on conflict, whether it is a fictional story between man and shark, as in *Jaws*, or a *60 Minutes* documentary on the concerned citizens of India versus their nuclear power industry.

- Cost. Unlike radio and print writing, film and video production is very costly, and scriptwriters must be very aware of this. A writer with a limited multimedia budget probably will have to either forget about blowing up that rocketship, do it as an animation, or write to stock footage that has already been created.

THE MULTIMEDIA PRODUCTION TEAM

The Designer

The role of the designer and the designer's relationship with the writer in a multimedia production are two of the biggest differences between interactive and linear writing. Because this is a young industry, there is no one way this relationship works and no clear division of duties between writer and designer. On a large project, there may be several types of designers (for example, instructional designers, graphic designers, and interface designers). These categories are sometimes lumped into one title: multimedia designer or just designer. Because of overlapping duties, these titles frequently become meaningless, but in most cases a head designer or interface designer's responsibilities include the overall visual look of the project, including the interface design.

The writer's participation in the design process varies considerably from project to project. Sometimes the interface designer develops the story idea and the basic structure of the piece before the writer comes on the project. It is the designer who determines what the player will be able to do and how the interactions will work. Sometimes the writer's role is even more restricted; the designer may do much of the writing and bring in a writer to handle just a few scenes. But even in this diminished role, the writers need to be aware of how the scenes they are writing relate to the overall piece. Other designers bring the writers in early and encourage their contribution to the overall design. Many writers feel this is the best way to go, particularly when dealing with stories.

As they gain experience in multimedia, many writers learn design and take more control of their material. This is actually a growing trend, particularly on small- and medium-sized projects in which the all-powerful interface designer is disappearing and being replaced by a team approach, which often includes the writer, graphic designer, project manager, and programmer. In other cases, the writer takes a dominant role and becomes a writer-designer. "A writer who can do interface design is a more valuable team player and more likely to be hired." (O'Meara)

The Project Manager

The project manager is the boss. He or she manages the budget, the personnel on the project, and the overall design and assembly of all the elements.

The project manager is similar to the producer in linear production who sees everything through from the beginning to the end. On some projects, the roles of project manager and designer are combined.

The Art Director

The art director determines the look of the production and creates or oversees the creation of all visuals: backgrounds, interface screens, graphics, and animations.

The Programmer

The programmer is the computer expert. He or she writes the code or uses the authoring program to make the dreams of the writer, designer, and other production members become reality on the computer screen.

The Writer's Relationship with the Programmer and the Art Director

A writer who is playing a strong role on a particular production needs to communicate his or her visions to the programmer and art director and needs to learn what is possible from the graphic artist and programmer. Particularly for the writer who is new to multimedia, these two individuals can be invaluable sources of technical information, creative ideas, and solutions to problems.

The Director

The video or film director is in charge of creating live-action video. The director may also be in charge of developing the original audio for stock footage. The writer's relationship to the director varies with each director, but in many cases it is a collaboration that starts with the director's commenting on early drafts of the script and extends into production, with the writer performing last-minute rewrites.

The Content Expert

The content expert is an important person in informational or educational multimedia because he or she can be an invaluable source of information. For example, medical pieces often have physicians as content experts. Nevertheless, content experts are not necessarily writers. Knowledge of a subject does not mean that one knows how to present it well. That is the job of the writer.

The Product Manager

The product manager works with the client and deals with marketing issues if the program is aimed at the mass market. Sometimes the roles of product manager and project manager are combined. A writer who is brought in early can test ideas with the product manager, who often knows the client's needs or the intended market best. But writers should never completely abdicate their creative vision in favor of market research. If the marketing people could always predict what will be successful, then they would all be rich.

The Hyphenated Writer

Understanding the roles of the other members of the multimedia production team is not always enough. In many productions, the writers are expected to be hyphenated. They are expected to have skills in addition to writing, such as writer-producer, writer-instructional designer, writer-content expert, writer-interface designer, or some combination of the preceding.

In the gaming field, writers often also produce. A writer will frequently write the script and then stay on as a producer or production manager, working with the designers, production team, and programmers to make sure that what is written appears on the screen. In the instructional and corporate fields, writers are more valuable if they have familiarity with certain types of content. It certainly doesn't hurt for a writer to have a specialty or several specialties, such as finance, medicine, or science. But all writers should be careful to maintain enough flexibility so that they don't get pegged into just one type of work.

REFERENCE

O'Meara, Maria. Notes to the author, February 1996.

3

FLOWCHARTING AND OTHER ORGANIZATIONAL TOOLS

On a very practical level, all of the interactive elements and multiple media discussed in the previous chapters are an organizational nightmare. The relatively simple structure of linear media has been replaced by multimedia's maze of interlocking options. To organize this maze the writer must learn new tools.

FLOWCHARTING

A key tool many writers use is the flowchart. Numerous examples of them appear in this book (pages 83, 84). A flowchart can have several functions and variations for the same production—for example:

- To design interactions. Lines with arrows drawn between the labeled boxes on a chart make it possible to understand what links with what and in what way. For example, does the link work in both directions? Is it viewer-initiated or automatic?
- To see the effects of revisions. Continuity is a monstrous issue in interactive media. In linear media, changes in one scene may affect only the scenes immediately following it, but in interactive, changes in one scene will affect all of the scenes that are linked to it. It is hard to determine these effects without a chart.
- To chart character development. Some writers create separate charts to track character development, particularly in parallel branching structures, where the writers must be sure that the character change is properly set up and consistent in each plot line.
- To present material to clients. A complex interactive script can be inscrutable to a client, particularly one who has no interactive background. A one-page flowchart overview can do wonders in explanation.

- To communicate with the production team. A production team chart is far more complicated than a client chart, especially a chart for the programmers, in which boxes are labeled with complicated programming code.
- To track large productions. Flowcharts combined with project management software can help chart the progress of a large production, keeping track of what has been accomplished and who is responsible for what lies ahead.
- To form the basis for the user map. Sometimes the chart itself is the user map, as in Fidelity Investments' retirement counselors' training program, where students can bring up the flowchart at any point and click on a labeled flowchart box to go to that section of the course.

Flowchart Symbols

A number of developers have suggested flowchart symbols to help make charts more useful. The medium being charted is usually distinguished by the shape of the boxes. The type of interaction is usually indicated by the types of lines and arrows. The symbols shown in Figure 3–1 are part of the list from Inspiration flowcharting software. (Inspiration)

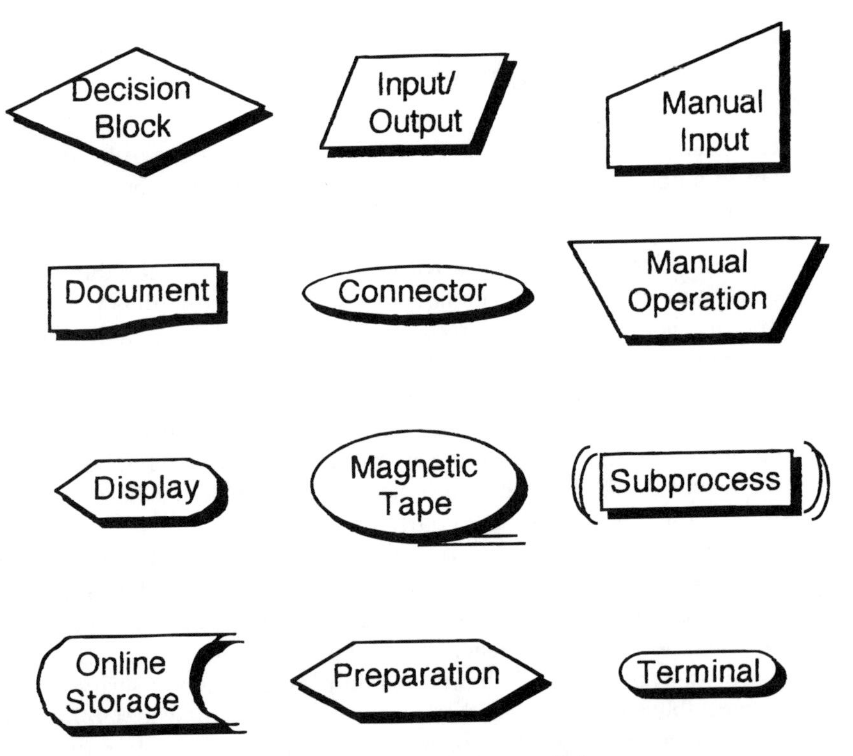

Figure 3–1 Flowcharting symbols.

Using symbols is a potentially helpful idea. The goal is to increase clarity, but if there are too many complex symbols, they may add confusion. In my experience, a universal set of symbols has not been accepted. Instead, writers and developers seem to adopt symbols that work well for them. For example, Aaron Conners of Access Software uses shaded boxes to distinguish characters in his interactive dialogue. (See *The Pandora Directive* flowchart, Figure 17-2, p. 276.)

With the great price drop in color printers, perhaps using different colors might be a more intuitive and more easily read way to go. Chart symbols could be coded in terms of how hot or active the media is: red = video, yellow = animation, green = audio, blue = still pictures, white = text. This hotness metaphor could be continued with the lines: red = most interactive paths, to blue = limited interactivity.

Gannt Charts

Instructional designer Rodger Gantt suggests labeling each box in a flowchart with a word symbol. These charts are often called Gantt charts. Some examples of Gantt code are:

INTRO = Introduction
DEMO = Demonstration
REV = Review

If there is more than one item of a type, such as demonstrations for a lesson or a product, a number is added before the code—for example:

1DEMO = Product 1, Demonstration

In this example, if there is more than one demo for a product, then a number is added after the code:

1DEMO2 = Product 1, Demonstration 2 (Iuppa, 34)

Writers don't usually go to this level of detail in their flowcharts, but if some variation of the Gantt code helps you clearly see the structure of your project, by all means use it.

Software for Drawing Flowcharts

Although some people prepare flowcharts by hand, it is usually easier to use software, particularly if the flowcharts will be part of a script presentation to clients. There are lots of choices. (See the Software section of the CD-ROM for software demos.)

Charting Software

A number of programs are designed for charting, including the following:

ABC Flowcharter
ABC Snap Graphics(included in Flowcharter)
Corel Flow
Visio
DeltaGraph Pro
Organization Charter(limited but included in MS Office's Powerpoint)
Inspiration (designed to chart the flow of ideas; it is the software used to draw the charts in this book)

Drawing Programs

Drawing programs can flowchart, although it may be harder to learn to use them than a dedicated charting program. A few examples include:

Corel Draw
Adobe Illustrator
Cricket Draw
Fractal Design Painter

Authoring and Presentation Programs

Major authoring and presentation programs also have the facility for flowcharting—for example:

Astound
Macromedia Director
Authorware Professional
IconAuthor

Combination Flowcharting\Script Formatting Programs

StoryVision. At this writing, this is the only dedicated program that combines flowcharting and script formatting functions. It is specifically designed for interactive writers.

Major Word Processing Programs

Word processing programs, such as Word, include drawing software. In Word, this software can draw callouts, which are boxes with lines attached. These can be combined to form flowcharts. (Dedicated flowcharting software is, of course, easier to use.)

OTHER ORGANIZATIONAL TOOLS

Outlines

Some writers prefer to start their project with a simple hierarchical outline, as in a linear piece. Some story writers find this one of the easiest ways to keep the story line and character development clear. Aaron Conners, whose interactive movies, *Under a Killing Moon* and *The Pandora Directive,* are among the most complex being written, uses an outline in the early stages of writing a game.

Storyboards

Storyboards are an excellent organizing tool. A storyboard contains images of the main screens of a program combined with text explanations of the elements and how they will work together. The storyboard is also a useful way to present a program to a client.

Some software creates pages that are quite suitable for this purpose. One is the database program FileMaker Pro. An advantage of using a database program such as this is that it has a built-in sort function, which can be helpful in rearranging scenes and designing a project.

Index Cards

A writer should also never be afraid of being low tech. A surprising number of authors still use pencil and cards, writing each scene on a card and then taking over the living room floor to arrange the links. The drawback with index cards is that they are hard to present to a client. Some software, such as Three by Five, has tried to solve this problem by creating computerized index cards. (Demo on CD-ROM)

CONCLUSION

Once the writer has organized the ideas for a multimedia program with the tools, it is time to write the script, the subject of the next chapter.

REFERENCES

Inspiration. Version 4.1. Portland, Ore.: Inspiration Software, Inc.
Iuppa, Nicholas V. *Interactive Video Design*. Boston, MA: Focal Press, 1982.

4

SCRIPT FORMATTING AND HTML

Multimedia's use of many media and interactivity makes script formatting difficult. Nevertheless, it is essential for writers to present their ideas visually on paper so that clients and production team members can see their ideas. At this point, there is no one set format for all situations. The format chosen depends to a great degree on the demands of the individual production.

TREATMENTS, PROPOSALS, AND DESIGN DOCUMENTS

Few projects start with a script. Most outline the basic story or information in some preliminary form. This is useful for clients who may have difficulty understanding an interactive script and also for a free-lancer who can pitch an idea without writing a complete script.

Treatments

Much of the preliminary writing in multimedia includes a description similar to the treatment used in linear film or TV writing. A treatment is written as if the writer were describing a program to someone who has not seen it. The structure of the information or story is described in a form similar to an essay or a short story.

There are some guidelines for treatment writing:

- Use third person (e.g., "He shambles," not, "I shamble" or "you shamble").
- Use the present tense ("shambles," not "shambled").
- Write visually. Be descriptive, but don't call shots.
- Capitalize:

- a) Character names when they first appear.
- b) Major sound effects.
- c) Technical directions, such as ZOOM, PAN, etc. (but don't use unless necessary)

- Usually summarize dialogue and narration, although a few bits of dialogue or narration are allowed if they help present the material.
- Usually double-space treatments, although sometimes they are single-spaced, with chapter headings or slug lines in all capitals.

Informational Treatment Sample

The following sample is from the conclusion of the treatment for *The Nauticus Shipbuilding Company*. (The entire treatment is in Chapter 7, page 76.)

> **Conclusion:** After the last component has been selected, a 3D animation sequence depicts the launching of the vessel. If the design is suitable for the mission, the visitor will see a depiction of their design successfully carrying out the mission. If the design is fundamentally flawed, the vessel will be shown sinking. Some evaluation will be provided as to the ability of the visitor's design to carry out the selected mission. Finally, the visitor will be given the opportunity to print out their design and evaluation.

Narrative Treatment Sample

A narrative interactive treatment is sometimes called a walkthrough. Following is a section of the walkthrough for *The Pandora Directive*. (The walkthrough appears on page 285.)

> In the introductory conversation with Gordon Fitzpatrick, you learn that he is looking for a Dr. Thomas Malloy, who recently stayed at the Ritz Hotel. Fitzpatrick and Malloy used to work together (where, unspecified). Fitzpatrick then says he saw a photograph of Malloy in the Bay City Mirror and found out that the photograph had been taken at a local university (San Francisco Tech). Fitzpatrick gives Tex a copy of the photo.

Proposals and Design Documents

A treatment is usually only one component of the first detailed description of an interactive project. This preliminary description is sometimes called a design document proposal, a design proposal, or just a proposal. Again, these names are not standardized.

Format for an Informational Design Document Proposal

(See Chapter 7, p. 76, for Complete Design Document.)

- Design objective. This is a short description of what the program hopes to accomplish. It is sometimes no more than a paragraph, but it is important because it is the first chance to grab the reader.

- Creative treatment. This is a detailed description of the entire program. It will run for many pages, depending on the length of the overall program.
- Navigation. This is a description of the interface and how the user will navigate through the program. It often includes a navigation flowchart. The navigation is also described in the treatment.
- Production and marketing. Design documents often have sections dealing with the project schedule or, if it is a mass market piece, ideas for marketing the program to the public. Biographies of the writer, designer, and other key personnel are sometimes included here.

Format for a Narrative Proposal A proposal for a multimedia program that includes a story would follow much of the same format as above. It may, however, call the treatment a "story summary." There may also be sections describing the characters.

LINEAR SCREENPLAY FORMAT

Once the preliminary design document or proposal has been approved by the client, it is time to write the script. Many approaches to formatting scripts for interactive multimedia use linear screenplay or teleplay format as their basis and then add variations.

Format is important because the running time of a script is judged by the number of pages. One page, if it is typed in proper format, is roughly, one minute of screen time. There are variations on the example below, such as greater use of double-spacing in television writing, but the example is a standard screenplay format that can readily be adapted to different situations.

Note that margins and line spacing are distorted in the example below to allow space for the directions.

DIRECTIONS	
Top margin = 1". Number pages in upper right-hand corner. No number on page 1.	THE MULTIMEDIA WRITER
Slug lines are typed in CAPS at the beginning of each scene, telling whether scene is INT. or EXT. (interior or exterior), location of scene, and day or night.	FADE IN: INT. ARNOLD'S BEDROOM DAY
Scene Description: Left margin 1.75", right margin 1" (7.5" if measured from left)	The room is a wreck. The floor is covered with papers and trash, the bed is unmade, and cigarette butts litter the desk and window sills.
Break long descriptions into several short paragraphs. The first time a character's name appears in the scene description, type it in CAPS.	ARNOLD throws the door open and stumbles into the room. CAMERA DOLLIES BACK with him. Arnold is in

his early twenties, thin, and unkempt. His once handsome features are contorted in agony. He clutches what appears to be a multimedia manuscript in his hand.

Single-space within scene description or dialogue. Add a blank line space between dialogue passages, scene description paragraphs, and slug lines.

He stumbles to the floor and falls to his knees, pulling the script to his bosom. He falls back with a scream and hits the floor in agony, dropping the script.

The title of the manuscript is revealed to be "The Great American Video Game."

Dialogue: Left margin = 3.0", right margin = 2" (or 6.5" if measured from left.)

ARNOLD (OS)*
(whispering)
Why me?
DISSOLVE TO:

EXT. ARNOLD'S APARTMENT DAY
LONG SHOT

The door of the apartment swings open and Arnold stumbles out clutching his script.

Name of person speaking dialogue is in CAPS and centered over the dialogue. No space between speaker's name and dialogue.

ARNOLD
I keep asking myself: What is the secret?

The booming, powerful, authoritative voice from the unseen NARRATOR of our film is heard.

Dialogue direction is typed in small letters, centered under speaker, and placed in parentheses.

NARRATOR (VO)**
(booming)
Arnold never did learn the secret. He should have read Tim Garrand's *Writing for Multimedia*.

Camera movements, such as tilt, pan, track, dolly, and zoom typed in CAPS in the scene description.
On right side of page are placed: Fade out and Dissolve to. On left is Fade in.

THE CAMERA QUICKLY ZOOMS IN TO Arnold. He tosses away his script in the trash and runs off.

His script sits on the top of the trash can, its pages fluttering sadly in the breeze.

Bottom margin = 1/2–1". It depends on how dialogue breaks. Don't break dialogue over 2 pages.

FADE OUT.

*(OS) next to the speaker means off-screen. The character is part of the action, but we do not see him or her in this particular shot. A character yelling from the bathroom while the camera focuses on the bedroom is an example of an off-screen voice. Or as in the example above, the camera could simply be focused on an object in the same room as the character, leaving the character nearby but off-screen.

**(VO) next to speaker means voice-over. This indicates that the speaker is not a part of the film or video's action. Peter Jennings narrating a World War documentary is an example of VO.

INTERACTIVE SCRIPT FORMATS

Single-Column, If-Then Interactive Format

This type of script can be used when the interactivity is fairly simple, usually scene branching. In the following example, part of an interactive museum piece located at the National Scouting Museum in Murray, Kentucky, the characters have to choose whether to search the school, the farm, or the neighborhood for a missing child. The situation is first outlined in a linear fashion, and then the options follow: first the school scene option, then the farm scene option. (This piece will be discussed in more detail in Chapter 14.)

BOY SCOUT PATROL THEATER

by Maria O'Meara

SCENE 2
TROOP HQ

2-1. WS GROUP

ALEX
Okay. We all know why we're here. Bob has divided the map up into areas. We're going to use the buddy system to cover each one.

BOB
Here's a map of the area we're searching.

2-2. MAP GRAPHIC

BOB (voice-over)
This is where she was last seen—the school. Here's where she lives. Between the two is the old Wilson Farm.

WHICH PART DO YOU WANT TO SEARCH?
A. THE SCHOOL
B. THE FARM
C. THE GIRL'S NEIGHBORHOOD

IF A. THE SCHOOL
SCENE 2A
2A-1. CU ALEX

ALEX
Chas and Don, you guys go see if she's not still hanging around the school.

M-1.
TRANSITION MONTAGE TO SCHOOL
1. POV HALLWAY
2. POV SCIENCE ROOM
3. POV POOL
4. POV STAIRS

SCENE 3
3-1. 2 SHOT BOYS enter a class room.

[Scenes have been deleted. The boys search the school and fail to find the girl. They return to scout headquarters and must choose again.]

WHICH PART DO YOU WANT TO SEARCH?
A. THE SCHOOL
B. THE FARM
C. THE GIRL'S NEIGHBORHOOD

[IF B. THE FARM]

2B-1. 2 SHOT ALEX AND BOB

ALEX
Greg and Hal—search the farm.

M-2.
TRANSITION MONTAGE TO FARM AREA
1. POV WOODS

They happen upon their science teacher who is looking for mushrooms in a field. He looks very scientific, and has a sample bag, note book, magnifying glass, etc. He is humming a little song.

Single-Column, Coded Interactive Format

A way to deal with a more complicated structure is by coding the scenes. Each scene starts on a new page and carries a number code at the top. Depending on the production, the code has various information, such as which story path this scene belongs to, what other scenes it is linked to, and when in the program it plays. (In the example below, the "Z3" indicates it is the third scene played simultaneously in the "Z" time zone; the 520 indicates it is Jessica's story path.) Once the scenes are coded, they are then presented in a linear fashion with a flowchart or some sort of guide to help the reader understand the possible paths of the story.

The following example is from *Voyeur*, an interactive narrative in which the player is a voyeur who lives across the street from the mansion of a corrupt politician, Hawke, who is preparing to run for president. The goal of the game is for the voyeur to expose Hawke's corruption without getting someone (including the voyeur) killed.

VOYEUR

by Lena Maria Pousette and Jay Richardson

Z3/115/520—Jessica exposes Reed Hawke
EXT.HAWKE MANOR/ALLEY—NIGHT—APPEARS ON PLAYER'S TV

Graphic SPECIAL BULLETIN appears on the TV screen.

Hand-held shaky-cam as the reporter and cameraman run to Jessica and Masa.

REPORTER #1
Excuse me, Miss Hawke, why are you leaving . . .

JESSICA
I have material that proves that Hawke Industries, with my father's knowledge, was responsible for poisoning an entire village in Japan.

REPORTER #1
Is this going to affect your father's decision to run for president?

JESSICA

Well, I intend to present this evidence at the highest level in Japan, where I am sure criminal charges will be filed. But that's all I have to say.

REPORTER #1

But what about the reports—

They exit.

Double-Column Format (Illustrated)

This format has two columns, with images on the left and audio and text on the right. An unusual aspect of this script is that it is illustrated, which works very well to present the feel of the completed project.

This program is displayed in an interactive kiosk at the National Maritime Center in Norfolk, Virginia. This production teaches shipbuilding principles by having the player build a ship. In the following section, users can choose to get information on various hull types and then must pick one of these hulls for the ship they are building. Because there is only a small amount of material on each hull, all the choices are listed sequentially. (See the end of Chapter 7 for the full script.)

IMAGES	AUDIO & TEXT
	"Press a number to learn about a hull"
	CHOICES:
	1) Air Cushion. —Flat hull rides on cushion of air —Capable of high speeds —Needs flat water conditions —Flat, rectangular deck, easy to load
	2) Planing Hull: —V-shaped hull capable of high speeds —Performs best in flat water conditions —High stress levels on hull

3) Displacement Hull
—Deep, rounded hull, very stable in all conditions
—Very large cargo capacity
—Stable platform for large propulsion systems
—Needs very large propulsion system

4) SWATH
—Small Waterplane Area Twin Hull
—2 submerged hulls, very stable
—Flat deck provides good work area

After selecting a hull to use, cut to Design Assembly screen, animation of hull rollout.

Loudspeaker VO: "Planing hull being moved into position."

Cut to POV animation moving to propulsion subassembly area.

Background sound of motors whirring and machinery clanging. "Next, you'll need to choose a propulsion system."

Triple-Column Format

Some writers like to use triple-column format, such as the one for the educational CD-ROM *Sky High* illustrated below. This approach separates the visuals in one column, the narration and dialogue in another, and the music, sound effects, and links in the third column. This type of format helps the production people clearly isolate the different production elements.

PANEL II—MEDIEVAL AND RENAISSANCE TIMES

CLOSE-UP—KING ARTHUR'S COURT—600 A.D.
Click on the castle and go inside!

VISUAL	NARR/SYNC	MUSIC/SFX
Animation [PHAZ.QT.ANM] Castle—On the wall, an ancient-looking calendar with moving phases of the moon	Narration [PHAZ.QT.NARR]	SFX [PHAZ.QT.SFX] [BK 2.2]
VISUAL	**NARR/SYNC**	**MUSIC/SFX**
Video [ECLP.QT.VID] CASTLE VIDEO—Méliès FOOTAGE, from "The Astronomer's Dream" will probably need to be speeded up a little ARCHIVE FILMS	Narration [ECLP.QT.NARR]	Music [ECLP.QT.MUS] Music [BK 02.3]
VISUAL	**NARR/SYNC**	**MUSIC/SFX**
Animation [CATP.QT.ANM] Castle—Ye Olde Gravity Lab—enter lab and play animated game catapulting different balls. Take catapult to the moon, Mars, and Jupiter to see differences.	Narration [CATP.QT.NARR]	Music [CATP.QT.MUS]

Two-Column Presentation Script

Multimedia presentations are often designed with a slide metaphor. Each screen, which might have pictures, video, animation, or text, is thought of as a slide that can be linked interactively with other slides if the developer wishes. Presentations often have limited interactivity, which is controlled by the presenter, and thus look similar to linear audio/video scripts. The following is part of a college promotional program.

PICTURE	AUDIO
(Words in all CAPS are printed on the screen)	
Slide 1	
Fade In:	
NEC Covered Bridge with white titles at top:	
NEW ENGLAND COLLEGE	
Soon after, Fade In bottom right Geena Davis still from QuickTime, speaking at commencement with her name titled underneath:	
GEENA DAVIS	
When audience has time to read her name and see who it is, start QuickTime video.	
	GEENA DAVIS The choice to make our own destiny is ours. Making that choice is not an event; it is a process. And for me, it began here at New England College. I really loved it here. This school is so much about being supportive, encouraging creativity, and helping you find your own path.
Keep QuickTime running, but dissolve background to:	
Slide 2	
Dissolve to:	NARRATOR
Student theater production upper right on blue screen.	New England College helped Academy

Award Winner, Geena Davis, find her destiny.

Let us help you find yours.

Fade in:
Student skier bottom left

Fade in:
Politician alum upper right

Fade in:
Scientist alum bottom left

Finally forming a collage of four possible dreams.

Dissolve to:

Other Interactive Script Formats

These are only a few of the interactive script formats in use. Be aware that many productions have limited use of traditional scripts and instead use combinations of flowcharts, dialogue lists, walkthroughs, and other types of written material. This material and other script samples are documented in the case studies in Parts II and III of this book.

SCRIPTING SOFTWARE

Dedicated Scripting Software

As of this writing, the only program specifically designed for writing interactive scripts is StoryVision, a flowcharting program that works directly with your word processing software to chart and test the options in an interactive script. There are, however, a number of programs for linear scripts that could be easily adapted to do formatting. A few of these are Movie Master, Final Draft, and Scriptware. (Demos of these programs are in the Software section of the CD-ROM.)

Word Processors

If you own one of the major word processing software programs, such as Word or WordPerfect, it is not necessary to buy dedicated scriptwriting software. Most major word-processing programs can do the formatting shown above. Learning how to use macros is the key.

Compatibility

If you are going to be working for a specific company, you should also consider compatibility. Don't use a Mac if everyone else is on a PC, because the script will ultimately perform many functions, such as sections being cut and pasted as text blocks in the multimedia program. Everyone on the production team needs to be able to use the script.

HTML AND THE WORLD WIDE WEB

The World Wide Web

A multimedia writer should be aware of the World Wide Web as a delivery site. At the moment it has by far the greatest potential audience for multimedia products. The Web is a network of computers (servers) all over the world that can present information graphically via the Internet. With a Web Browser, a modem, and an Internet connection, users can access text, pictures, video, and sound from Web servers and display them on their home or office computer screen. The information on the Web is organized on Web pages. These pages are interactive. A simple mouse click on a "hot" spot can instantly link a viewer of one page to a different section of the same document or to another Web page continents away.

HTML

The most commonly used tool to write Web pages is HTML (HyperText Markup Language). HTML is text with a series of markup tags that describe how the various elements on the Web page are supposed to be displayed and what interaction is allowed. HTML is easy to learn and is a tool multimedia writers should know. It is also used to create disc-based multimedia programs, such as the CD-ROM attached to this book.

The Web Page

A browser, such as Netscape or Mosaic, presents the Web page shown in Figure 4–2 on a monitor by finding and interpreting an HTML file, which resides on a Web server. The HTML text file for this page contains two types of information: (1) the on-screen text of the document and (2) the HTML tags that tell the browser what other elements (e.g. pictures) are included in the page and how these elements and the text should be displayed. Below the picture is the HTML file for the Web page in Figure 4–2. An explanation of the tags follows the HTML example.

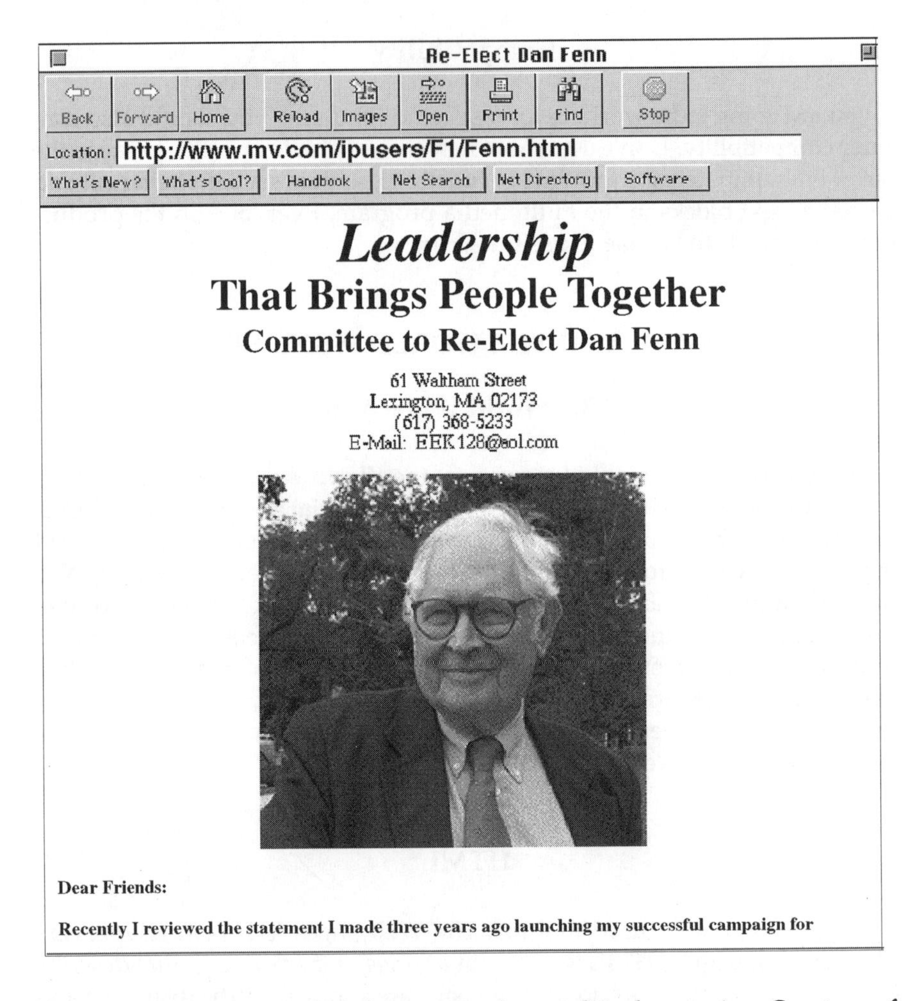

Figure 4–2 World Wide Web home page for a political campaign. Courtesy of Interwrit Designs © 1996.

HTML For the Example Shown in Figure 4–2

```
<HTML><HEAD><TITLE>Re-Elect Dan Fenn
</TITLE></HEAD>

<H1 ALIGN=CENTER><EM>Leadership</EM><BR>
That Brings People Together</CENTER></H1>

<H2 ALIGN=CENTER>Committee to Re-Elect Dan Fenn
</CENTER></H2>
```

```
<P ALIGN=CENTER>61 Waltham Street<BR>
Lexington, MA 02173<BR>(617) 368-5283<BR>
E- Mail: EEK123©aol.com<BR><BR>
<IMG SRC="Dan.gif" ALIGN=CENTER><P>

Dear Friends, <P>Recently I reviewed the statements I
made three years ago launching my successful campaign
for
```

HTML Tags Explained

The TITLE tag = the name of the page, which is displayed in the bar at the top of the browser. In this case, the title is "Re-Elect Dan Fenn."

H1 = heading 1, which is usually displayed larger in size, followed by heading 2–6
EM = display this text with emphasis, usually italics
BR = break to a new line
P = new paragraph
CENTER = center this material
IMG SRC= "Dan.gif" = tells the browser that there is an image here and gives the name of the file. In this case it is "Dan.gif" which is an image file separate from the HTML document.

Using markup tags in a similar way, HTML can create interactivity by linking words or pictures on one document with different sections of that same document or a totally new document on a computer thousands of miles away.

More complex interactivity demands greater technical knowledge and programming skills than is usually required of the writer. However, writers primarily interested in writing for the Web should at least familiarize themselves with the creative potential of such tools as CGI (Complex Gateway Interface) programming, Macromedia's Shockwave, Sun's HotJava, VRML (virtual reality modeling language), and many other programs that allow true multimedia on the Web. (Amdur 42) It also wouldn't hurt the writer to learn basic imaging tools such as Photoshop and Illustrator. A "writer" for the Web rarely just writes. Image creation and manipulation skills are a plus.

HTML Standards and Technical Considerations

An understanding of HTML standards is helpful before deciding which HTML software to use. An HTML standard is a universally accepted group of HTML tags. The current standard accepted by most browsers is HTML 3. This means that if a Web page is written using HTML 3 tags, most browsers will be able to properly present the pages. Some browsers, such as Netscape, have their own tags, which may not be supported by all browsers. Some older browsers may read only HTML 2. What HTML standard you use will be determined by what browser your intended audience uses. Some Web authors create two versions of their pages to accommodate viewers with less sophisticated browsers.

If you are going to use an HTML editor or other Web authoring program, first make sure that it supports the same level of HTML that is used in the browser(s) you are writing for. If, for example, your HTML editor includes only HTML 2 tags, you will have to type all your HTML 3 tags in by hand.

Another consideration before deciding on software is maximum file size. A number of HTML editors restrict file size to 32 KB, which is too small for a large Web site.

HTML SOFTWARE

HTML software can be broken into four major categories (demos of several of the programs listed below are on the CD-ROM):

- Word processors and text editors. Because HTML is a text document, it is possible to write it on a word processor or text editor, such as Word, WordPerfect, or SimpleText. This requires that the writer type in all of the tags. Just a glance at the HTML document above proves that this could be tedious business.
- HTML editors. HTML editors, such as Hot Dog and HTML Assistant Pro have menu listings of HTML tags that the user can insert into the document by clicking a menu choice. Many of these editors also include a browser to show what an HTML page will look like on the Web.
- HTML converters. Many major word processors, such as Word, include extensions that will turn word-processed text into HTML, automatically inserting the HTML tags. These extensions are usually free to current owners of the software. There are also converters that will translate simple text and RTF (rich text format) into HTML.
- Drag and drop authoring. These programs try to make authoring a Web page as easy as using your favorite presentation program. Such tools as Adobe Page Mill allow the user to drag images into place, resize them, align text with images, and create links simply by dragging items or clicking menu choices.

The bad news is that none of these tools will perform all the HTML tasks that you want. After you use your favorite tool, it will usually be necessary to go back in with a text editor and fine-tune the pages by manually typing or deleting HTML tags. The good news is that many of the programs mentioned are inexpensive, and they are constantly being updated.

The above is meant to be a brief introduction to HTML. It is not meant to teach how to do Web pages. There are many excellent books on this subject, such as Laura Lemay's *Teach Yourself Web Publishing with HTML 3.0 in a Week*. There is also much free information on the Web, such as that available at the National Center for Supercomputing Applications site. (This site and others are listed on the attached CD-ROM.)

REFERENCE

Amdur, Dan. "The Scene Is Set for Multimedia on the Web." *New Media* (November 1995).

5

KEY POINTS FROM PART I: MULTIMEDIA AND THE WRITER

Interactive multimedia is a communication medium that uses any combination of sound, pictures, video, and text to communicate to the user interactively. The multimedia writer creates proposals, treatments, walkthroughs, scripts, design documents, and all the other written material that describes the content of a multimedia production.

INTERACTIVITY AND THE WRITER (CHAPTER 1)

Unlike linear media in which the writer must limit options, in multimedia, the writer must have a feel for all the possible interactions in a narrative scene or all the different ways that information can be linked together in an informational program. Complicating the interactivity is the need to anticipate user input—the different ways that users will want to take advantage of the interactive options the writer has provided.

LINKS (CHAPTER 1)

A link is the way that one element of a program is connected to another element in the same program or a completely different program. There are three basic types of links:

1. Immediate or direct links: An action.
2. Indirect links: A reaction.
3. Intelligent or delayed links: A delayed reaction.

INTERACTIVE DEVICES (CHAPTER 1)

The designer and writer must develop interactive devices that will make the players aware of the links and other interactive possibilities that have been created. These devices include on-screen menus, help screens, icons, props, other characters, and cues imbedded in the story itself.

INTERFACE DESIGN (CHAPTER 1)

Interface design is the face the program presents to the user—the basic way the user is allowed to interact with the content. An interface can be as simple as a clickable text menu that organizes the information into content categories, or it can be as complex as a navigable town rendered in 3-D. Interface design also affects the navigation of the piece—how the viewer can travel through the information or story and the order in which the information will be presented. Key elements affecting interface design are the map, metaphors, and the input device.

WRITING FOR MANY MEDIA (CHAPTER 2)

Multimedia can easily incorporate many types of media into a single production or even a single screen, and multimedia can manipulate these media in ways not before possible. Therefore writers of multimedia must be expert in a variety of techniques: writing to be read (journalism, poetry, copywriting), writing to be heard (radio, narration), and writing to be seen (presentations, film, and video).

WRITING AS PART OF THE MULTIMEDIA PRODUCTION TEAM (CHAPTER 2)

The participation of writers in the design process varies considerably from project to project depending on their creative relationship with the designer. With experience in multimedia, many writers learn design, take more control of their material, and become writer-designers. Other key members of the multimedia production team include the project manager, the art director, the programmer(s), the video director, the content expert(s), and the product manager.

FLOWCHARTING AND OTHER ORGANIZATIONAL TOOLS (CHAPTER 3)

To organize the complex elements of a multimedia production, the writer must learn organizational tools. Flowcharting is a particularly useful way to visualize an interactive program for clients and production team members. Other organizational and visualization tools commonly used by writers are outlines, storyboards, databases, and index cards.

MULTIMEDIA SCRIPT FORMATTING (CHAPTER 4)

The preliminary forms for many multimedia programs are proposals and design documents. The elements of an informational design document include design objective, creative treatment, navigation, and production and marketing. A narrative proposal might also include a story summary and characters. There is a wide variety of script formats including: single column, double column, and triple column.

HTML AND THE WORLD WIDE WEB (CHAPTER 4)

The World Wide Web is a network of computers (servers) all over the world that can present information graphically via the Internet. At the moment it has the greatest potential audience for multimedia programs. The most commonly used tool to write for the World Wide Web is HTML (HyperText Markup Language). HTML is text with a series of markup tags that describe how the various elements on the Web page are supposed to be displayed and what interaction is allowed.

PART II
WRITING NONNARRATIVE INFORMATIONAL MULTIMEDIA

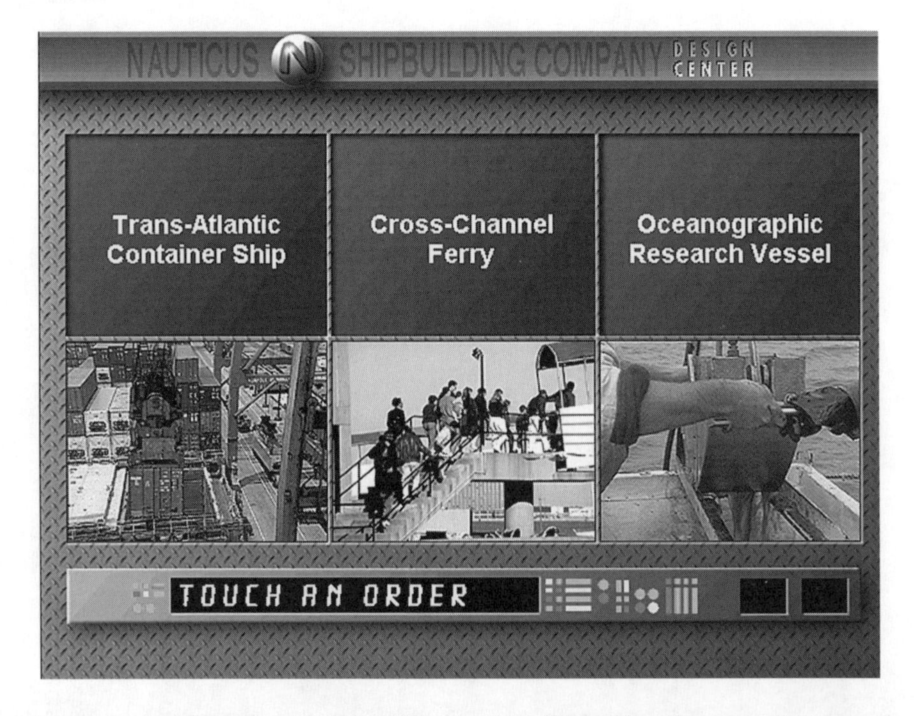

A menu screen from the simulation, *The Nauticus Shipbuilding Company*. Courtesy of Chedd-Angier Production Company. © 1994 Chedd-Angier Production Company.

6
INTRODUCTION TO NONNARRATIVE INFORMATIONAL MEDIA

Most people think of film and TV as primarily fictional stories. Most people think of multimedia as primarily video games. Most people are wrong. The majority of film, TV, and multimedia produced is designed to communicate information. In multimedia, informational titles range from general consumer references, such as *Microsoft Encarta*, to classroom educational programs, such as D. C. Heath's *Sky High*, to corporate training programs for most major companies. Informational multimedia programs are already big business; experts predict that revenues from these products will shortly exceed $20 billion or approximately 10 percent of the worldwide information industry, dwarfing the $7 billion feature film box office revenue. (Aston, 19)

In most cases, informational multimedia follows the documentary tradition of presenting its information through the actual locations and individuals studied. For example, *"Compton's Interactive Encyclopedia"* shows a video of Babe Ruth hitting a home run in Yankee Stadium as opposed to having an actor portray Ruth in a studio.

There would be nothing wrong with an informational program that used an actor to play Babe Ruth, and many informational programs are created using narrative fiction. Examples include dramatic re-creations of historical events or character-driven training programs in which an actor takes on the role of a typical employee. Narrative fiction and informational programs using narrative have special concerns of their own and will be dealt with in Part III of this book.

The focus of this part of the book is multimedia whose primary goal is to communicate information clearly and accurately and without using fictional storytelling techniques. The aspects of informational multimedia examined include: types of programs, goals, and key concerns of informational multimedia writers, such as video structure, instructional theory, and persuasive techniques. The section closes with five informational multimedia case studies.

INFORMATIONAL MULTIMEDIA COMMUNICATION GOALS

Informational multimedia is now a pervasive part of everyday life, used in the home, school, business, and public sites, such as museums. It is delivered in a variety of ways, including CD-ROM, kiosks, laser discs, large screen presentations, interactive television, and online in networks, such as the World Wide Web. The material covered includes general reference, infotainment, education, interactive magazines and newspapers, sales and marketing, training, public relations, and much more.

The good news for the individual trying to comprehend this wide array of informational programming is that to a large degree these programs all share one or more of the following goals:

- To entertain.
- To inform.
- To teach.

These are not hard categories; rather, they often overlap and combine, but they give a useful way to examine the communication goals and methods to achieve those goals used by individual programs.

One could argue that there could also be a fourth category: to persuade. But persuasion is really a metacategory that affects all types of media. The key principles of persuasion for linear media hold true for interactive media. These principles have been well described elsewhere and will not be repeated in this book. (If you are not familiar with basic persuasion theory, check out the persuasion article in the Chapter 10 supplementary material on the attached CD-ROM.)

Entertain: Getting Beyond Click and Read

To entertain is to present information in an amusing way that engages the audience. All programs must entertain or engage their audience to some degree. Even if a program had the greatest information, it would have limited communication value if it was boring.

Entertainment Continuum

A project can be viewed on a continuum, with a plain listing of the information at one end to a piece that is pure entertainment at the other end. But most pieces do not exist at one end of this continuum; rather they fall somewhere along the line, embracing elements of both entertainment and information. Where a specific project sits on this continuum is an important consideration for the writer.

Misjudging where a program should fall on the information-entertainment continuum can mean complete failure for a program. This happened in a corporate piece designed to solve communication problems for a large electronics manufacturing firm. The problem was that different departments of the company were not communicating well, and the result was redundancy and inefficiency. The writers for this project decided to use the metaphors of "barriers and walls" and a framework of sketch comedy similar to *Saturday Night Live*. The final project consisted of a series of comedy skits dealing with barriers separating people. It was very entertaining, but the basic information that the company wanted to communicate was lost in the jokes. This is not to say that humor cannot communicate information, but in this case, the writer moved too far toward the entertainment end of the continuum and failed his clients.

Examples: Getting Beyond Click and Read

Too many interactive writers gravitate toward a hierarchical navigation structure that requires the viewer to click and read through a series of menus to get the information they want. This is perhaps a functional way to access information, but it keeps the viewers distant by not making them use or think about the information. For example, Figure 6–1 shows a click-and-read approach to a museum kiosk interactive project about shipbuilding. In this case, the writer simply organized the information according to categories and subcategories, so users can click to their area of interest. This information is perhaps presented in a clear manner, but it is not very engaging.

With a little thought, however, the writer-designer can go beyond click and read and develop a program on the same subject that truly involves the user interactively. The flowchart in Figure 7–3 on page 84 is from *The Nauticus Shipbuilding Company*. In this program, the user becomes a shipbuilder and is asked to assemble a ship by choosing from a variety of components. At the end of the program, the completed ship is evaluated. As it leaves the dock, it floats or it sinks. This approach teaches the same information as the click-and-read hierarchical approach but does so in a much more exciting fashion.

The answer to getting beyond click and read is to involve the user in some way. (This is, after all, **interactive** multimedia.) Even if this can't be done for a complete program, at least sections of the program can be developed in this way. Other approaches beyond click and read follow:

- *Problem solver:* This was the approach *The Nauticus Shipbuilding Company* used. It set up a problem and asked the user to solve it with the information in the program, using the simulation structure.
- *Gamer:* In this case the user is a player in a game. Playing this game teaches certain principles. A game can be inserted into a program that is otherwise click and read. This is somewhat similar to the problem-solver approach except it usually operates with more clearly defined game rules. An example from *Sky High* is the Gravity Lab Game in which users must discover what type of ball (basketball, tennis, etc.)

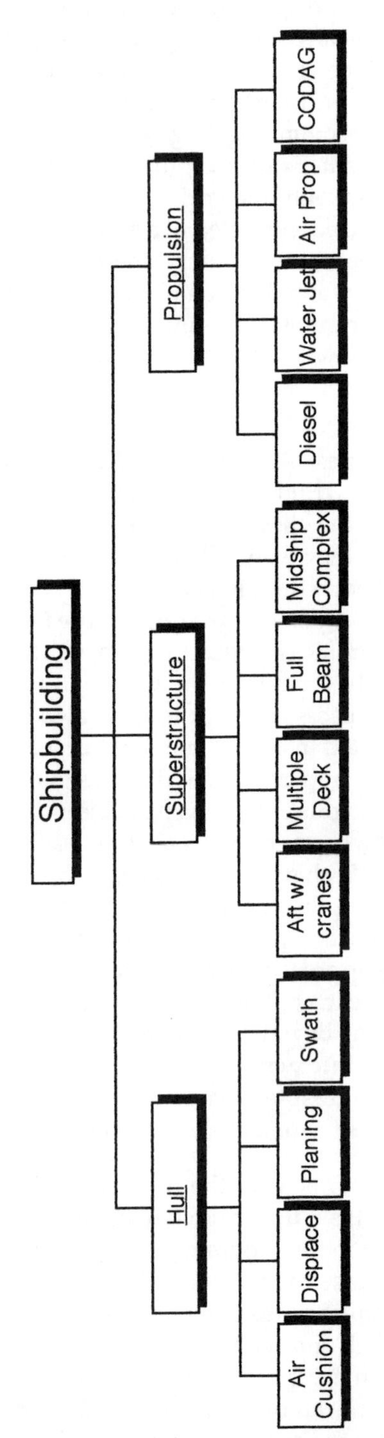

Figure 6–1 Click-and-read hierarchical shipbuilding chart.

can be catapulted through a hoop on each of the planets of our solar system.

- *Reporter:* A number of educational programs, including *Sky High,* allow users to report on their multimedia experience by using a virtual camera and a word processor to write a journal.
- *Explorer:* Here the user explores a physical space in either a complete program or a component of a program.

Another option is to make the user a character in a story, an approach dealt with in Part III. These are only a few options. The correct approach should emerge from the information to be presented and the intended audience.

Inform

A writer whose goal is to inform wants to provide users access to a large body of information in a reference work, such as an encyclopedia. The viewers need not and usually are not expected to access all of the information. Instead they simply take what they need. The information is usually presented clearly and structured into discreet units with limited manipulation of the material by the writer.

The database is the most common form of a program whose main goal is to provide access to a large body of information. General reference works, such as *Grolier's Multimedia Encyclopedia* and *Britannica Online,* and more focused references, such as *Microsoft Cinemania,* are essentially databases. The multimedia database also has many uses in business. Real estate companies often have databases of homes for sale, and some major multinational corporations have databases of managers, complete with videos and photos, to help executives make personnel decisions.

Approaches—Creating the Accessible Database

The major challenge with a database is to organize the information in a way that allows users to access the information that they want easily. There are a number of ways to do this.

Grouping by Categories The simplest way is to group by categories, that is, putting all the same types of items together—for example, *Cinemania* groups, movie listings, biographies, awards, and media. Media includes the subgroups of movie stills, portraits, dialogue, music, and film clips.

Content categories are the most obvious grouping, but material can be organized according to numerous criteria, such as place, time, or theme. For example, *Cinemania* could have a feature that allows searching by place so a user could search for all the material that originated in New York. By time, a search could include all material before 1930. By theme, it could include all material involved with crime.

Even more useful is to combine categories into what is sometimes called a complex query. Combine the movie listing with the place listing, and get all the movies made in New York. Add the time criterion, and get all the movies made in New York before 1930. Add the crime theme criterion, and get all the movies made in New York before 1930 that deal with crime.

The limitation of this approach is that the categories that the writer comes up with may not be the ones that the user would come up with, given a free hand. The ideal product would help users create their own categories and customize the database to their use.

Concept Maps Concept maps are a way to visualize categories in a database according to a visual image or map. The museum and journey approach are fairly common. The museum approach allows users to enter a virtual museum, enter exhibit rooms in their area of interest, and view exhibits about a particular subject. The journey allows users to travel along a certain sequence.

A danger with concept maps is combining incompatible maps. An early draft of the program *Sky High* attempted to combine the temporal map of journeying along a time line with the spatial map of the stars and planets. These two different types of maps did not work smoothly together and had to be abandoned. (See Chapter 8 for a full discussion of this issue.)

Guides and Agents One of the most promising approaches for making a database accessible is by creating guides or agents to lead users through the material. These guides could be software creations that are part of the program. For example, *The Mayo Clinic Family Health Book* includes an on-screen character who introduces material and helps to guide users in the direction that they want. This type of a guide is limited by the material that was written for the screen character to present, but there is much research into how to create a truly intelligent agent who could be told by the user what information he or she needed, and then the user could go get a cup of coffee while the helper searched the world and delivered the information to the user's desktop computer. Agent technology is already in place in some of the more sophisticated web search programs.

Guides could be real people, which becomes possible with online communication. The Electronic Emissary Project at the University of Texas links experts with K-12 classes or individuals. These experts guide the students through the maze of online data. Some human guides are specific to a certain site. The Argonne National Laboratory allows students to leave questions for scientists at the site.

Cognitive Overload—Controlling Complexity Guides are one way to keep students who are browsing a vast database from getting confused by the diversity and complexity of the unsequenced material they encounter. Browsing a database is quite a different experience from reading a textbook, where the information is carefully explained and structured to build understanding of an overall topic gradually. In a database, just the opposite can occur. Topics of varying degrees of difficulty can be encountered and only partially understood by the student. "A failure to control this complexity can lead to cognitive overload and failure to learn." (Ambron 127)

Cognitive load can be reduced in a number of ways—for example:

- Reduce the number of choices available on the screen at any one time ("seven plus or minus two" is optimal). (Ambron 128)
- Reduce the level of difficulty available to the student at any different time. Students must have viewed crucial introductory material before they are allowed to access advanced concepts.
- Build a note-taking function into the program so students can track their progress and note partially understood concepts. (Note-taking can include text and pictures).
- Give students the opportunity to "mark" a section of the program that they can return to later.
- Build in a clear orientation so students can understand where they are and that the various pieces of information are connected. Navigation maps and consistent interface design help with this.

Teach

A database provides access to a wide body of information. Exactly what information the user accesses and learns is up to the individual. In a teaching program, however, the information may be more narrowly defined and the writer has a clearer goal of what information he or she wants the user to take away from the program.

The Integrated Media Group's *Video Producer* is a good example of a teaching program at the college level. Its goal is to teach the basics of video production. It is carefully structured to do this with mini-lectures, examples, reviews, and quizzes. Fidelity Investments' training program for retirement counselors is similarly focused on teaching a skill.

Instructional theory is a complicated subject that must be studied in depth if one is to become an instructional designer, but it is important to be familiar with some of the basic concepts of instructional design before writing educational or training programs.

Interactive Multimedia Instruction as Interpersonal Instruction

Some experts in interactive instruction claim that effective interactive instruction should include the characteristics of interpersonal instruction: immediacy of response, nonsequential access of information, adaptability, feedback, options, bidirectional communication, and interruptibility. (Schwier 175–176)

- Immediacy of response. In practical terms, this means that an action the learner takes should get a response immediately. It is psychologically important for the learner to feel connected. For example, when a student clicks on an answer in a quiz, he or she should get some sort of response even if it is just a sound. Similarly, if there is going to be a wait after a student clicks an icon to access a large file, something should be happening on the screen—preferably something more interesting and tied to the program than an hourglass or a watch. Wait-state and other responses should be in tune with the program. Rodney's *Wonder Window*, a humorous children's educational CD-ROM, has funny wait-state text messages: "Please wait, Rodney is putting on clean underwear," and visual images, such as the heads on the character icons spinning around or their hair curling.
- Feedback. Immediacy of response does not mean complex feedback to every action. Deciding what kind of feedback to give and when to give it to the learner is a difficult question. There is no consensus on this subject. There is even disagreement on simple types of feedback. For example, some writers provide only a minimal response, such as "Correct" to correctly answered test questions, and reserve complex feedback for questions answered incorrectly. Others include detailed feedback for correct answers as well, to reinforce the message and to guard against students' guessing the right answers and not learning the material.
- Bidirectional communication. Clearly related to immediacy of response and feedback is bidirectional communication and interruptibility. A well-designed learning program gives the user ample opportunity to communicate with the program as well as for the program to communicate with the user. This includes letting the learner communicate through various methods, including typing text, manipulating images, and sound. This is essential if maximum learning is going to happen for the maximum number of students, because studies have proved that we all learn in different ways—some by watching, others by doing, and yet others by analysis. Thus it is important to present the message in a variety of ways.
- Interruptibility. Students should be able to interrupt the program at any point and go in the direction that is useful for them. They should, for example, be able to return easily to earlier material for review. If they feel comfortable with the material, they should be able to jump ahead to a more advanced part of the program.

  Programs that do not allow this movement can be frustrating. *Video Producer*, an otherwise excellent education program on video production, requires that students complete a series of quizzes on video production techniques before they are allowed to create a video in the program's studio. This defeats the purpose of interactive multimedia and incorporates the drawback of linear media and classroom instruction where all levels of students must progress through the material in the same way.

Inclusion of standard navigation tools can also improve interruptibility. Many programs respond to standard quit commands, such as command Q on the Macintosh. When users quit, they should be able to leave a bookmark at the spot they left and return to it when they start again and not have to start at the beginning.

- Help. Excellent help programs are now included in basic productivity programs, such as word processors, but a surprising number of educational programs do not provide a constant helping hand for the student. And as discussed with wait-state messages, a writer who can make the access to help more interesting and in tune with the particular program than a help button will contribute to the program's effectiveness. It's important to build the help function into the interface design from the beginning and into the writer's schedule. Writing help pages can be extremely time-consuming.
- Personalizing instruction: Nonsequential access to information, adaptability, and options. Multimedia's ability to access information in the order that the user finds most useful allows a writer to personalize a program and make it adaptable to the learner. Many programs allow learners to personalize the program at the beginning by filling out a user profile based on such criteria as educational level, job, and familiarity with the subject. Once entered into the computer, this profile might cause the program to take the learner down a completely different instructional path, or it might just alter the text on certain screens.

Personalizing the program continues beyond the beginning by tracking the learner's progress and adapting to his or her needs. For example, a learner who consistently has difficulties in a certain area might be directed to special remedial sections geared to that particular problem. The program might also alter the way it presents the instructional material in the rest of the lesson. If the student learned best from the video segments, the video might be increased and text minimized.

A simple way to personalize is to allow students to choose the level of difficulty and thus advance at their own rate. Another adaptation is the degree of control allowed the student over the learning material. Some studies have suggested that weaker students can benefit from more structure. (Schwier 186)

The way subject matter is approached also personalizes a program. Someone learning marketing should be able to choose various contexts designed into the program in which to practice their new skills, such as marketing a virtual baseball team, video store, or rock group.

Learning to Learn: Educating Tool Makers

In addition to teaching a specific skill or subject matter, multimedia is also very successful at teaching students how to learn. A generation ago, the standard structure for most elementary school classrooms was a teacher standing in front of a sea of students at desks and delivering knowledge from his or her information-packed brain to the empty-headed students.

A visit to most classrooms today would find a different structure. The sea of desks is gone. Students are grouped in fours or fives around smaller tables and are engaged in activities. The teacher moves about the room, facilitating their learning. This different structure reflects current learning theory, which rejects the concept of empty heads waiting to be filled and replaces it with the goal of teaching students how to learn. Some theorists have used the metaphor of tool maker (Reddy 284–324)—that is, teaching students how to create the learning tools that will serve them throughout life.

A big reason for this major change is the rapid explosion in knowledge. A hundred years ago, the body of knowledge was relatively stable. Individuals could learn a trade and successfully perform that trade until retirement. Today, however, information is expanding so rapidly that education has become a lifelong pursuit. Students have no assurance that the information they are learning will be valid in a few years or even that the careers they are training for will exist after graduation. To thrive in this type of a world, students must be excellent learners and have a full bag of learning tools to take with them for the rest of their life.

Teaching Tool Makers with Interactivity—Playing As If

One of the best ways to develop these tools, to learn how to learn, is through hands-on learning, an opportunity to interact with the subject under study. One way to do this is through interactive multimedia programs. However, as Edith Ackerman of the MIT Media Lab points out, "we should not assume that 'hands-on' activities alone will make for a meaningful experience of constructive learning. . . . Any activity remains essentially undirected and non-controllable, blind, and meaningless, if it is just acted out without any evaluation of its consequences." (Ackerman 1–3)

Approaches to evaluate these consequences include reliable feedback and giving the learner the ability to reconstruct the experience. There should be some way to reconstruct and replay the learning experience in a safe environment, because the major way learners incorporate new material is not through the experience itself but through the ability to recreate the material in some fashion, thus making it their own. In short, "Interactivity is important, not because it allows the direct manipulation of real objects, but because it fosters the construction of models or artifacts, in which an intriguing idea (thought and feeling) can be run or played out 'for good' in a make believe world." (Ackerman 6)

In an interactive multimedia program, this construction of models can range from trying out different marketing techniques learned by managing a virtual candy store or building an entire city in the simulation *SimCity 2000*. Such game elements allow the students to explore "what" will happen "if" they try various options. And as Ackerman points out, "Scientific inquiry, as much as other forms of cognitive investigation, indeed requires playing 'what if.'" (Ackerman 6)

INFORMATIONAL MULTIMEDIA STRUCTURE

Many of the advantages of multimedia, such as the ability to get the information you want when you want it and the opportunity to explore the interconnection of complex ideas, are directly related to interactive structure. There are two key aspects of interactive structure: the types of links or individual connections between different parts of a program or different programs and the navigation pattern or flow of the overall structure.

Types of Links

Chapter One defined the three basic types of interactive links: direct, indirect, and intelligent. All three are used in informational multimedia.

In informational multimedia, the direct link (an action) is probably the most common. By clicking on a menu choice or an icon, the user is directly and instantly connected to the information that they want. The advantage of this approach is obvious: It is directly responsive to the user's needs.

Indirect links (reactions) are common in instructional pieces, where a student who is fumbling the questions in a certain area may be automatically routed to easier review material, as opposed to being advanced to the next level. For example, a student failing an arithmetic question in a math tutorial might be sent back to an arithmetic review module instead of advancing to the algebra module. (See Figure 1–1 in Chapter 1.)

Intelligent or delayed links (delayed reactions) are fairly common in training and education programs. An intelligent link is a connection that can learn from the way someone uses a program. In an instructional program, the user often logs on with a name or number. The program then tracks the learning pattern of each user. The program gradually understands the learning pattern of each user, changing the links accordingly. For example, if a student consistently does poorly on the long division portion of a math program, when the student logs on again, he or she will be linked to a review page with additional long division problems.

Delayed links are also used in informational simulations. For example in *SimCity 2000*, a program that allows the user to build a city, the choice to build a new subway may not have immediate impact. It could, however, set off a series of delayed reactions that eventually bankrupt the city administration.

Structure

This ability to link in a number of ways gives multimedia a wide variety of possible structures. Rarely do these structures exist in a pure form. Most programs have some combination of these structures. A key question the writer must ask when developing a program is which structure will best achieve the communication goals. Initial structure is often planned with flowcharts, called navigation maps. Flowcharts and navigational metaphors are used to make the structures clear. Every possible interactive structure is not listed here, merely those that are most commonly used by the writer and designer of nonnarrative, informational multimedia.

Linear Structure

Defined: Linear structure can be compared to a desert highway with no crossroads. It is the structure of most motion pictures and television programs.

Use: It makes it possible to integrate into multimedia some of the standard linear informational structures, such as the problem–solution structure and the dialectical structure. The problem–solution structure is used by setting up a problem linearly and then asking the user to solve it interactively. Dialectical structure, a favorite of *60 Minutes*, sets up a dialogue between two different points of view. First we hear from the bureaucrat who loves Indian nuclear power; then we hear from the doctor who hates it. This a/b, love/hate pattern is repeated until a conclusion emerges or we can draw our own conclusion. This can be done interactively with the viewer controlling the sequencing of the different points of view. A simple use of linear structure in interactive is presenting key information that should not be interrupted. This is often used as introductory material.

Linear Structure with Scene Branching

Defined: This structure can be compared to the desert highway that has a few detours. (See Figure 6–2.) The detours, however, always return the trav-

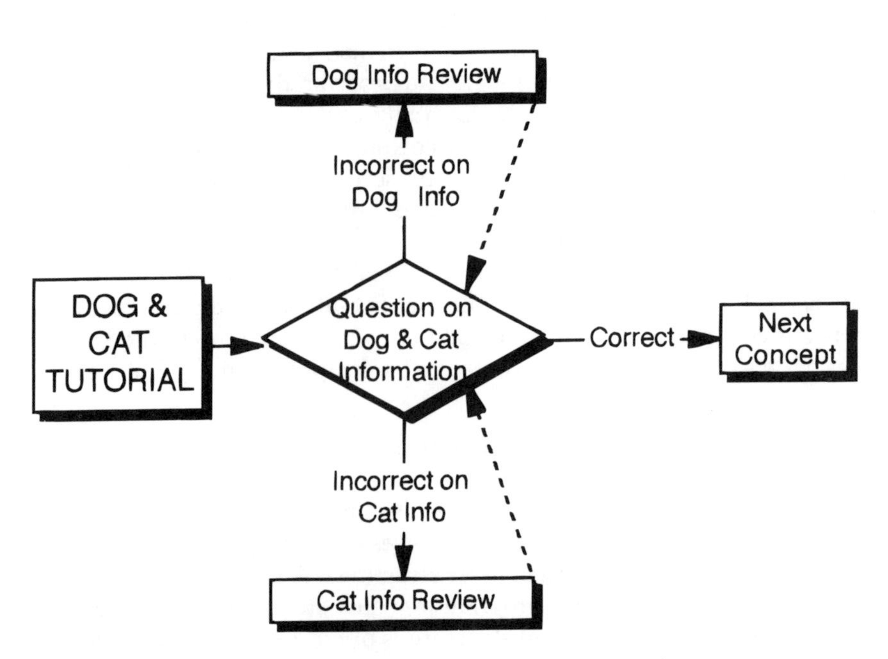

Figure 6–2 Linear structure with scene branching.

eler to the same highway. This is basically a linear structure with a few limited choices as to how certain scenes will play out.

Use: This could be used in a training piece that was following a linear structure of explaining a concept, giving an example, and posing questions. There might be the option of detouring for a review of the concept before answering the questions, but after the review, the user would be returned to the question that he or she had left. Outside of training, this approach has limited use because it is too restrictive on the user seeking the information he or she wants.

Hierarchical Branching

Defined: This approach could be compared to going to a mall searching for an Italian cookbook. At the first fork in the mall, you can choose left for the department store, straight ahead for for the bookshop, or right for the electronic shop. You want a cookbook, so you choose straight and go to the bookshop. Now you must choose between nonfiction, fiction, and magazines. You choose nonfiction, which includes many choices, ranging from biography to cookbooks to zoology. You choose cookbooks. The cookbook section has French cookbooks, Indian cookbooks, and Italian cookbooks. You choose Italian and, phew, you are finally done.

Use: Hierarchical branching in a multimedia program works exactly this way with a hierarchy of ever-narrowing choices, except your finger does the clicking instead of your heels. It is easy to see why electronic malls are a natural.

This approach has several potential pitfalls, however. One is branching explosion, which means creating too many user options. Increasing either the number of decision points or the number of choices for each decision point means that the number of possible endings increases exponentially. In Figure 6–1, page 56, the options quickly jump from three, to twelve, and, by adding one more level, to forty-eight. The amount of material quickly expands to a volume difficult for a writer to create and prohibitive to produce. Branching explosion is kept under control by limiting options and creatively reusing the same program components.

Another danger with hierarchical branching is that if there are too many levels of information, the user can get lost and find it difficult to make connections with material on the same hierarchy. There is also a practical limitation to the number of choices at any one branch (some studies say that five to seven choices is the most people can easily comprehend). Hierarchical branching is an effective way to narrow informational choices, but it is pure click and read and not very exciting. It is nevertheless probably the most common structure in informational multimedia.

Single-Level Linking

Defined: As opposed to hierarchical branching, which looks like a well-organized mall, single-level branching is like wandering into a chaotic flea market. At a flea market you can go any number of places and talk to anyone in any order.

Use: There is no hierarchy in this approach. Usually the user is presented a problem and given a number of possible resources for solving this problem. In the interactive documentary *A Right to Die, The Case of Dax Cowart,* Dax Cowart has a serious illness. He wants to refuse treatment and die. His doctors and others feel differently. The user of this program can access video interviews, text, and other material about this case in order to answer the question, Does Cowart have the right to choose his death? (The irony of this piece is that Dax was not allowed to choose his death; the therapy was successful, and he went on to live a happy life.) Although single-level linking structure is useful, it is fairly rare because it must be limited to a focused topic with limited options. If there are too many options, then a hierarchical structure or another approach has to be used to organize the material.

Worlds Structure

Defined: This structure (also called virtual structure) is similar to the single-level structure but more complex. In this case our metaphorical traveler is dropped into a complex world to explore. The worlds structure organizes the options available to the viewer not in a linear fashion or in a hierarchy but in a graphic spatial representation. *Myst* is the most famous example of a worlds structure, where the viewer can explore an island and discover prescripted situations and locations. An advantage of this approach with complex information is that it can be less easy to get lost than with a hierarchical structure.

Use: This structure is most useful if there is a large body of information that can be incorporated in a location. It does not have to be a physical location that we normally visit. The museum interactive piece *Into the Cell* allows viewers to take a fantastic voyage into a living cell. A writer approaches a project like this by first deciding on a list of locations in the virtual world that he or she is creating, then determining what will happen in each location, and finally how the user will be able to discover these events. A flowchart is not that useful here. More useful is a graphical illustration of the world and a list of the locations and events that will occur there.

Simulation

Defined: In a simulation, the user does not merely visit a world and discover what is there; rather, the user creates (or destroys) a world from a series of components that have been built into the system.

Use: This is great for communicating a body of information that is best learned by doing. This can be a single skill, such as flying a jet in *Flight Unlimited,* or as complex as building a city, as in *SimCity 2000.* In this program, the user is given the power to build a city by altering the landscape, adding parks, schools, railroads, power plants, and other components, but it must be done within budget and the user must cope with disasters, such as flood, fire, and alien invasion.

The writers Brian Sawyer and John Vourlis suggest the best way to write a simulation is to start with the "most basic categories, 'Characters' and 'Locations,' then break these down into sub-categories, and so on. . . . After laying out the categories, the next step is to fill in the details of each object: 1) its attributes and 2) its rules of behavior." (Sawyer 101)

For example in the ship-building simulation, *The Nauticus Shipbuilding Company*, the attributes of the air cushion hull are that it is capable of high speeds, needs flat water conditions, and has a flat deck that is easy to load. Its behavior, if chosen for the oceanographic research vessel, is that it will sink because it can't withstand the rough seas off New England.

ATTRIBUTES AND BEHAVIOR OF THE HULLS IN *THE NAUTICUS SHIPBUILDING COMPANY* SIMULATION

ATTRIBUTES	BEHAVIOR OF HULLS IF USED FOR OCEANOGRAPHIC RESEARCH VESSEL
Air Cushion:	
Flat hull rides on cushion of air	Non-functional
Capable of high speeds	Can't withstand rough seas
Needs flat water conditions	
Flat, rectangular deck easy to load	
Planing Hull:	
V-shaped hull capable of high speeds	Functional
Performs best in flat water conditions	Capable of high speeds
High stress levels on hull	Not very stable in rough seas
	Limited work and living space
Displacement Hull:	
Deep, rounded hull very stable in all conditions	Functional
	Stable in rough seas
Very large cargo capacity	Plenty of work and living space
Stable platform for large propulsion systems	Deep draft limits access to shore areas
Needs very large propulsion system	
SWATH (Small waterplane area twin hull):	
Two submerged hulls very stable	Optimal
Flat deck provides good work area	Very stable in rough seas
	Plenty of protected work and living space
	Shallower draft provides access to shore areas

Multisite Branching

CD-ROM and museum kiosks are closed systems. The user has access to the program material in that system and nothing more. On the World Wide Web and other networks, however, it is possible to link from words or images on one site to related information on other sites all over the world.

When Web technology comes of age, it will allow the possibility of linking all of the above structures in one unlimited search for information. A user might start at one site that is hierarchical, link to another site with a linear video, and yet another that involves him or her in a simulation. A graph of this would look like a mad combination of all of the examples above. With multisite branching, the individual creator has the resources of the world to present his or her information, but the writer gives up much of the control in so doing.

Multisite branching involves researching other sites that have links that would amplify the information on your site. For example, the city of San Diego's Web site allows users to link to the Planet Earth Home Page—Welcome to California. This site allows a link to Other California Resources, which includes a link to Going Places—United States National Parks. Once the user gets to another site, however, the writer of the original Web site (San Diego) has no control over what information the user will access at the new site or if he or she will ever return to the original Web site. In this example, does information about U.S. National Parks achieve the goals of the designers of the San Diego site?

INTRODUCTION TO THE INFORMATIONAL MULTIMEDIA CASE STUDIES

The case studies in the chapters that follow demonstrate how various goals were achieved and challenges were met in specific multimedia programs:

- *The Nauticus Shipbuilding Company*, a museum kiosk shipbuilding simulation located at Nauticus: National Maritime Center, Norfolk, Virginia.
- *Sky High*, an elementary school CD-ROM on the subject of flight and space.
- *Clinical Support Staff Interactive Certification Program: Vital Signs*, an interactive video disc training program for medical assistants at a health maintenance organization (HMO) on the process of taking medical vital signs: temperature, pulse, respiration, and blood pressure.
- *ZD Net Personal View Online Ad Campaign*, a World Wide Web advertising campaign produced by Ziff-Davis Interactive to promote its free customized news service: ZD Net Personal View.
- *T. Rowe Price Web Site*, a commercial Web site from the investment firm T. Rowe Price that offers interactive information for new and seasoned investors.

An understanding of how the writers of these programs dealt with informational multimedia issues will give you insight into how to deal with similar issues when they arise in your work. Each case study answers the following questions:

- Program Description and Background. Is the program a typical example of its genre or is it unusual? Who commissioned, developed, and wrote the program? What was the preproduction process?
- Goals. What were the writers and designers' goals in creating this project? What information or experience were they trying to communicate?
- Challenges. Which goals were particularly difficult to achieve? What approaches were successful in achieving these goals and which were discarded?
- Response to the Project. Did the program achieve its goals? Was it a critical and/or commercial success?

The case studies are documented with script examples, screen shots, and flowcharts. Additional script samples and other material are available for many of the programs on the CD-ROM.

REFERENCES

Ackermann, Edith. "Tools for Constructive Learning: Rethinking Interactivity." Cambridge, MA: MIT Media Lab, October 1993.

Ambron, Sueann, and Kristina Hooper, eds. *Learning with Interactive Multimedia: Developing and Using Multimedia Tools in Education*. Redmond, WA: Microsoft Press, 1990.

Aston, Robert, and Joyce Schwarz. *Multimedia: Gateway to the Next Millennium*. Boston: AP Professional, 1994.

Reddy, M. "The Conduit Metaphor—A Case of Frame Conflict in Our Language about Language." In Andrew Ortony, ed., *Metaphor and Thought*. Cambridge: Cambridge University Press, 1979.

Sawyer, Brian, and John Vourlis. "Screenwriting Structures for New Media." *Creative Screenwriting* 2 (Summer 1995): 95–103.

Schwier, Richard A., and Earl R. Misanchuk. *Interactive Multimedia Instruction*. Englewood Cliffs, NJ: Educational Technology, 1993.

7

MUSEUM KIOSK CASE STUDY: *THE NAUTICUS SHIPBUILDING COMPANY*

Summary

Name of Production: *The Nauticus Shipbuilding Company*
Writer: Steven Barney
Developers: Tarragon Interactive, Chedd-Angier Production Co.
Audience: General
Medium: Computer hard drive in kiosk setting
Location: Nauticus: National Maritime Center, Norfolk, Virginia
Subject: Shipbuilding
Goals: Entertain, teach
Structures: Simulation, hierarchical branching

PROGRAM DESCRIPTION AND BACKGROUND

Program Description

The Nauticus Shipbuilding Company is an interactive museum kiosk program that introduces users to basic concepts of shipbuilding. The program is run on an Intel 486-based computer's hard drive accessed by users' touching images or menu items on the touch screen monitor. The computer and monitor are housed in a stand-alone kiosk in the museum's main exhibit hall. Near the kiosk is a wall of graphic and text information on shipbuilding that supports the kiosk program. *The Nauticus Shipbuilding Company* is also being used in classrooms as part of the museum's curricular outreach.

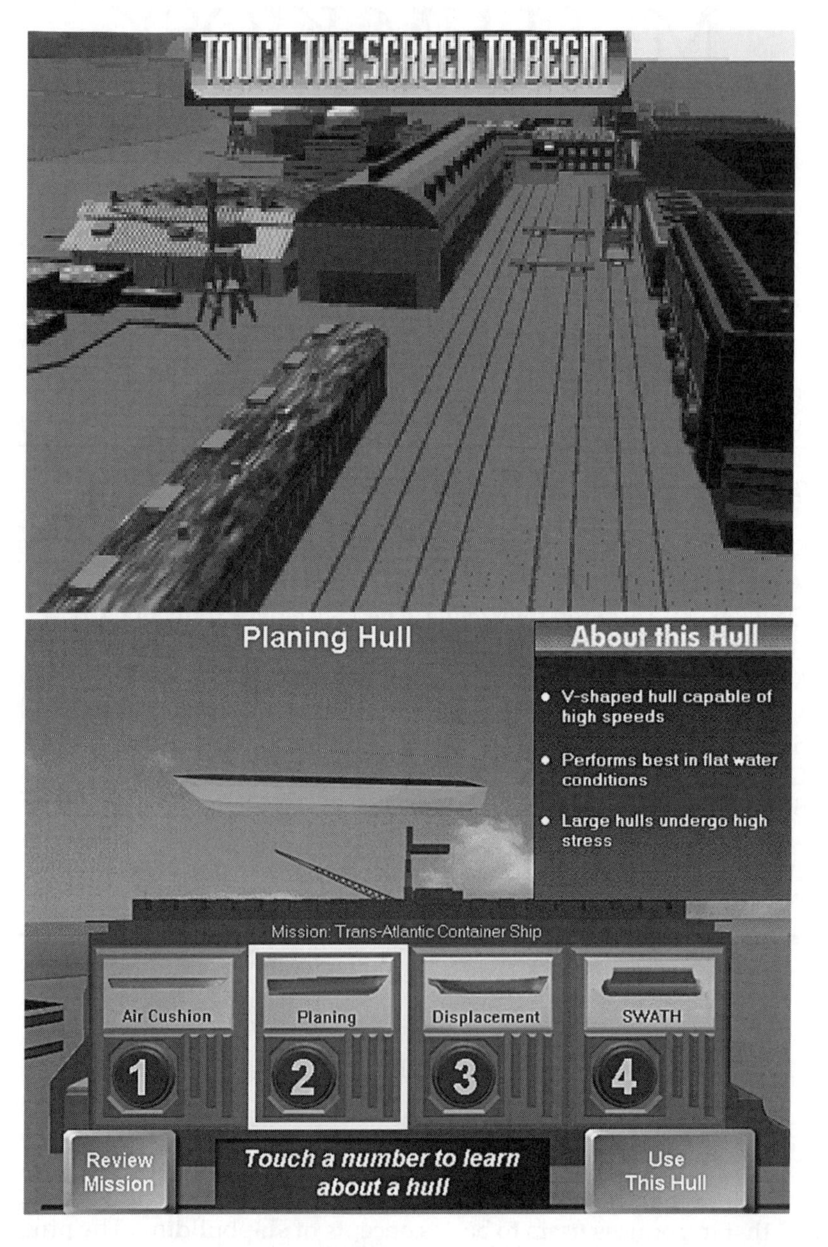

Figure 7–1 Top screen: From the attract program for *The Nauticus Shipbuilding Company*. Bottom screen: Where the user chooses hulls. (The original color images for these screen shots and others in the book are available on the attached CD-ROM.)

Multimedia in Museums

A single-user kiosk presentation, such as *Nauticus*, is a common way to present multimedia in a museum. Because of the need to accommodate large groups, multimedia is also presented in a group format, where a number of people control the action on the screen. An example is the National Scouting Museum's *Boy Scout Patrol Theater*, which allows eight users to take on the role of the individual Boy Scouts portrayed in the multimedia program. (See Chapter 14.)

In addition to exhibits, many museums also have learning centers, which house a variety of multimedia "edutainment" programs for groups or individuals. Larger museums are active in educational outreach, providing curricular support for schools. The old fossils-on-wheels programs, which brought artifacts to schools, is now being supplemented by multimedia programs, such as *Nauticus*, and by online programs from museums, such as the Museum of Science in Boston, the Exploratorium in San Francisco, and the Franklin Institute Science Museum in Philadelphia. (See the Chapter 7 supplementary material section of the CD-ROM for links to these sites.)

Production Background

The Nauticus Shipbuilding Company was jointly developed by Chedd-Angier Production Company and Tarragon Interactive for Nauticus: National Maritime Center. The National Maritime Center, located on the Norfolk, Virginia, waterfront, offers exhibits, films, and multimedia programs dealing with shipping, the navy, and the sea.

Chedd-Angier Production Company is a Boston-based media production company that Nauticus hired to develop a number of the media productions for the museum. Chedd-Angier in turn recruited Tarragon Interactive to develop *The Nauticus Shipbuilding Company* project. Tarragon is a custom developer of multimedia titles for marketing and sales, training, and "infotainment" (museum and CD-ROM titles). The writer of this program is Steven Barney, president of Tarragon Interactive. He is a designer-programmer with a background in instructional design.

WRITING AND DEVELOPING *THE NAUTICUS SHIPBUILDING COMPANY*

The Development Process

At Tarragon Interactive the writer's primary involvement occurs during the first two stages of development, project definition and design/preproduction, but the writer is also often called in during production to make last-minute changes.

The project definition identifies:

- Design objective
- Target audience
- Delivery platform/location

Design/preproduction documents include:

- Proposals. Outlining the program's approach
- High level design document. A text-based content treatment and a program navigation flow diagram
- Scripts. Program navigation flow plus narration, dialogue, screen text, and full description of visuals

Development Challenges

Many of the challenges facing the developers of *The Nauticus Shipbuilding Company* are common to media development for museums and other public sites.

Design Objective

The design objective of *Nauticus* is to provide museum visitors with an interactive environment in which to explore how ships are built for specific missions. This piece uses technical information that must be precisely accurate. The project was reviewed for accuracy by the faculty of MIT's Department of Naval Engineering and members of the National Board of the Society of Naval Architecture and Marine Engineering. The entertainment aspect of this piece was tested through focus groups and through placing a test exhibit at a museum and evaluating viewers' reactions.

Another objective of this program is that users will go through the game and return to play it again. This means that diversity and depth must be designed into the experience, but because of run time, size limitations, and turnaround time (the amount of time it takes someone to complete the program and a new user to begin), this diversity cannot create a huge program. Long turnaround time would mean long lines and frustrated museum visitors.

Target Audience

Developing a program like this for the typical museum audience poses a number of challenges:

- Diversity. Museum audiences include people of all ages, backgrounds, education, and levels of interest in the subject. An exhibit has to have a little something for everyone.
- Short attention spans. Because there are so many exhibits competing for their attention, museum goers generally will not play a program for more than 2 minutes (60–90 seconds is the typical experience time). A program has about 5 seconds to capture a user, but even when cap-

tured, many leave after 30 seconds. A complex subject puts demands on the developer to present the material succinctly or to create a piece, such as *Nauticus,* that is so appealing it can lure users into longer than typical play times.

Delivery Platform and Locations

The nature of the delivery platform and location has a significant impact on what is creatively possible. A kiosk program running off a fast hard drive allows the use of video, 3-D graphics, and other features that would be difficult to deliver on media with slower access time. But because most museums are nonprofit organizations, money is often tight, and complex challenges must be met by the writer inexpensively. New museums or new wings of museums tend to be better funded than renovations of existing exhibits.

Meeting the Challenges

The program's objectives and the challenges must be met by the writer-designer's proposals, high-level design documents, and scripts. There were many revisions of the written material. Here are a few of them.

The Proposal

The initial proposal is the earliest stage of a project. Compare the proposal with the treatment that follows it and consider what changes were made before reading the analysis.

INTERACTIVE MODULE — #5,7
SHIP BUILDING:

Objective

To simulate modular ship construction at work.

Treatment

Visitors will use a stylus to draw any kind of ship on a pressure-sensitive platen. Children might sketch out a simple shape. Others can create more sophisticated designs. When the drawing is complete, the user will push a button. The ship will disappear from the platen and will then be "built" on the video screen.

To do this, the program will divide the ship drawing into modular sections (based on the platen's grid and predetermined guidelines). These modules will then be "constructed" on screen, to the accompaniment of appropriate sound effects, such as hammering, riveting, and perhaps even the shouts of work crews. When all the modular sections are complete, they will be united, forming a replica of the visitor's original design.

The video game will be, in effect, a simulation of the CAD/CAM process, whereby ships are designed on screen and then built with the aid of computers—in separate modules.

If feasible, the computers can be linked to a printer, and visitors can take home sketches of their creations.

Technique/Method

Visitor-activated platen with video monitor.

High-Level Design Document

After the initial proposal was revised several times and the basic concept refined, the high-level design document, which includes a design objective, creative treatment, and a navigation flowchart, was prepared:

1.0 Design Objective

The objective of the program is to provide museum visitors with a fun, interactive environment to explore how ships are built to accomplish specific missions. Visitors will be able to experiment by building custom ships from a variety of components. Through this experience, visitors will learn to apply the principle of "form follows function" to the process of building ships. Visitors will learn about the major design components of a ship: hull, hold, engine, and special equipment. Visitors will learn how variations in these design components affect a ship's ability to carry out a specific mission.

2.0 Creative Treatment

Attract Routine When no one is using the program, an attract routine will invite visitors to come explore the program. The attract routine will contain a brief glimpse of one of the mission introductions, picked randomly. This will be followed by a series of snapshots of components being selected, and a ship being built by the program. Text overlays will repeat continuously. Sample text: "Build a Ship to Accomplish a Mission," "Touch the Screen to Begin."

Introduction Immediately upon touching the screen during the attract routine, the visitor is greeted with a brief sequence introducing the program with audio and text. Sample text: "Pick one of the five missions; then go to the shipyard to build your own custom-designed boat. When you are done, see if your boat succeeds in accomplishing the mission." "Let's go to the briefing room to choose a mission."

Briefing Room The metaphor of a briefing room will be used to allow the visitor to select from a menu of missions, and then to review each mission. Upon selecting a mission from the menu, the visitor is briefed. Each briefing will consist of a full-screen graphic with text. A 1/4 screen video clip with a talking head keyed over stock footage will introduce the mission. Design criteria for the mission will appear on a checklist. At the conclusion of the briefing, the visitor can either select this mission or return to the mission menu.

Mission 1. North Sea Fire Fighter
The North Sea is full of gigantic oil-drilling platforms that use mile-long pipes to drain oil from under the sea floor, then store it in tanks until tankers come to take it to the mainland for processing and distribution to the general public. Sometimes these platforms catch on fire. Your job is to design a ship that will be able to put out these fires. The ship must be stable enough to remain near the platform until the fire is put out, and must have pumps powerful enough to drive large amounts of water through its hoses. It must also be able to withstand the rough seas and weather of the North Sea.

Mission 2. Alligator Census
Many years ago, the Everglades were viewed as a wasteland, home to millions of potentially disease-spreading mosquitoes. Because of such concerns, the Everglades were drained to create farmland. People now recognize that the Everglades is a beautiful, but fragile ecosystem that was greatly disrupted by the drainage and dredging projects. Many birds and other creatures died as a result. These species are believed to be making a comeback, but the only way to know for sure is to go into the Everglades by boat and count them. The ideal boat for this mission must be quiet so as not to disturb the wildlife, and it should be able to navigate shallow waters and swamp.

Mission 3. Coast Guard Drug Interdiction
Undercover police and FBI investigators routinely attempt to infiltrate suspected drug rings and break up shipments of drugs from South America and other countries. They have just ordered a ship from your shipyard that will be able to intercept shipments of drugs coming into Miami, Florida. It must have a high top speed, be able to travel at or near that speed for long distances, and be outfitted with weapons sufficient to threaten and subdue vessels operated by suspected criminals. It should also have a low profile, making it difficult to spot from a distance.

Mission 4. Trans-Pacific Freighter
Exports account for an increasingly large portion of our country's economy. Trade with the Far East is expected to double by the year 2000. Efficient freighters are needed to transport the large flow of goods to and from this important economic region. The design should be cost-efficient, have enough range to travel to Korea, Japan, Singapore, and Taiwan, and be able to carry large quantities of cargo. Speed is a secondary design consideration.

Mission 5. Arctic Ice Breaker
The "Land of the Midnight Sun" is an accurate name for the Arctic. Due to the Earth's orbit and tilt, the region experiences six straight months of darkness, followed by six straight months of light. This prolonged darkness contributes to temperatures as low as negative 70 degrees Fahrenheit, more than sufficient to freeze Hudson Bay and the rest of the Arctic Ocean. Ice breakers are needed to clear shipping channels otherwise blocked for months. You must design such an ice breaker to clear a path from Churchill, Canada, to Barrow, Alaska. It must be heavy, as indestructible as possible, and be able to remain at sea for months.

After the user selects a mission, he or she is told: "You have selected a difficult mission. Now let's go to the shipyard where you can design and build your own custom boat to accomplish the mission."

The Shipyard
Opening animation: A 3D animation sequence will give an overview of the shipyard, then zoom in to the point of view of a shipbuilder entering the gates.

After the opening animation, the visitor selects components from a series of menus. The design features for each component are summarized upon selection. After selecting each component, the partially completed boat moves along a track to the next component selection area.

Components

Hulls

Single V:
Efficient, stable, with a large amount of room for supplies, cargo, fuel, and passengers, they make an excellent choice for almost any ship. Single V-shaped hulls are by far the most common.

Double V:
Double V-shaped hulls are far less common than single V's, but they also make a good choice for ships where the main hull not being penetrated is of the utmost importance, such as oil tankers.

Single Flatbottom:
Single flatbottom hulls are used mainly for riverboats and other craft where a shallow draft is important. They are less efficient and stable than other designs, but sometimes a shallow draft is the top consideration.

Hydrofoil:
Hydrofoils are radically different than the other three designs. The boat is fitted with several projections with angled metal plates on the bottom. They lift the boat out of the water when it runs at high speed. This design works only for small boats.

Hold

Cargo:
Cargo holds are used for holding large amounts of goods while on the ship. These range from weapons to cars to food, frequently packaged in the railroad cars which transported them to the harbor.

Passengers:
Passenger space usually consists of many small rooms, of which the interior varies according to type of ship. Cruise lines commonly have rooms to rival the best hotels, where military ships often just have four hammocks.

Ballast:
Ballast is used as a stabilizer for ships with little weight in their hulls. It is usually just a room that has sea water pumped into it.

None:
Small boats infrequently have ballast, as there is not a huge need for it.

Engine

Nuclear:
Nuclear powerplants in ships work much like their electricity-generating counterparts on land. Steam is heated passing next to radioactive material, usually U-235. It is then used to push turbines connected to the propellers, giving the ship its power. The shielding around nuclear plants is very heavy, making them efficient only for large ships.

Gas:
Gas powerplants are much the same as jet engines, just on a larger scale. Their advantages are high speed and short start-up times, but they are noisy, inefficient for large ships, and require many men to run.

Diesel:
Diesel engines have many of the same characteristics as their counterparts in vans and trucks. They are efficient, low-maintenance engines with an ability to run at low revolutions per minute (RPMs). They are ideal for moving large ships at moderate to low speeds.

Steam:
Steam engines burn oil or gasoline to heat water until it is steam, and then use that to drive turbines.

Special Equipment

Weapons Mounts:
Turrets and mounts with machine guns and small cannon, from .50 caliber to 5 inches.

Cranes, Booms, and Winches:
Equipment for lifting cargo from the decks and holds of ships.

Pumps and Hoses:
Used for spraying water on burning vessels, docks, and other objects in or near the water. Water is drawn from the ocean or river that the boat is in.

Reinforced Hull:
An extra layer of reinforcements to increase hull integrity in certain areas. Useful for ships with a high potential of running into reefs and other obstacles.

Grappling Hooks:
Lines and hooks for latching on to other ships or objects while at sea.

Conclusion After the last component has been selected, a 3D animation sequence depicts the launching of the vessel. If the design is suitable for the mission, the visitor will see a depiction of the design successfully carrying out the mission. If the design is fundamentally flawed, the vessel will be shown sinking. Some evaluation will be provided as to the ability of the visitor's design to carry out the selected mission. Finally, the visitor will be given the opportunity to print out the design and evaluation.

3.0 Project Schedule

High-Level Design	completed
Research/Scripting	September 1–October 1
Detailed Design Approved	October 1
Prototyping/Initial Graphics Development	October 1– October 31
Initial Graphic Design Approved	November 1
Graphics and Program Production	November 1–December 15
Final Graphics Approved	December 15
Programming/Integration Completed	January 15
Final Delivery	February 1

4.0 Budget

High-Level Design	1 week @	$ #
Research	2 weeks @	$ #
	2 weeks @	$ #
Scripting	2 weeks @	$ #
Video	1 week @	$ #
	2 weeks @	$ #
Graphics	12 weeks @	$ #
Programming/Integration	6 weeks @	$ #

QA/Revisions	2 weeks @	$ #
Total Budget:		$ #

(Budget dollar amount deleted for this book)

Proposal and Design Document Compared

Comparing the design document's treatment to the proposal shows some striking changes in the evolution of this project. The proposal's initial idea, to have a computer "build" a ship based on a user's rough sketch, was replaced in the treatment by the more structured approach of having the viewer build a ship to achieve a specific mission based on defined ship components. Another key aspect of the treatment is that the user's design is evaluated at the end of the process, and the user is encouraged to play the game again to improve the design.

Although the initial proposal is fun, it illustrates the importance of balancing interactivity with control to teach a specific subject. The proposal provides a rough demonstration of CAD/CAM, but the more controlled approach in the treatment accomplishes much more. It allows users to utilize well-defined principles concerning hulls, engines, and other components to build a ship. The evaluation function suggested in the treatment allows users to learn from their efforts and build on them in repeat plays. With no evaluation function in the proposal, the user does not even know if his or her ship would float.

There are also some practical concerns here. It is important to give the general museum audience a positive experience. The treatment approach of assembling parts means that even a young child can piece together an impressive boat. This may not be true with the proposal approach. What will the CAD/CAM process be able to do with the rough squiggles of a seven year old? There could be a few default ships automatically rendered from unintelligible sketches, but this would not be the ship the user drew, and on repeated plays, he or she could be disappointed if the same ship was produced from different drawings.

Navigation Program/Flow

The creative treatment of the design document lays out the basic content of the production; the navigation/program flowchart defines how that content will be accessed interactively. Compare the flowcharts in Figures 7–2 and 7–3, and consider the changes that were made before reading the analysis that follows.

Changes in Navigation/Program Flow

Different flowcharts serve different functions. Some, such as that shown in Figure 7–2, lay out the possible navigation flow early in a project. Because this chart will be read by clients who may not be sophisticated in multimedia navigation, there is an advantage to keeping it as simple as possible. Detail is limited, particularly in the component section, where the multiple choices under each component are reduced to one broad category.

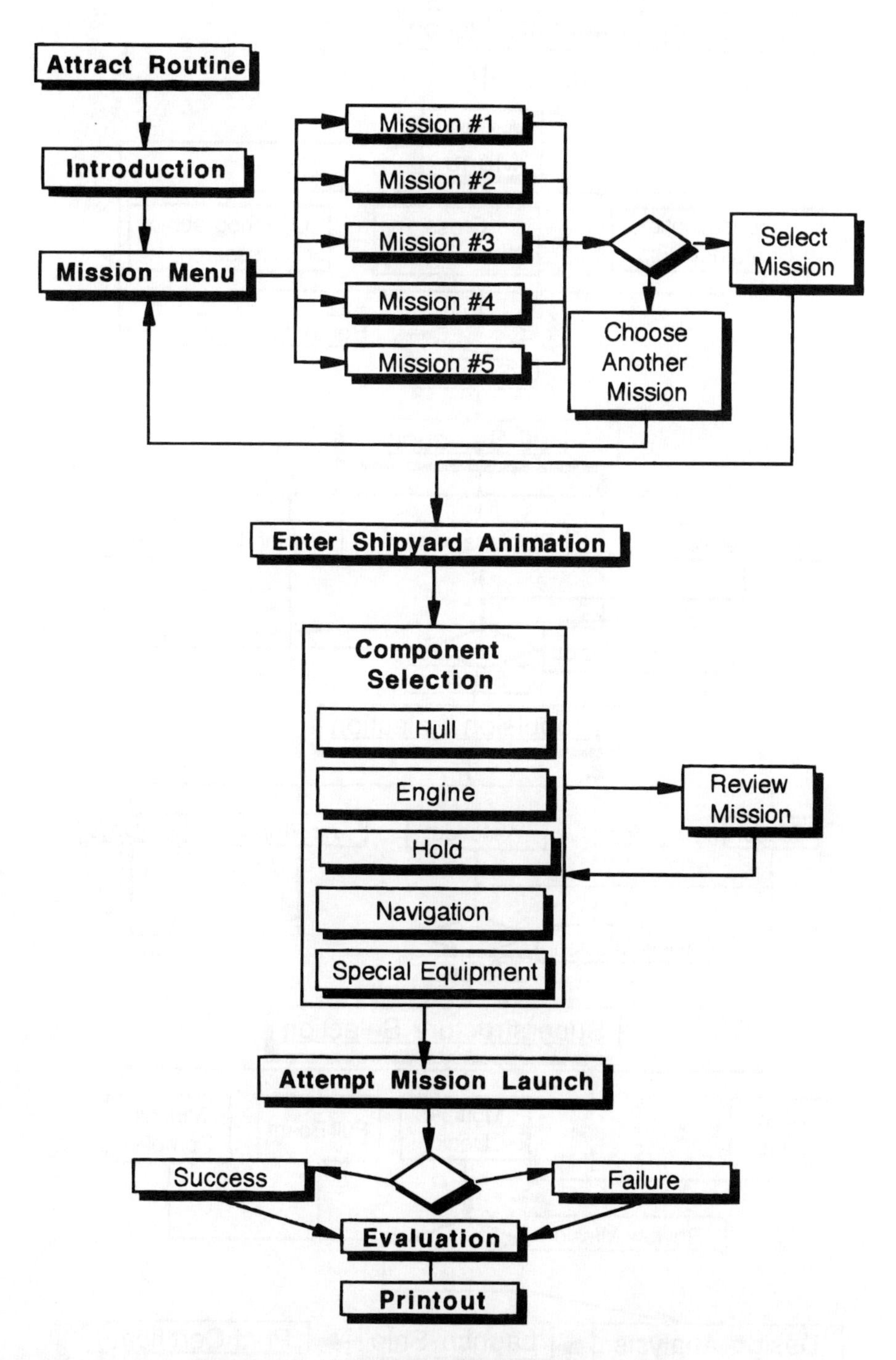

Figure 7–2 First draft navigation/program flow.

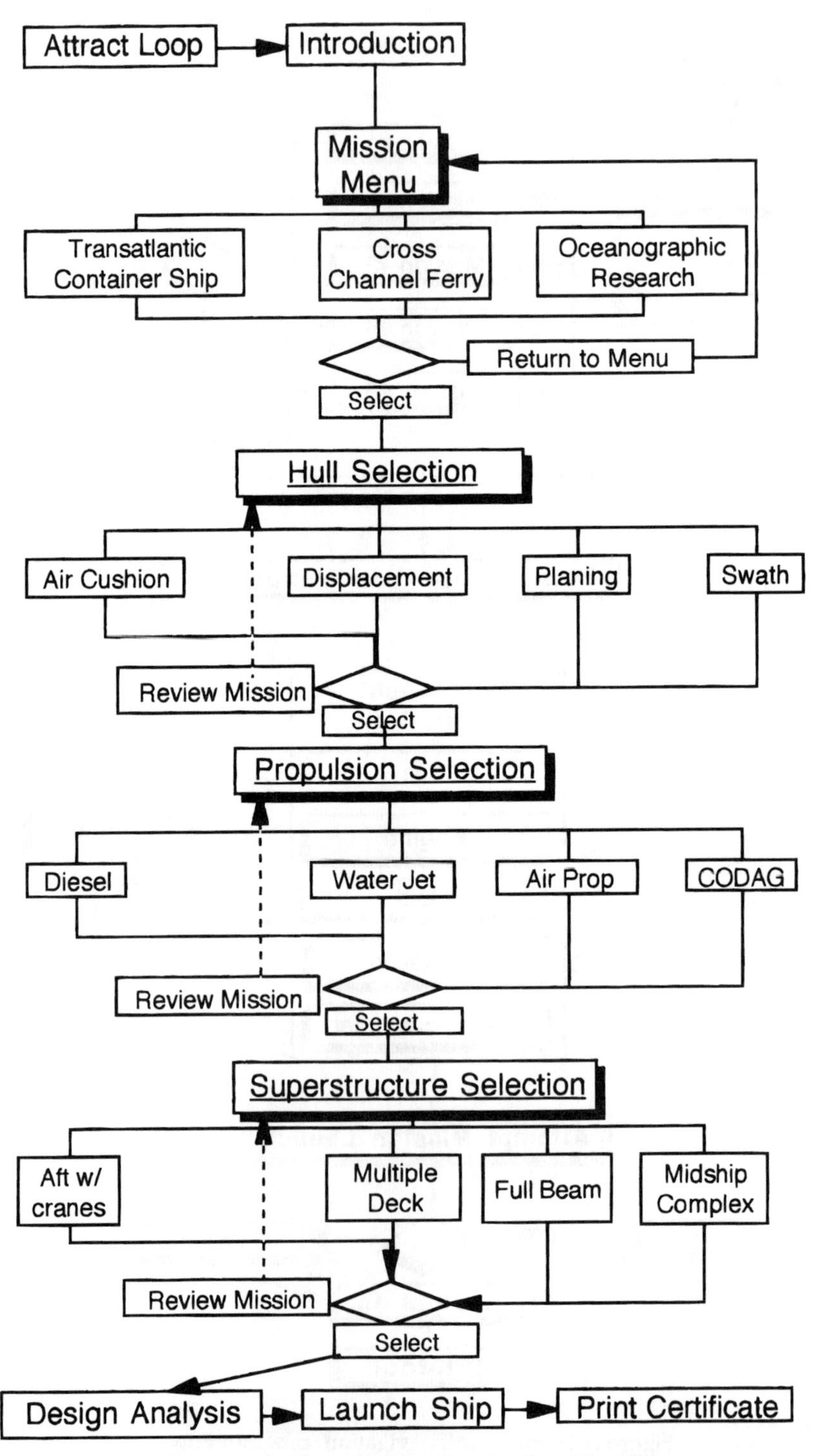

Figure 7–3 Final draft navigation/program flow.

The second chart comes when the program is more defined. At this point, it is possible to chart all the paths in the project. A chart like this is useful to a sophisticated client and can also be the basis of a planning document for the production team.

Both of these charts are designed very simply, but there are a few conventions in the second chart worth noting. The small square set on a corner suggests that this is a point where the user can make a choice. The text in main categories is underlined. The first program flow uses arrows and lines to suggest directions. Some designers also use arrows to suggest a link where the viewer has no choice, such as the Attract Routine to the Introduction. No arrows indicate a place where the viewer has multiple choices as in the Missions.

The Final Script

The script is the complete and detailed description of the program on paper. A well-written script also communicates the look and feel of the project. This is usually done with formatting and descriptive writing, but the writer of this script took a novel approach to achieve this goal. He included small illustrations of the ship components, which help present the visual experience to the viewer.

After reading the script, consider what changes were made from the design document before reading the analysis.

SCENE	**NARRATION**
ATTRACT ROUTINE	(Note: The following text banners are repeated throughout the attract routine:)
When no one is using the program, an attract routine will invite visitors to come explore the program.	1. "The Nauticus Shipbuilding Company" 2. "Urgent: Naval Architect Needed" 3. "Touch the Screen To Begin"
Attract Routine steps 1. Flyover of shipyard in 3-D 2. Cut to rotation of planing hull.	"The Nauticus Shipbuilding Company—the most highly advanced shipbuilding facility in the world." "Touch the Screen To Begin"

3. Cut to assembly area with planing hull rolling in.	"Urgent: Naval Architect Needed" "Touch the Screen to Begin"
4. Cut to launch area, showing ship launch.	

INTRODUCTION

Immediately upon touching the screen in the attract routine	Background sound of helicopter rotors
Flyover of shipyard in 3-D	
Cut to helicopter descending and landing on heliport.	"Welcome to the Nauticus Shipbuilding Company. Thanks for being our visiting naval architect on such short notice. The Nauticus Shipbuilding Company is the most highly advanced shipbuilding facility in the world. We can custom-build many different types of ships. Each ship we build is unique and is designed to efficiently meet our client's nautical mission requirements." "Let's go to our Design Center to see what ships are on order."
Cut to POV [point-of-view] animation leaving the heliport, past office building to Design Center.	Loudspeaker *VO*: "Naval architect on premises. Ready production facilities."

DESIGN CENTER

Doors of Design Center open, wipe to interview of the briefing room.	"We currently have a backlog of orders for 3 ships":

1. "a trans-Atlantic container ship which will sail out of Norfolk."
2. "a ferry that will transport passengers and cars between England and France."
3. "an oceanographic research vessel that will operate off the coast of New England."

"Touch an order to learn more about its mission and design requirements."

TRANS-ATLANTIC CONTAINER SHIP:

Map animating the route between Norfolk and several European ports

"A large shipping company has asked us to design and build a ship which can safely and economically transport large amounts of cargo between their home port, right here in Norfolk, Virginia, and several European ports. The ship:
—must be able to withstand the rough seas of the Atlantic
—have a very large cargo hold with container handling facilities
—be moderately fast
—have a long cruising range."

Dynamically build mission checklist.

Container Ship Checklist
1. Ability to withstand rough seas of Atlantic
2. Large cargo hold with container handling facilities.
3. Moderately fast
4. Long cruising range

Visitor is prompted to build the ship or review another mission.

"Press the flashing panel to build a ship for this mission or select another order."

PASSENGER AND CAR FERRY:

Map animating the route between Dover and Calais	"An English ferry operator has asked us to design and build a ship which can quickly cross the English Channel between Dover, England, and Calais, France. The ideal design: —will be very fast —have a cargo capacity for 200 passengers and 50 cars —be easy to load —be able to navigate shallow, crowded harbors."
Dynamically build mission checklist.	Ferry Requirements: 1. Very fast 2. Cargo capacity for 200 passengers and 50 cars 3. Easy to load 4. Able to navigate shallow, crowded harbors
Visitor is prompted to build the ship or review another mission.	"Press the flashing panel to build a ship for this mission or select another order."

OCEANOGRAPHIC RESEARCH VESSEL:

Show map animating area of research.	"A marine research institute requires a new flagship for its exploration of the ocean floor. The ship should: —be a safe platform for working with complex equipment —be able to withstand rough seas —have good performance at all speeds —have accommodations for extended research work at sea

Dynamically build mission checklist.

Research Ship Requirements:

1. Safe platform for working with complex equipment
2. Able to withstand rough seas
3. Good performance at all speeds
4. Accommodations for extended research work at sea

Visitor is prompted to build the ship or review another mission.

"Press the flashing panel to build a ship for this mission, or select another order."

ORDER SELECTED

After selecting an order to build, scene cuts to POV animation leaving the Design Center, past building to hull subassembly area.

"You'll need to make 3 major design decisions to build the ship, all affecting the ship's performance and ability to carry out its mission. You must choose:
—a hull shape
—a propulsion system, and
—a superstructure."

CHOOSE A HULL SHAPE

Hull subassembly area, 4 compartments are shown.

Loudspeaker VO: "Hull type being selected."

After a compartment is selected, 3-D hull appears above the subassembly area and rotates around 360 deg. in y-axis, then 360 deg. in x-axis. As hull is rotated, text describing characteristics appears on data screen.

"Touch a number to learn about a hull."

After learning about the characteristics for a particular hull, the visitor is prompted to use this hull or examine one of the others.

"Use this hull or press another number."

Air Cushion:
—flat hull rides on cushion of air
—capable of high speeds
—needs flat water conditions
—flat, rectangular deck easy to load

Planing Hull:
—V-shaped hull capable of high speeds
—performs best in flat water conditions
—high stress levels on hull

Displacement Hull
—deep, rounded hull very stable in all conditions
—very large cargo capacity
—stable platform for large propulsion systems
—needs very large propulsion system

SWATH (Small Waterplane Area Twin Hull)
—2 submerged hulls very stable
—flat deck provides good work area

After selecting a hull to use, cut to Design Assembly screen, animation of hull rollout.

Loudspeaker VO:
"Planing hull being moved into position.

Cut to POV animation moving to propulsion subassembly area.

Background sound of motors whirring and machinery clanging.

"Next, you'll need to choose a propulsion system."

PICK A PROPULSION SYSTEM

Propulsion subassembly area, 4 compartments are shown.

Loudspeaker VO: "Propulsion system being selected."

"Touch a number to learn about a propulsion system."

After a compartment is selected, 3-D propulsion system appears above the subassembly area and rotates around 360 deg. in *y*-axis. As propulsion system is rotated, text describing characteristics appears on data screen.

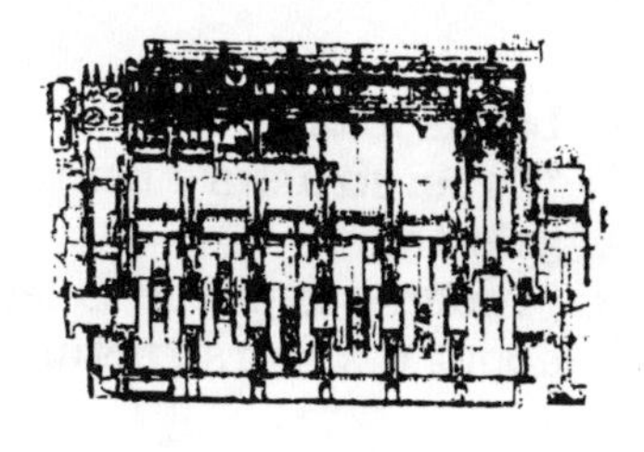

Diesel
—best performance at lower speeds
—fuel efficient
—infrequent maintenance

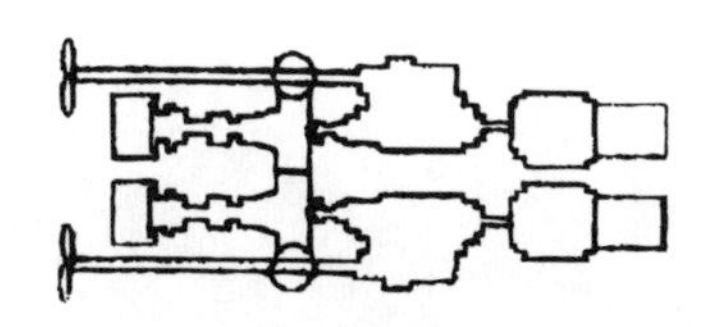

CODAG (Combination Diesel and Gas)
—good performance at all speeds
—improves maneuverability
—frequent maintenance

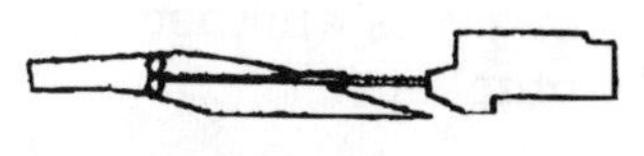

Water Jet
—low to moderate power
—high speed for right hull
—few underwater projections

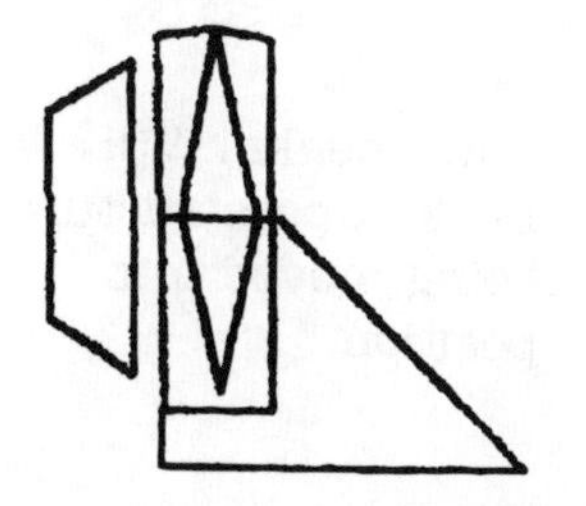

Air Prop
—low to moderate power
—high speed for right hull
—no underwater projections
—affected by bad wind conditions

After learning about the characteristics for a particular propulsion system, the visitor is prompted to use this propulsion system or examine one of the others.

"Use this propulsion system or press another number."

After selecting a propulsion system to use, cut to Design Assembly screen, animation of propulsion system being dropped into selected hull.

Loudspeaker VO: "Air Prop propulsion system being moved into position."

Cut to POV animation moving to superstructure subassembly area.

Background sound of motors whirring and machinery clanging. "Next, you'll need to choose a superstructure."

CHOOSE A SUPERSTRUCTURE

Superstructure subassembly area, 4 compartments are shown.

Loudspeaker VO: "Superstructure being selected."
"Touch a number to learn about a superstructure."

After a compartment is selected, a 3-D superstructure appears above the subassembly area and rotates around 360 deg. in *y*-axis. As superstructure is rotated, text describing characteristics appears on data screen.

After learning about the characteristics for a particular superstructure, the visitor is prompted to use this superstructure or examine one of the others.

"Use this superstructure or press another number."

After selecting a superstructure to use, cut to Design Assembly screen, animation of superstructure being lowered onto selected hull.

Loudspeaker VO: "Multiple Deck superstructure being moved into position."

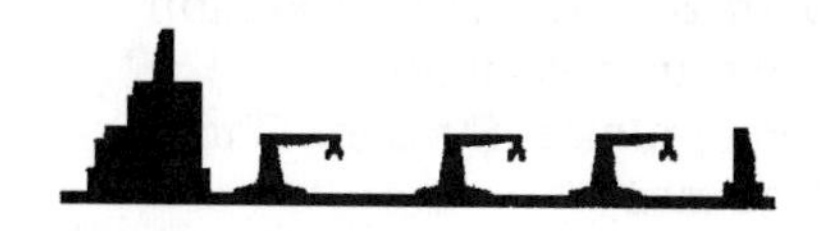

Bridge with Cranes
—shipboard crane system for container handling
—high bridge provides good visibility

Multiple Deck
—forward bridge provides excellent visibility
—sleek structure reduces wind drag

Full-Beam Bridge
—very high bridge house provides excellent visibility
—work spaces and accommodations close together

Complex Amidships
—compact and integrated work area
—good deck space fore and aft

DESIGN ANALYSIS

Animation of completed designs rotating 360 deg. in *y*-axis.

"Completed design ready for inspection and evaluation."

1 of 3 possible completed design outcomes:
"Very good! You have chosen an optimal design!"
"You have chosen a functional design."
"You have chosen a non-functional design."

Animation of hull choice rotating 360 deg. in *y*-axis.

1 of 3 possible hull outcomes:
"Hull Choice: Optimal"
"Hull Choice: Functional"
"Hull Choice: Non-functional"

followed by mission-specific feedback for chosen component (see Feedback below).

Animation of propulsion system choice rotating 360 deg. in *y*-axis.	1 of 3 possible propulsion system outcomes: "Propulsion System Choice: Optimal" "Propulsion System Choice: Functional" "Propulsion System Choice: Nonfunctional" followed by mission-specific feedback for chosen component (see Feedback below).
Animation of superstructure choice rotating 360 deg. in *y*-axis.	1 of 3 possible superstructure outcomes: "Superstructure Choice: Optimal" "Superstructure Choice: Functional" "Superstructure Choice: Nonfunctional" followed by mission-specific feedback for chosen component (see Feedback below).
User is prompted to touch graphic of champagne bottle.	"Press the champagne bottle to launch your ship."
After button press or 5 seconds, animation of completed design being launched.	"Ship being launched."
If design was optimal, user is prompted to touch graphic of certificate to receive his/her printout of Optimal Design Certificate.	"Press the button to print your Optimal Design Certificate!"

DESIGN ANALYSIS FEEDBACK

Selected Mission:
Trans-Atlantic Container Ship

Hulls:

Air Cushion	"Hull Choice: Nonfunctional —Can't withstand rough seas of Atlantic

	—Can't support heavy bridge and crane system —Cargo capacity too small"
Planing	"Hull Choice: Non-functional —Can't support heavy bridge and crane system —Cargo capacity too small"
Displacement	"Hull Choice: Optimal —Very stable in rough seas —Very large cargo capacity"
SWATH	"Hull Choice: Non-functional —Cargo capacity too small"

Propulsion System:

Diesel	"Propulsion System Choice: Optimal —Fuel efficient —Performs well at low to moderate speeds —Infrequent maintenance"
Air Prop	"Propulsion System Choice: Nonfunctional —Not powerful enough —Needs flat water conditions"
Water Jet	"Propulsion System Choice: Nonfunctional —Not powerful enough —Needs flat water conditions"
CODAG	"Propulsion System Choice: Functional —Performs well at many speeds —High maintenance —Gas turbine features not necessary"

Superstructure:

Bridge with Cranes	"Superstructure Choice: Optimal —Cranes allow easy handling of containers —High bridge provides excellent visibility"
Multiple Deck	"Superstructure Choice: Nonfunctional —No way to handle containers"
Full-Beam Bridge	"Superstructure Choice: Nonfunctional —No way to handle containers"
Complex Amidships	"Superstructure Choice: Nonfunctional —No way to handle containers"

Selected Mission:

Cross-Channel Ferry

Hulls:

Air Cushion	"Hull Choice: Optimal —Capable of high speeds —Shallow draft allows easy access to harbors —Rectangular deck perfect for loading cars"
SWATH	"Hull Choice: Non-functional —Requires large propulsion system for speed —Deck shape makes car loading difficult"
Displacement	"Hull Choice: Non-functional —Requires very large propulsion system for speed —Deep draft limits access to harbors"

Planing	"Hull Choice: Non-functional —Requires very large propulsion system for speed

Propulsion System:

Diesel	"Propulsion System Choice: Nonfunctional —Performs best at lower speeds —Hull projections increase draft"
Air Prop	"Propulsion System Choice: Functional —Needs large power plant —Affected by bad wind conditions"
Water Jet	"Propulsion System Choice: Optimal —Good for high speeds —No hull projections keep draft shallow"
CODAG	"Propulsion System Choice: Nonfunctional —Hull projections increase draft —Diesel features not necessary"

Superstructure:

Bridge with Cranes	"Superstructure Choice: Nonfunctional —Cranes not necessary for cars and passengers —Reduces deck space for cars"
Multiple Deck	"Superstructure Choice: Optimal —Multiple levels perfect for cars and passengers —Forward bridge good for high speeds"

Full-Beam Bridge	"Superstructure Choice: Nonfunctional —Can't handle lots of passengers comfortably"
Complex Amidships	"Superstructure Choice: Nonfunctional —Can't handle lots of passengers comfortably —Reduces deck space for cars

Selected Mission:
Oceanographic Research Vessel

Hulls:

Air Cushion	"Hull Choice: Non-functional —Can't withstand rough seas"
Planing	"Hull Choice: Functional —Capable of high speeds —Not very stable in rough seas —Limited work and living space"
Displacement	"Hull Choice: Functional —Stable in rough seas —Plenty of work and living space —Deep draft limits access to shore areas"
SWATH	"Hull Choice: Optimal —Very stable in rough seas —Plenty of protected work and living space —Shallower draft provides access to shore areas"

Propulsion System:

Diesel	"Propulsion System Choice: Functional —Fuel efficient —Infrequent maintenance —Performs best at low speeds"

Air Prop	"Propulsion System Choice: Nonfunctional —Not powerful enough —Needs flat water conditions —Affected by bad wind conditions"
Water Jet	"Propulsion System Choice: Nonfunctional —Not powerful enough —Needs flat water conditions"
CODAG	"Propulsion System Choice: Optimal —Good performance at all speeds —Makes hull more maneuverable"

Superstructure:

Bridge with Cranes	"Superstructure Choice: Nonfunctional —Container handling system not necessary"
Multiple Deck	"Superstructure Choice: Nonfunctional —No work space on deck"
Full-Beam Bridge	"Superstructure Choice: Nonfunctional —Too big for appropriate hull —Too far aft"
Complex Amidship	"Superstructure Choice: Optimal —Good work space on deck —Well-integrated space for labs"

Script and Design Document Treatment Compared

There were a number of substantial elements changed from the design document's creative treatment to the final script. These changes illustrate solid interactive writing principles.

Attract Routine Attract routines play when no one is using the kiosk. Clearly they are very important as bait to lure or attract the players. Without a strong attract routine, a kiosk program is ineffective because no one will play it.

Treatment: The attract routine in the treatment suggests showing one of the program's ships being built and the text: "Build a Ship to Accomplish a Mission."

Script: The script starts with a 3-D animation flyover of the shipyard and the text: "The Nauticus Shipbuilding Company—the most highly advanced shipbuilding facility in the world. Urgent: Naval Architect Needed."

The script changes give a much better introduction to the program by using the shipyard flyover, a standard cinematic establishing shot of the location. The location is extensive and impressive (see Figure 7-1). The script's text also helps build the simulation and the excitement of the program. We are now dealing with the most advanced shipbuilding company in the world. Players are also asked to assume the role of architect and become a part of the world of *The Nauticus Shipbuilding Company*, and they are needed urgently!

Briefing Room Treatment: The treatment includes a video clip of a talking head of the shipyard president keyed over stock footage to explain the mission.

Script: The script eliminates the video talking head and the footage, replacing this material with more graphic elements, such as maps showing where the ship would travel.

There are several good reasons for this change. One is that the video talking head and documentary footage in a world of 3-D animation creates a conflict in style, one of the effects of which is to point out the artificiality of the animation. By eliminating this conflict, the program has stylistic consistency, and it is raised up one level of abstraction. The user can now more easily enter this fantasy world where he or she is the only real person.

The graphic elements, such as the maps, also ground the user visually into the mission, as opposed to being told about it by the talking head. Finally, the talking head video expanded the number of elements on screen, creating clutter and confusion for the viewer.

Missions Treatment: The treatment has five missions ranging from North Sea Fire Fighter to Arctic Ice Breaker.

Script: The script has three missions: Transatlantic Container Ship, Cross-Channel Ferry, and Oceanographic Research Vessel.

The script reduces the number and changes the types of missions. Three factors motivated these changes:

1. The budget and running time of the program.
2. The particular missions that best presented a wide view of naval architecture.

3. The missions that best suited the game design. The ideal missions had to present shipbuilding problems where the answers weren't obvious but not impossible. The information had to allow clues that could be subtle.

Components Treatment: The treatment's ship components include hulls, hold, engine, and special equipment.

Script: The script's ship components include hulls, propulsion, and superstructure.

The special equipment was combined into the superstructure, and the hold was eliminated to reduce one variable in building the ship. It is important that the overall experience be as short as possible and still be effective. This has an impact on production cost and the time that the user would have to interact with the program.

Evaluation of Design The script increased the amount of evaluation of the ship design at the end of the program. The goal here was to encourage the user to go back and try the process again. This is ultimately a more successful learning approach than a one-shot deal where the user gets it right or wrong. The chance to try, fail, and redo something without penalty is an important learning feature of interactive multimedia.

CONCLUSION: RESPONSE TO THE PROJECT

The response to *The Nauticus Shipbuilding Company* has been positive in both the museum and in classroom use. It makes strong use of the simulation model and hierarchical structure to accomplish its goals of teaching a subject to a general audience in an entertaining fashion.

REFERENCE

Barney, Steven. Interview with the author, Watertown, MA, September 1995.

8

EDUCATIONAL MULTIMEDIA CASE STUDY: *SKY HIGH*

Summary

Name of production: *Sky High*
Writers: Maria O'Meara, Ruth Nadel, Ron McAdow, and Beth Chapman
Developer: D. C. Heath and Company
Subject: Space and flight
Audience: Elementary school children
Medium: CD-ROM
Presentation location: Schools
Goals: Inform, teach, entertain
Structure: Hierarchical branching, worlds, simulation

PROGRAM DESCRIPTION AND BACKGROUND

Program Description

Sky High is a CD-ROM aimed at an elementary school audience on the subject of manned flight and space exploration. Its main interface is a 360-degree panoramic landscape built along a time line from antiquity to the present. Only a portion of the landscape is visible on the screen at one time. The user accesses the hidden parts of the landscape by moving the mouse to one edge of the screen. This causes more of the landscape to appear as the viewer travels forward or backward in time.

At the bottom of the screen is a time line of dates. Above the dates are screen images and text. These hot spots can be clicked with the mouse to reveal an animation, text, video, and/or graphic on an aspect of flight during that time period. Some hot spots in a panel are grouped into explorable spaces, such as King Arthur's Castle, Leonardo DaVinci's Workshop, the Wright Brothers' House, and the Visitor's Center. Each of these spaces can be entered by clicking.

Inside these spaces are many more hot spots to click on for more information, such as a photo of the Wright Brothers, a trophy, or "books" on various aspects of flight. There are also games and quizzes in several of these spaces. The students can take notes and snap screen shots for their on-screen journal, which pops up by clicking "Your Journal" in the bottom right of the main interface. (See Figure 8–1.)

Multimedia in Schools

CD-ROMs are a major way that multimedia is used in schools. Some titles, such as *Sky High*, are produced primarily for the classroom; other programs, such as *Adi's Comprehensive Learning System*, are designed for the

Figure 8–1 Medieval and Renaissance panel of main interface with Dragon, Brother Eilmer, and King Arthur's Castle.

school and the home; and consumer edutainment titles, such as *Sim-City* and *Carmen Sandiego*, are also popular with educators. For larger groups, multimedia is often presented with a computer projection system that allows teachers to instruct an entire class in a fashion far superior to "chalk talk."

There are also numerous World Wide Web sites geared for children and elementary school teachers. The Learning Resource Server at the University of Illinois provides links to a number of useful sites, as does The Global SchoolNet Foundation. Another useful spot is the Busy Teacher's WebSite, which features a collection of resources for teachers presented in alphabetical order. (Links to these sites are listed under this chapter on the CD-ROM.)

Production Background

Sky High was developed by the Educational Technologies Department at D. C. Heath and Company, a major publisher of textbooks for the primary grades through college. *Sky High* is part of the Discoveries Series of CD-ROMs that also includes *In the Desert, Into the Forest,* and *The Nature Connection.*

The *Discoveries* project was developed as part of *Heath Literacy,* D. C. Heath's theme-based elementary reading program. The goal of the project was to support the idea that literacy is more than the ability to read. It is the ability to connect ideas that come through a variety of media—sounds and visuals, as well as text. In addition, the feeling was that children should be in charge of their learning as much as possible, making choices about what to study in greater depth.

Students can explore the *Discoveries* CD-ROMs independently or use them to support work on projects involving collaboration and communication with others. Each CD in the series reflects one theme covered in the literacy program. *Sky High* is connected to a third-grade theme of space and flight. The plan was that the CDs could be sold and used with Heath literacy or sold separately and used alone or with other subject areas and in a wider range of grades than the original target market. (Astudillo) The project manager on the series was Deborah Astudillo, and the director of educational technologies was Roland Ochsenbein. The writers were Maria O'Meara, Ruth Nadel, Ron McAdow, and Beth Chapman.

CHALLENGES IN WRITING AND DEVELOPING *SKY HIGH*

The key challenges writing and developing *Sky High* were these:

- Organizing and making accessible a large database of loosely related material.

- Reaching a broad elementary school audience.
- Writing to archival material versus creating the content.

Organizing a Large Database of Loosely Related Material

Unlike the previous case study *The Nauticus Shipbuilding Company,* which was tightly focused, *Sky High* covers a wide subject area: manned flight and space exploration. Whereas *Nauticus* is designed to be played in a few minutes, *Sky High* contains hours of material on the subject that can be browsed or searched in the books of the virtual library. This vast amount of material could potentially cause organizational problems for the development team and access problems for the user, who could get lost in such a large database of material.

Script Format

In a project of this magnitude, the writers and other team members need to use various tools to keep material organized. The script format itself is important. This project used tables in Microsoft Word to separate and label the different types of material.

Sky High's media (text, graphics, video, etc.) are accessed by clicking hot spots, which are grouped on the monitor screen according to a time frame called a panel, such as "Panel IV—Early Aviation." The hot spots in a panel can be further grouped into a location that can be clicked on and entered, such as the Wright Brothers' House.

In the script, the location of the media is first introduced in standard screenplay fashion in single-column format. Then the individual hot spots and their media in that location are explained in a three-column coded format. (The following three-column example does not follow immediately after the description in the script.)

PANEL IV—EARLY AVIATION

IV A. Wright Brothers Close Up

A Victorian style house on the panorama opens to a Wright brothers close up. Note bike leaning on fence outside. This is a nice touch.

Once inside, Katherine, the Wright brothers' sister, narrates. The walls are covered with wallpaper. There are ferns on plant stands, and other Victorian doodads. Photos on the walls and in frames standing on the tables highlight family members, the Wrights as children and adults, and a shot of the bike shop.

VISUAL	NARR/SYNC	MUSIC/SFX
Animation **[BUZZ.QT.ANM]** ANIMATED BUZZARDS Lace curtains in window, clicking on window activates buzzards outside to circle. [1.2]	**Narration** **[BUZZ.QT.NARR]** KATH NARR Wilbur and Orville studied soaring buzzards and observed how they turned by moving their wings.	**Music** **[BUZZ.QT.SFX]** SFX MUSIC Music, subtle underscoring LIBRARY LINK 01.3 HOW THINGS FLY—GLIDING

The first column lists the clickable hot spot. It is written in caps and separated from the other material by a double space. In this case, the hot spot that can be clicked is an animation of buzzards outside the window of the house.

The buzzard hot spot gets its own code name: BUZZ.QT.ANM. The first word identifies the buzzard image; QT stands for Quick Time, the digital video format used to present the animation; and ANM means it is an animation as opposed to a STL (still picture) or VID (video). The number at the bottom (1.2) indicates that it has a link to Book 1, topic 2 in the Visitor's Center library. The viewer can click on this library link and get more information about gliding.

The second column follows a similar coding procedure, letting us know that this is connected to the BUZZ image and that this is voice-over narration (NARR) as opposed to synchronized sound (SYNC). Synchronized sound usually refers to a sound that appears to be produced by the image on screen, such as a person talking on camera. The next line also lets us know that KATH (Katherine Wright) is the narrator.

The code at the top of the third column labels MUSIC or SFX (sound effects), any sound other than music or speech. This column also clearly defines the link for more information, which in this case is to the "book" in the on-screen "library" titled HOW THINGS FLY. The specific section is GLIDING.

Organizing the Screen Format for Cards and Book Pages: Technical Limits on the Writer

Each animation in the panorama calls up a card with more information in the form of a video and text, which links to a library "book." The large amount of material in this project necessitated the use of four standard screen formats for these cards:

Format 1: Picture or video on top of the page, with title and text below.
Format 2: Picture or video on top of the page with text below.
Format 3: Text.
Format 4: Text at the top and still picture at bottom.

These standard formats facilitated production because the graphic designers and programmers did not have to design a new screen for every page. The consistency of screen interface also helped the viewer access the material. The viewer could quickly learn that each page had its own rules—for example, no hot spots on all-text screens and hot spots in certain places on other screens.

Format 1 always had to be first in a sequence because it carries the title panel. The other formats could follow in any order.

These formats created a restriction for the writers, who had to write to one of the specific formats and be sure to flag in the script which format was being used. The writers were limited to the specific number of lines available on each card. This meant writing in journalistic, inverted-pyramid style, with the least important information at the bottom so that it could be trimmed if necessary.

Another limitation on the writer was text that was bitmapped and displayed as an image. This allowed more control over the text's visualization, but as the following example shows, the writers had to write the text in the correct font size and the exact number of lines. This also helped to flag the text as artwork for the production team.

Text	**Narration**
[CD.TXT.SPUT]	**[CD.SPUT.NARR]**
When the Russians sent Sputnik into orbit, it was the first time humans had ever sent anything into outer space. People around the world were surprised. They thought that America would do it first.	When the Russians sent Sputnik into orbit, it was the first time humans had ever sent anything into outer space. People around the world were surprised. They thought that America would do it first.

Information Card Text (F1) **[CD.ART.SPUT]:**

When the Russians sent

Sputnik into orbit, it was the

first time humans had ever

sent anything into outer

space. People around the world were surprised. They thought that America would do it first.

Making the Database Accessible to Users

Once the writing process was organized, ways had to be found to make this large database of loosely related material accessible to users. This was accomplished through focusing the scope of the project, using concept maps, and moving beyond click and read in a number of ways, including simulations, games, and explorable spaces.

Focusing the Scope of the Project

The project was made more accessible to users by focusing the content and limiting the technical complexity of the program. Originally the series was going to hook into the Internet. It was also going to include the capacity for drawing and recording voice. Eventually all of these approaches were abandoned as too elaborate and expensive. Instead, it was decided to concentrate on presenting content in the most engaging way possible.

The next decision was to narrow the very broad topics of flight and space to flight firsts: the first person to fly a plane, the first person to fly across the Atlantic, the first man on the moon, and so on. The treatment of space focused on a visit to each planet and a history of its discovery and exploration.

Organizing with a Concept Map

Concept maps are a way to organize the material in a database according to a visual image or map. The museum or journey approaches are fairly common. The basic interface of *Sky High,* which tracks the development of flight from antiquity to the present, is a time-journey concept map.

A danger with concept maps is combining incompatible maps. For example, in *Sky High,* one of the original ideas was to be able to pan up from the earthbound time line to see the stars and planets in the sky. This idea had to be abandoned because the panorama journey is time-based, and the stars and planets would have been space-based. The problem would have been ensuring that the right element in the sky was in the right place in relationship to the time line. For example, if a user was in the 1960s time frame and studying the moon landing, he or she should be able to pan up to the sky and see the moon. But when the user is in 1903 and looking at the Georges Méliès film *A Trip to the Moon,* he or she should also be able to pan up to the sky and see the moon. But the moon can't be in two places: above 1903 and 1969.

Because of this conflict as well as technical limitations, the sky spatial concept map was dropped from the main panorama interface and instead included as a planetarium in the Visitor's Center, an explorable building on the map that can be clicked on and entered.

Organizing the Material With Explorable Spaces

The Visitor's Center or planetarium is just one example of an explorable space in this program. An explorable space uses the world's structure. The interface for this structure is a space that the user can enter and explore, such as a room, a house, or even an entire world. Information related to that space can be accessed by clicking on hot spots, such as photographs on the wall, trophies on a table, or books on a shelf.

Some of the explorable spaces in this project include King Arthur's Castle, which contains medieval flight information; Leonardo DaVinci's Workshop, which contains his drawings and writings; the Wright Brothers' House, which has material about their contribution to flight; and the Visitor's Center, which includes a library, observatory, and trivia games. The Visitor's Center can be entered at any time through its image, which is always located at the edge of the screen between the present and the past or through its menu bar icon.

Following is a portion of the Wright Brothers' House sequence, a good example of an explorable space. Note the effort to make the media as engaging as possible, such as camera movements and zooms on still pictures, highlighting parts of a plane as the parts are mentioned in the narration, and including entertaining animations, such as the doodly drawing of a kite. Within this "house" the information is also organized into a subcategory with a scrapbook metaphor that can be viewed like a real book.

Wright Brothers' House Sequence

IV A. Wright Brothers Close Up

A Victorian-style house on the panorama opens to a close-up of a room. Note bike leaning on fence outside. This is a nice touch.

Once inside, Katherine narrates. The walls are covered with wallpaper. There are ferns on plant stands, and other Victorian doodads. Photos on the walls and in frames standing on the tables highlight family members, the Wrights as children and adults, and a shot of the bike shop. (Samples from the room sequence follow.)

VISUAL	**NARR/SYNC**	**MUSIC/SFX**
Video **[BIKE.QT.VID]** IV A. WALL PHOTO #6 VIDEO-EXT. SHOT OF BIKE SHOP Zoom into front door, slowly dissolve to inside (p. 12) INT. BIKE SHOP Wilbur working. Still from Wright Collection	Narration **[BIKE.QT.NARR]** KATH NARR Back then bikes were all the rage. Wilbur and Orville started out riding bikes, and then repairing them. . . Soon they were making bikes and selling them.	SFX **[BIKE.QT.SFX]** Machine noise in shop grows louder as we enter. MUSIC SFX, exterior birds, wind
Still **[GRAD.QT.STL]** IV A. WALL PHOTO #7 KATHERINE graduation still from Wright Collection	Narration **[GRAD.QT.NARR]** KATH NARR There I am, Katherine Wright. In this picture, I was graduating from Oberlin College. I was the only child in the family who went to college. Orville was so wrapped up in his printing business, he never went. Wilbur stayed home to care for Mama, when she was dying of tuberculosis. After Mama died, I came home and took care of the family.	Music? **[GRAD.QT.SFX]**
Animation **[BUZZ.QT.ANM]** ANIMATED BUZZARDS Lace curtains in window, clicking window activates buzzards outside to circle [1.3]	Narration **[BUZZ.QT.NARR]** KATH NARR Wilbur and Orville studied soaring buzzards and observed how they turned by moving their wings.	MUSIC? **[BUZZ.QT.SFX]** SFX MUSIC Music, subtle underscoring LIBRARY LINK 01.3 HOW THINGS FLY-SOARING

(table continues)

VISUAL	NARR/SYNC	MUSIC/SFX
Animation **[TOYH.QT.ANM]** IV A. TOY HELICOPTER spins when activated	Narration **[TOYH.QT.NARR]** KATH NARR That's a toy helicopter Orville made after he and Wilbur wore out the toy one Papa had given them.	SFX **[TOYH.QT.SFX]** Rubber band helicopter sound

Photo Album on Coffee Table

A photo album lies on a coffee table. Clicking opens it. Each page has a voice-over which is activated when clicked. Katherine's voice-over narrates a brief history of her brothers' yearly trips to Kitty Hawk. Viewer may page backwards or forwards. STILLS, Wright Collection.

PAGE 5 & 6 (of photo album).

VISUAL	NARR/SYNC	MUSIC/SFX
Art **[ALBM.QT.ART]** (combine pp. 44 and 126 "See Them Flying")	Narration **[ALBM.QT.NARR]** Orville and Wilbur decided that a flying machine would need three things.	SFX **[ALBM.QT.SFX]** SFX air, whoosh
ART Basic diagram of a flying machine, with words "wings," "engine," "rudder" written next to appropriate piece	Wings, to lift it into the air—an engine to move it through the air—	SFX 12 hp engine
HIGHLIGHT the wings HIGHLIGHT engine HIGHLIGHT rudder	and a rudder to steer it.	SFX turning rudder, creak noise

PAGE 7, (L) SKETCH/KITE.

VISUAL	NARR/SYNC	MUSIC/SFX
Art **[ALBM.QT.ART]** SKETCH Drawing of kite, biplane with 5 ft. wingspan, show	Narration **[ALBM.QT.NARR]** To test their theories, my brothers built a	SFX **[ALBM.QT.SFX]** SFX Wind, laughter, children's voices

VISUAL	NARR/SYNC	MUSIC/SFX
in proportion to a brother, doodly style, make sure to put cap & bow tie on him. Maybe have doodle with two brothers flying it, kids watching?	huge kite. Every child in the neighborhood showed up to watch them fly it! Delighted at their ability to control the kite, Wilbur and Orville set to work immediately on a glider big enough to carry a person.	

Organizing the Material with a Book Metaphor

The last part of the above example uses a photo album as a way to organize the material. Books are a handy metaphor to organize information. *Sky High* uses this metaphor again in the library of the Visitor's Center with books on a variety of topics. To read a "book," the user clicks on the book, and it comes off the shelf; more clicking turns the pages. Following is a page from the library's working table of contents to show how the material is organized and labeled. To sample the contents of one of the books, read the shuttle example at the end of this chapter.

SKY HIGH Labeled Library Table of Contents

[BK.HOW] How Things Fly
[FLAP] Flapping (QT)
[GLID] Gliding (QT)
[HOVR] Hovering (QT)
[JPRO] Jet Propulsion (ANIMATION)
[BK.MOON] The Moon
[ORBT] Orbit—ANIMATION
[PHAZ] Phases—ANIMATION (Day, Month)
[ECLP] Eclipses—ANIMATION
[BK.WHY] The Book of Why about the Sky
[RAIN] What Makes Clouds? (ANIMATION)
[THUN] Why Is There Thunder and Lightning? (ANIMATION)
[RBOW] Why Are There Rainbows? (ANIMATION)
[BK.FFLY] Famous Fliers
[WBRO] The Wright Brothers (QT)
[LIND] Charles Lindbergh (QT)
[EAR] Amelia Earhart (QT)
[BESS] Famous Person (QT)

[BK.GAZE]	Stargazers
[ANGZ]	Ancient Stargazers (STOCK/QT)
[COP]	Copernicus (STOCK/QT)
[GAP]	Celia Gaposhkin (STOCK/QT)
[NOVA]	Stephen Hawking (STOCK/QT)

Simulation as a Way to Present Material

Most of the above approaches simply organize the material into categories that can be explored in an interesting way through a concept map or a book. There are other ways to present material, however, that are more interactive. Perhaps the most engaging is the simulation approach, which was demonstrated in depth for *The Nauticus Shipbuilding Company*. A simulation structure, however, does not have to be used for an entire piece. As in the next example, it can also be used as part of a larger piece that follows another structure.

"Ye Olde Gravity Lab" is a simulation that can be played by clicking on a castle and entering King Arthur's Court. Ye Olde Gravity Lab is meant to teach principles of gravity by showing what would happen if you catapulted various sizes of balls at a bull's-eye while on different planets or the Earth's moon. Following is the scripted content of the Court followed by a description of the "Ye Olde Gravity Lab" simulation.

PANEL II: MEDIEVAL AND RENAISSANCE TIMES

CLOSE-UP: King Arthur's Court—600 A.D.

Click on the castle and go inside!

VISUAL	**NARR/SYNC**	**MUSIC/SFX**
Animation **[PHAZ.QT.ANM]** Castle—On the wall, an ancient looking calendar with moving phases of the moon	Narration **[PHAZ.QT.NARR]**	SFX **[PHAZ.QT.SFX]** [BK 2.2]
VISUAL	**NARR/SYNC**	**MUSIC/SFX**
Video **[ECLP.QT.VID]** CASTLE VIDEO— Méliès FOOTAGE, from "The Astronomer's Dream" will probably need to be speeded up a little (ARCHIVE FILMS)	Narration **[ECLP.QT.NARR]**	Music **[ECLP.QT.MUS]** Music [BK 02.3]

VISUAL	**NARR/SYNC**	**MUSIC/SFX**
Animation **[CATP.QT.ANM]** Castle—Ye Olde Gravity Lab—enter lab and play animated game catapulting different balls. Take catapult to the moon, Mars, and Jupiter to see differences.	Narration **[CATP.QT.NARR]**	Music **[CATP.QT.MUS]**

Ye Olde Gravity Laboratory

When you click on the castle in the panorama, you see a close-up of a wall inside the castle. There are three hot spots on this wall, leading to a moon, an eclipse, and to Ye Olde Gravity Lab. If you click on the catapult, you enter the laboratory.

The laboratory fills the screen except for the Discoveries control bar on the bottom. The initial laboratory screen contains the following elements:

- Catapult—base with hinge, arm with basket for ball, and compression spring to power the "throw." The base and hinge can be part of the background art, but the arm + basket + spring is separate artwork. In order to do the animation with the arm + basket we need five different positions between the starting position and the ending position. There is a release mechanism, such as a string that you "pull" to fire the catapult.
- Target supported by post or tripod.
- Balls (with labels): ping-pong, golf, baseball, and bowling. Each ball is a separate piece of artwork, and each has a labeled resting place that is part of the background art.
- A control panel with radio buttons for four places: Jupiter, Earth, Mercury, Earth's Moon, and an Exit Lab button. These buttons can be painted into the background art BUT there must be an alternate version of each gravity button that is highlighted (radio button on).
- Prompter's booth. The guy who changes the place backgrounds is in this booth. Although you don't see him do it, he also grabs thrown balls as they roll in front of him.

- An Exit Lab button.
- A curtain or other wall covering that appears to be behind the control panel. On the curtain is an instructions box:

  Ye Olde Gravity Lab Welcomes

  You
  Click to Choose a Place

  When you click a place button, a voice says:
  "So, you want Jupiter."
  "Okay, here's Earth."
  "All right, you get Mercury."
  "Here's the moon."
  A hand reaches from the prompter's booth to the top of the screen and pulls down a backdrop representing the place requested.
- Jupiter sign: "Jupiter. Twice the gravity of Earth."
- Earth sign: "Earth."
- Mercury sign: "Mercury. One-third the gravity of Earth."
- Moon sign: "Moon. One-sixth the gravity of Earth."

SFX: "WHAPWHAPWHAPT" as backdrop unrolls.

The instructions box says: "Drag a ball to the end of the catapult." When the catapult is loaded, the instructions box says: "To fire the catapult, pull the string."

There are seventeen different throwing possibilities, one for each combination of ball and gravity, plus one for an unloaded catapult. If the ball flies over the target, you hear a SFX "WHOOSH." If it hits the target but misses the bull's-eye, you hear SFX "THUMP," then as it bounces on the floor you hear SFX "BOUNCE." If it hits the bull you hear a loud bell. If the bowling ball goes directly to the floor you hear SFX "CRASH." If the catapult is fired without being loaded, you hear SFX "THWANGGGGG."

After a throw, there is a two second delay; then the program resets. The place does not change, but the balls return to their starting points and the catapult is drawn back into ready position (SFX "SPRING COMPRESS"). The directions box says "Load the catapult or change the place."

At any time you can click a different place. A hand from the prompter's booth pushes up the old background (SFX "WHIROOP"), then pulls down the new one while you hear its narration. The instructions box returns to "Drag a ball to the end of the catapult." You can change the gravity or exit at any time. Clicking the Exit Lab button takes you back to the close-up through which you entered. As you exit, the guy sticks his head out of the prompter's booth and looks at you.

If you click on the prompter's booth, the "guy" peers around at you and says "Huh."

Quizzes as a Way to Present Material

Another way to present material is through quizzes, as in the next example. Notice that there is feedback for every answer and amusing sound effects aimed at this young audience.

Question 14 [CD.QZ.CSNA 1—BG.PAN]

VISUAL	**NARR/SYNC**	**MUSIC/SFX**
Question 14 **[CD.QZ.CSNA.1]** Charles Lindbergh named his plane The Spirit of. . . . St. Louis. Ammonia. New York.	Narration **[CSNA.1.Q.NARR]** Charles Lindbergh named his plane The Spirit of. . . . St. Louis. Ammonia. New York.	
Answer **[CSNA.1.A]** St. Louis		SFX **[CSNA.1.Q.SFX]** Right answer SFX
Distracter 1 **[CSNA.1.D1]** ammonia.	Narration **[CSNA.1.D1.NARR]**	SFX **[CSNA.1.D2.SFX]** Whew! No!
Distracter 2 **[CSNA.1.D2]** New York.	Narration **[CSNA.1.D1.NARR]**	SFX **[CSNA.1.D2.SFX]** loud honking car

Matching Games as a Way to Present Material

Matching games, which use images that viewers can move with the mouse, are another way to get the user to interact with the material. *Sky High* used two basic types of matching games:

- Put things in the right sequence—for example, place planets in order, starting from the closest to the sun (see Figure 8–2).
- Place in the proper group—for example, choose all elements that fly straight up, such as a hummingbird, helicopter, and hot air balloon, or drag planets that have moons into the boxes.

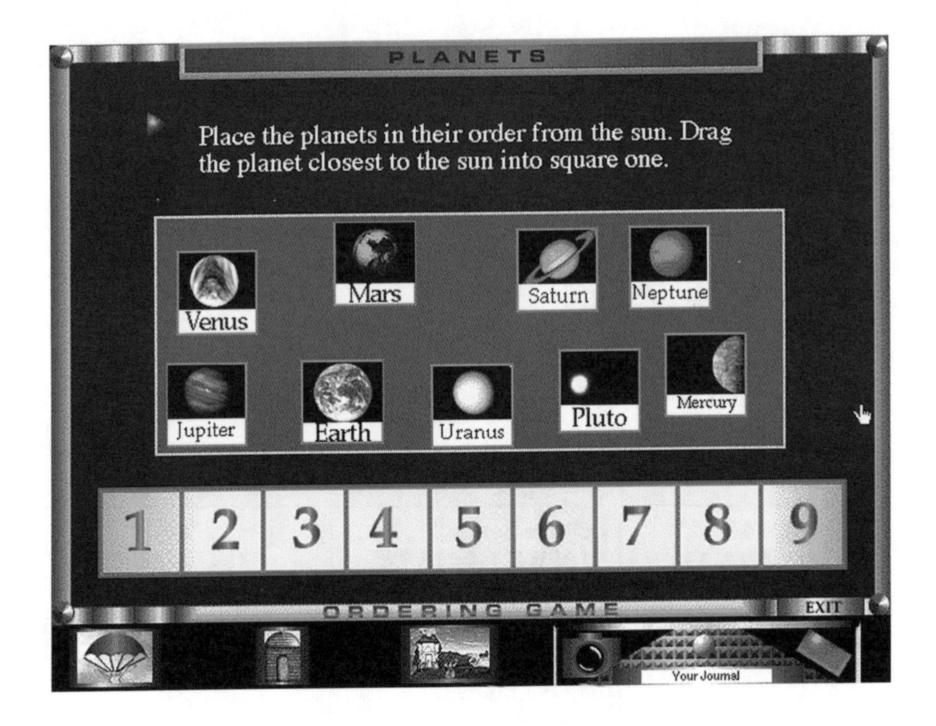

Figure 8–2 Ordering game.

Reaching a Broad Primary School Audience

In addition to the key challenge of *Sky High*, which was organizing and making accessible a large database of material, the writers also had to maximize the program's use by making the material appealing to a broad primary school audience.

This was done by:

- Using the many media in this program to make the basic information comprehensible to a wide age group
- Including entertaining elements
- Expanding the basic subject material to make the program multidisciplinary

Using the Many Media in This Program to Make the Basic Information Comprehensible to a Wide Age Group

Although the *Sky High* CD was aimed primarily at third graders, multimedia can appeal to a wide audience, because the same information can be communicated in multiple ways and can be replayed by the user. This feature helps both younger children and students with disabilities. For example, on this CD, students have the option of having text read out loud. They can take notes and snap screen shots for their on-screen journal for later review and questions for the teacher. In general, the images also provide a context to understand information. Because of this multimodal communication, the finished CD-ROM has a wide appeal, ranging from grades 1 through 8.

Presenting information in an entertaining way or simply choosing entertaining material is also important with a school-age audience. This can be done in a number of ways—for example:

- Feedback: There's a trivia game in the Visitor's Center in which the user's correct answers are rewarded with different animations of a flying stunt, such as a barnstormer on the wings of a biplane.
- Text and audio quotes: It's important to keep an eye out for quotations that might especially appeal to children. This vivid description of life at Kitty Hawk by Orville Wright has gotten chuckles in the classroom:

VISUAL **(Super Quote Still)**	**NARR/SYNC**	**MUSIC/SFX**
TEXT **[CSNA.QT.VID]** There was no escape [from the mosquitos.] The sand and grass and trees and hills and everything was fairly covered with them. They chewed us clear through our underwear and socks. Lumps began swelling up all over my body like hen's eggs. Your brother, Orville	**NARR TEXT** **ORVILLE** There was no escape [from the mosquitos.] The sand and grass and trees and hills and everything was fairly covered with them. They chewed us clear through our underwear and socks. Lumps began swelling up all over my body like hen's eggs. Your brother, Orville	**SFX** Buzzing mosquitos

- Audio. The buzz of mosquitoes sound effect in the above script sample is an example of how audio can be used to liven information.
- Pop culture material. Using material from pop culture can also be effective. For example, a Flash Gordon video illustrates some early ideas about vertical flight, and a clip from the TV series *Lost in Space* portrays visions of space travel.

Expanding the Basic Subject Material to Make the Program Multidisciplinary

The audience for this program was broadened by expanding the subject matter beyond pure science issues concerning flight. An example is the inclusion of the story of Bessie Coleman, the first black person to earn a pilot's license. Because of racism, no one in the United States would teach her how to fly. There was, however, less prejudice in France, so she learned French, got her pilot's license, and later returned to the United States and started her own air shows.

Important popular culture material was also included, such as *A Trip to the Moon*, by Georges Méliès. This is a significant work in film history and the first movie about a trip to the moon. It was made the same year the Wright brothers made their flight. General historical context is also available to the *Sky High* user. Clicking on the date on the bottom of the time line reveals a description of other events happening at that time.

Writing to Archival Material versus Creating the Content

Writing a broad database project, such as this one, means using primarily archival material to present information. Writers can approach this challenge by acquainting themselves with existing archival material and then developing their concepts based on this information, or they can form a general concept of what they want to say, then find (or have a researcher find) the photo, video, quotation, or other element that will best present their idea.

In either case, writers are always adjusting their original conceptions to the archival material that is available. It is important for writers not to become too rigid about their original ideas because sometimes they must abandon them when available media supports a totally different approach.

Below are the first and second drafts of the Space Shuttle section from the "book" in *Sky High's* Visitor's Center titled *Space Firsts*. The original concept in the first draft was to present a serious piece about repairing the Hubble telescope. Unfortunately, the footage received from NASA was about the shuttle crew eating breakfast! The sequence had to be completely rewritten to accommodate the new footage. See what you think of the results.

SPACE SHUTTLE: First Draft

VISUAL	NARR/SYNC	MUSIC/SFX
VIDEO **[CSNA.QT.VID]** NASA, shots of space shuttle #1 TAKE OFF #2 Hubble being repaired	**NARR VIDEO** **[CSNA.QT.NARR]** The crew of this space shuttle went up to repair the Hubble, a powerful space telescope. The crew worked hard to fix the Hubble.	SFX take off

VISUAL	NARR/SYNC	MUSIC/SFX
#3 Hubble being repaired	Many people watched them on TV.	Mix in wild sound of astronauts & ground control
#4 Crew leaving Hubble	Now the Hubble can bring us pictures and information about the stars so we can learn more about how our universe was formed. The shuttle comes back ready to go on another mission.	
#5 Shuttle landing		SFX shuttle landing

SPACE SHUTTLE: Second Draft

VISUAL	NARR/SYNC	MUSIC/SFX
VIDEO **[SHOT.QT.VID]** #1 SPACE SHUTTLE TAKE OFF	**NARR VIDEO** **[SHUT.QT.NARR]** A day in the life of a space shuttle crew member is a lot like yours.	**MUSIC** Skater's Waltz
#2 Floating astronaut putting on pants. #3 Banana spins into mouth #4 POV floating thru tunnel	You get up in the morning . . . get dressed . . . have a little breakfast . . . and find your way to school or work.	
#5 3 astronauts stacked up doing push ups, then flying toward camera #6 ECU hand holding candy, then letting go. #7 Wide shot, woman eating M & M's that are floating in air	Now you're ready to get down to business. Time for some exercise! Feeling a little hungry? Then it's time for a snack . . .	

(table continues)

VISUAL	NARR/SYNC	MUSIC/SFX
VIDEO **[SHUT.QT.VID]** #8 EXT. Astronauts working outside shuttle, floating in space. #9 INT. Astronauts in bunk area, writing, notebooks floating all over. #10 ECU red globs breaking apart.	NARR Now for some outdoor activities . . . Of course, everyone has homework to do . . . and some experiments to finish.	**MUSIC** Skater's Waltz
#11 Long shot of earth in distance. #12 Astronauts asleep in bunk, arms floating around. #13 EXT. Shuttle going thru space.	Then it's time to kick back and just watch the world go by. It's been a long day. Time to get some rest. Goodnight.	

CONCLUSION: RESPONSE TO THE PROJECT

The project was very popular in its testing stage in the classroom. In some cases, it was hard to tear students away to give a classmate a chance to play—testament to the skillful way this development team took a large body of loosely related information and fashioned it into an informative and engaging multimedia program.

REFERENCES

Astudillo, Deborah. Interview with the author, Lexington, MA, November 1995.
James, W. R. "Multimedia Goes to School." *Digital Video*, V3 (November 1995).
McAdow, Ron. Fax to the author, November 3, 1995.
O'Meara, Maria. Interviews with the author, Brookline, MA, November 1995.

9

TRAINING CASE STUDY: *VITAL SIGNS*

Summary

Name of production: *Clinical Support Staff Interactive Certification Program: Vital Signs*
Writers: Instructional designer, John Cosner; writer, Fred Bauer
Developer: MediaViz Productions
Audience: Trainee medical assistants at a health maintenance organization
Medium: Interactive video disc
Presentation location: Work
Subject: The process of taking medical vital signs: temperature, pulse, respiration, and blood pressure
Goals: Teach
Structures: Linear, hierarchical branching, simulations

PROGRAM DESCRIPTION AND BACKGROUND

Clinical Support Staff Interactive Certification Program: Vital Signs is a training program designed to teach trainee medical assistants at Harvard Community Health Plan (HCHP), a Boston-based health maintenance organization, how to take vital signs—temperature, pulse, respiration, blood pressure—and (for the OB/GYN assistants) urine analysis. Figure 9–1 shows the program's interface. It has the main image area in the center frame, text to the right, and buttons on top of the page that take the student to each sec-

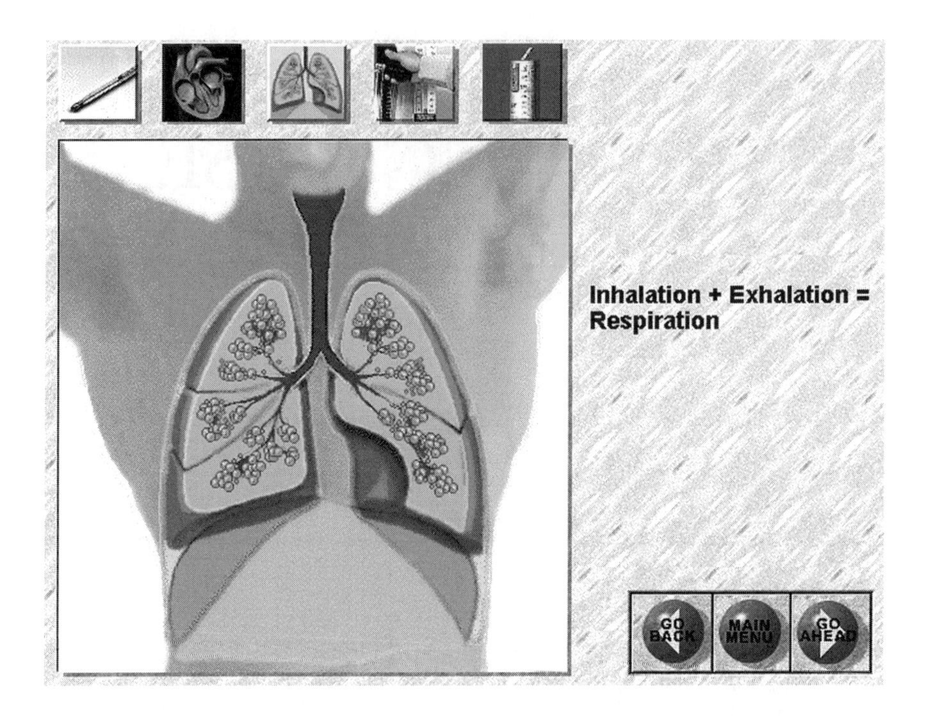

Figure 9–1 The main interface for *Vital Signs*.

tion of the program: thermometer = temperature; heart = pulse; lungs = respiration; manometer = blood pressure; and dip stick = urine analysis.

Vital Signs presents a classic example of straightforward, effective, computer-based training. One of the ways it differs from the two previous case studies is that its goal is to teach a specific skill to a clearly defined audience. Properly learning this skill has life-and-death importance. Because of this, entertainment value is stressed far less than it is in the kiosk for the general public, *The Nauticus Shipbuilding Company*, and the sequencing of the information is far more structured and precise than *Sky High*, which provides general information about a broad subject.

Multimedia Training Programs

Training programs are the bread and butter of most small- and medium-sized production companies. Training is a multibillion dollar business, because in order to keep current, employers must constantly train and retrain employees. Training includes the traditional classroom, print material, and linear media, such as film and video. However, computer-based multimedia training is becoming an increasingly popular part of this mix because it has been proved to be faster, cheaper, and more effective in many cases than other types of training.

Vital Signs was developed in traditional CBT (computer-based training) tutorial style: present the topic, test, and retest. This is a highly effective and common approach in CBT. Some CBT can, however, use more elaborate metaphors and simulations, such as creating a story or a game that the user plays to learn the material or a discovery program where learners explore their environment. Among the recent trends in training are:

- Increased customization. More information about the user is taken at the beginning of the program so that the course material can be focused precisely to the user's needs.
- Increased networking. More training programs are being made available over networks.
- Just-in-time training. Instead of presenting entire programs, just-in-time (JIT) training presents small snippets of information when they are needed. With this approach, an employee with a question about a particular process can jump on the computer and get immediate help. This is similar to help programs in some applications, such as Wizards in Microsoft Office. The formal name for JIT training is employee performance support system (EPSS).

Production Background

Why the Client Produced This Program in Multimedia

Vital Signs was commissioned by HCHP, a New England-based staff model HMO. A staff model HMO has its own health centers staffed by its own medical personnel, who see only patients who belong to that HMO. The *Vital Signs* training program was aimed toward HCHP medical assistants, who help the physicians and other clinicians by greeting patients, bringing them into the examining room, taking vital signs, and generally assisting with any other work that the physician needs to have done. In order to improve the training of the medical assistants, HCHP instituted an in-house certification program, of which the *Vital Signs* project is one component.

HCHP decided to teach these skills through interactive media for many of the same reasons that many companies choose multimedia for training:

- Students are dispersed. It was difficult to gather students together for a traditional group class, because they worked in many different departments all over the area, and they were usually hired only a few at a time. With a multimedia program, individual students could view the program as they needed it and did not have to wait for a group and a teacher.
- Students have varied backgrounds. The background of trainee medical assistants ranges from high school graduates to individuals with master's degrees. For some of the trainees, English was their second

language. This wide mix of educational levels would make a traditional class nearly impossible to pace without either confusing the slow learners or boring the more advanced students. With multimedia, each student can learn at his or her own pace. Some can skip material; others may want to replay certain sections several times.

- Importance of keeping information consistent. Taking vital signs is an essential skill in all medical departments. It was important that all medical assistants perform this service in the same way and with the latest techniques. If all assistants watch the same multimedia program, this is ensured.
- Cutting training time. It was difficult to take a large group of medical assistants out of their jobs at any one time. It was much easier if they could come individually at slow times in their departments. In addition, for skills such as these, independent studies have documented that students complete multimedia courses more than 30 percent faster than covering the same material in a traditional course. (Bank Technology News 25)
- Cutting expenses. Once the program is completed, major training costs are over until the program has to be updated. This is far cheaper than hiring teachers for every new group of students. Studies have documented that "multimedia cost an average of 64 percent less to develop, maintain, and deliver than traditional training." (Bank Technology News 25)

Program Development

This piece was developed by MediaViz productions, a production company specializing in the design and production of multimedia training programs for corporate clients. This project was designed by instructional designer John Cosner of MediaViz and written by Fred Bauer. Cosner also functioned as project manager along with HCHP's Comma Williams, who served as client contact and in-house project manager.

The development of this project followed a standard training model. The information in the program was based on several print training documents that HCHP had already produced. Using this material and additional research, the designer developed a design document. This document included a content outline, which laid out the structure of the course in standard hierarchical outline form. There was no flowchart for this project, although more complicated training programs commonly use flowcharts.

The design document was refined in several design meetings with the writer, the client, the instructional designer-project manager, and eventually the graphic artist. The writer developed several drafts of the treatment based on these meetings and, when the final treatment was approved, wrote several drafts of the script.

The Instructional Designer

The instructional designer is an important figure in multimedia training. According to John Cosner, the instructional designer on this project, there are different conceptions of what an instructional designer is. Many instructional designers have an advanced degree in instructional design and/or a teaching background. Other instructional designers have not been formally trained in the field.

On some projects, instructional designers don't write the script but instead deal with high-level instructional design, such as audience analysis, needs, and goals. In these cases, once the treatment and outline are taken care of, the project is handed over to the writer, with the instructional designer editing the material after it is completed. The role of the instructional designer depends on the attitude of the developer, the type of content, and the complexity of the project. Sometimes, there is no formal instructional designer, and the writer assumes the duties normally assigned to that position.

GOALS AND CHALLENGES IN WRITING AND DEVELOPING *VITAL SIGNS*

Challenges

The key challenges developing this project arose from the type of content, the time limitation on the program, and the nature of the students.

Content

The goal was to teach a specific process: taking vital signs. This process is an essential part of health care and the first thing the physician wants to know about the patient. Because of this, a serious approach was in order.

Time Limit

The client wanted the students to be able to complete this program in less than an hour. This was the amount of time that the stand-up class in the same subject took, so if the interactive program took longer, it would defeat the purpose of limiting the amount of time training takes from work. This time limit restricted the amount of material that could be placed into a program and meant that students wouldn't have time to learn rules of an elaborate game or simulation. The program would have to be simple and clear.

Audience Issues

A number of issues affected the design of this project:

- Some students had English as a second language.
- This was the first introduction to this kind of material for many of them.

- Most were not college graduates.
- There were three different types of students: internal medicine, pediatrics, and OB/GYN. After the introductory material, each student needed specialized information for his or her department. This meant a greater variety of information in the program and a need to identify and track each individual student clearly.

Writer and Instructional Designer's Goals

Instructional Designer

Although the writer and the instructional designer shared many concerns, the instructional designer's primary focus was the overall content and design of the program. The instructional designer, John Cosner, had the following concerns on this project:

- Content driven. The serious nature of the content set the tone of this piece, and the process of taking vital signs set the sequencing of information. The importance of a precise understanding of the information dictated that the same material be presented in a number of ways.
- Clear navigation. A primary goal for any training piece is to make the navigation clear and easy to use for the student. If the program feels complicated to a user, then it has failed. In a good training program, the students should be learning the material, not the program.
- Humanize. In a piece dealing with human interaction, such as this, it's a good idea to put a human face to most of the procedures. For example, the pediatrics section uses the same young girl through several scenes.

The Writer

The writer, Fred Bauer, had input into the overall design of the program. For example, he agreed with the instructional designer that clear navigation was a primary concern; students cannot learn if they are lost. His major concern, however, was with successfully realizing the overall design by achieving the following goals:

- Pace. A key to interactive multimedia is to pace the program in a way that keeps people involved. Users should not passively watch the screen for longer than 25 to 30 seconds before they are asked to interact with the program in some way. It's also important to vary the length and tempo of scenes and the length of time between actions that people are asked to do.
- Humor. In education, humor can be effective in a number of ways: as a reward for a successful performance, as a memory aid, and as a way to help people relax. The opening of this piece, reproduced on page 130, is a good example.

- Emotion. It is essential not only to present information but also to present feelings and elicit an emotional response. In *Vital Signs,* it was important for the students to feel that, as medical assistants, they are a crucial part of the medical service provider team. Another goal was to make the students aware of the feelings that the patient has and to help the students look at the patient as a human being and not just part of the job. The pediatric section of this piece was particularly effective in achieving this.
- Aligning program's voice with viewer. The writer thought that users would feel more comfortable if he could match the program's voice with the users' emotions and expectations. The voice of a program is basically who seems to be talking to you through the program. A voice can be neutral, simply presenting the information without attempting direct contact with the viewer. A neutral voice is fine for an informational program, but in a training piece, it helps the user if the voice can be separated from the content and align itself with the user. For example, in this project, text on the screen frequently questions what was said in the dialogue or the narration. Sometimes the screen text will even attempt to sympathize with a student's confusion if the student got a question wrong. Actual tone of voice also helps here; it should never talk down to or lecture the student.
- Style of presentation. A multimedia program is usually experienced as up close and personal. A student sits inches away from a screen and is connected via keyboard or other input device. It is also usually a one-on-one experience. Because of this, the writer said that multimedia programs should be more intimate. They should not be developed in the same style as a film or a TV program that will be viewed in a group from a much greater distance. Ways to increase this intimacy include more close-ups and using the screen as more of a window on the world than an artificial stage. With a window, characters' entrances and exits are framed in such a way that the users get a sense that there is a larger world beyond the borders of the screen. This is the same experience as looking out a window of a house. Some critics call this "open form framing." Intimacy is also increased through the quality of the program's voice.

MEETING THE CHALLENGES AND ACHIEVING THE GOALS

Overall Design

As you read the descriptions and script samples that follow, be aware of the overall design. One of the strongest aspects of this piece is how the same information is introduced numerous times, but each time the information is presented, it is demonstrated in a more challenging manner. The program builds from simple linear demonstrations and definitions to highly interactive simulations and testing as described in the following outline of the program (there are also additional script samples included on the CD-ROM):

1. Registration
2. Pretest
3. Humorous Introduction
4. Overview
5. Basic Terms
6. Detailed Instruction
7. Practice
8. Case Study Experience
9. Posttest

Registration, Pretest, and Humorous Introduction

Students register for the program with their employee number and department. This information helps to focus the material to their needs. For purposes of demonstration, you, the reader, will register in the pediatric department. This means that after the general instruction, the program will link you to pediatric information.

After registration, students take a multiple-choice pretest on vital signs. The purpose of this test is to get them thinking about the subject. This test is not numerically graded. Instead the subjects are listed with a bright bulb or dim bulb next to the topic, depending on how well the students knew that specific material. This feedback makes them aware of their strengths and weaknesses.

The pretest is followed by a humorous introduction in which users monitor the vital signs of Norman. (Light lines divide sections; heavy lines divide pages.)

Humorous Introduction Script Sample

Unit: Vital Signs Introduction (Video)
Lesson:
Topic:
Title:

Screen: I1.1
Type:
Graphic File:

(**GRAPHIC/VIDEO:** Photograph of a young man, mid-twenties, asleep. A panel opens in the upper right of the frame. It contains four running graph lines labeled:

"Temperature," "Pulse," "Respiration," "Blood Pressure." All are moving, but quiescent. Temperature and pulse are steady, respirations peak with each inhalation, blood pressure shows almost no variation.) (NOTE: In general, 4 heart beats per 1 respiration. Pulse is usually constant during sleep.)

Text:

NORMAL VITAL SIGNS: SLEEPING

If we wake Norman, will his vital signs . . .

Remain the same
All show an increase
Some remain the same, and some increase

AUDIO: NARRATOR (VO): (SOFTLY, SO AS NOT TO WAKEN NORMAN) Shhh—Normal Norman is sleeping. His normal vital signs—temperature . . . blood pressure . . . pulse . . . and respiration—are flowing along in that panel to the upper right. These values reflect body changes you can't always see just by looking at a patient. We take vital signs to spot early warnings, like high blood pressure—often, these warnings allow us to give preventative care. Norman's vital signs are normal for sleeping. What do you suppose will happen to them when we wake Norman up? Will his vital signs remain the same, all show an increase, or some remain the same and some increase? SELECT your choice, and we'll see.

Feedback: (AUDIO + Text) **NARRATOR (VO):**

Same = Close but not quite. Watch.
All = A good guess, but not quite. Watch.
Some = Very good. Watch
After all answers = (CALLING) Wake up, Norman!
(SFX: snorts and grunts from Norman.)
Branching:

I1.2
Special Instructions:

Unit: Vital Signs Introduction (Video)
Lesson:
Topic:
Title:

Screen: I1.2
Type:

Graphic File:

(**GRAPHIC/VIDEO:** Photograph of young man sitting up in bed and yawning. Vital signs show waking norms.)

Text:

NORMAL VITAL SIGNS AWAKE

Button = "Breakfast, Norman!"

AUDIO: (SFX: Music assumes a more upbeat tempo.)
NARRATOR (VO): (IN REGULAR SPEAKING VOICE) In the morning, our temperature is at the lowest point of the day. Norman's waking pulse, respiration, and blood pressure are higher than when he's asleep. No surprises there. Well, time for breakfast. SELECT the breakfast button and we'll see what happens to Norman next.

Feedback:

Button = **NARRATOR (VO):** Breakfast, Norman! (SFX: clanging triangle, as in Western movies chuck wagon call.)

Branching:

Button = I1.3
Special Instructions:

(In the following scenes, Norman's temperature rises as he drinks hot coffee. When Norman suddenly realizes he's late for work, his blood pressure goes up and his pulse increases. When he gets a flat tire, his vital signs go crazy.)

Analysis of Humorous Introduction

The major function of this sequence is to introduce the topic in a light manner to initiate users' interest and get them relaxed and ready to learn. This sequence also gives students a chance to concentrate on learning how the program operates without having to learn complex course information. This makes program navigation clear to the students.

In the audio on the first page, the writer quickly sets up a friendly voice for the program and connects directly to the user. By creating the character Norman, whose vital signs the user monitors, the writer puts a human face on the information.

Under the feedback section on the same page, the user is asked to guess what will happen next, adding interactivity and greater audience involvement to what is essentially a linear sequence. The breakfast button on the next page works the same way and helps to maintain pace.

Overview

After the humorous introduction, the piece turns more serious, outlining the importance of the topic and the objectives of the program. This is followed by a video overview showing an experienced medical assistant taking a patient's vital signs.

The overview puts a human face on the experience by creating characters for the patient and medical assistant. It also gives the students a general view of what they will be learning in a nonthreatening environment in which little is being asked of them in terms of answering questions and providing information. It is, however, more serious and fact-filled than the humorous introduction. This is part of the slow and careful buildup of the information presentation.

Basic Terms

After the overview, it is time for users to roll up their sleeves and start learning the nuts and bolts of taking vital signs. The lessons are first listed in the following interactive menu, which gives users an option of what to study first:

- Temperature
- Pulse
- Respiration
- Blood pressure

If the user clicks on Blood Pressure, a series of screens that define this topic's basic concepts appear.

Basic Terms Script Sample

(**GRAPHIC/VIDEO:** Repeat animated diagram of heart showing flow of blood.)

Text: Blood Pressure Lesson (small heart symbol)
(CALL OUTS)

Right Atrium Left Atrium
Right Ventricle Left Ventricle
The pressure of blood—
at height of wave from ventricles
as heart relaxes between beats

AUDIO: NARRATOR (VO): While pulse and respiration are taken directly, blood pressure is measured indirectly using a device called a manometer. It is actually two values. Blood pressure is the measurement of the highest force of the blood on the walls of the blood vessels, at the height of the wave from the ventricles, and the lowest force of the blood on the walls of the blood vessels, as the heart relaxes between beats.

Feedback:

Branching:

u1.4.2

Special Instructions:

Unit: u1
Lesson: Blood Pressure
Topic:
Title:

Screen: u1.4.2
Type:
Graphic File:

GRAPHIC/VIDEO: (Animated diagram of artery with red dots flowing left to right, and vein, with blue dots flowing right to left.)

Text:

Blood Pressure Measurements:
Systolic and Diastolic

Artery
(Muscle)
Vein
(Valves)

AUDIO: NARRATOR (VO): Blood flows from the heart in arteries, which have muscles to help keep it moving. Blood returns to the heart through veins, which don't have muscles, but do contain valves that prevent blood from flowing backwards. Blood pressure consists of two measurements—systolic and diastolic. SELECT each to learn more. (When you've finished, SELECT "GO AHEAD" to continue.)

Feedback: (AUDIO + Text)
Highlight term when chosen

Systolic = **NARRATOR (VO):** (ARTERY AND VEIN FREEZE AT HEIGHT OF FLOW) Systolic values measure the pressure at the height of the pulse wave.
Diastolic = **NARRATOR (VO):** (ARTERY AND VEIN FREEZE DURING PAUSE) Diastolic readings measure the pressure during the relaxation period between beats.

Branching:

ul.4.3

Special Instructions:

Analysis of Definition of Basic Terms

Because of the audience for this program, no scientific knowledge is assumed. Basic terms are explained clearly and simply. The interactive animation on the second page of the example is a particularly good use of instructional multimedia.

Detailed Instruction

Once basic terms and processes are explained, the program moves to the next level of complexity, which focuses on the medical assistant's specialty, such as pediatrics or OB/GYN. For example, a user who registered from the Pediatric Department, would receive detailed instructions on how to take vital signs from a child.

Practice

Immediately following the detailed instruction is a highly interactive sequence in which the user takes a little girl's blood pressure. It starts off with the challenge: "Now it's your turn." Enough sitting around watching, it's time to do it.

Practice Script Sample

Unit: u1
Lesson: Blood Pressure
Topic:
Title:

Screen: u1.4.13p
Type:
Graphic File:

(**GRAPHIC/VIDEO:** Colette looking apprehensive)

Text:
Meet Colette, age 7.
You're going to take her blood pressure. You've explained the procedure to her. What do you use next?

(CAPTIONS)
Cuff Ball Pump Valve on cuff Doll

(AUDIO: NARRATOR VO): Now it's your turn. Meet Colette, age 7. You're going to take her blood pressure. You've explained the procedure. What do you use next—the cuff, the ball pump, the valve on the cuff, or the doll? SELECT your choice now.

Feedback: (VO and text)

Cuff, Ball Pump, Valve = (SFX: Little Girl's Voice) **(VO audio ONLY):** No. I don't want that. It's going to hurt!
NARRATOR (VO): Apparently, Colette didn't buy your explanation. Try again.
Doll = **NARRATOR (VO):** You're good. That's right. From the look on her face, you can tell Colette didn't buy your

explanation, so you demonstrate on a doll. (SELECT "GO AHEAD" to continue.)

Branching:

ul.4.14p

Special Instructions:

Unit: ul
Lesson: Blood Pressure
Topic:
Title:

Screen: ul.4.14p
Type:
Graphic File:

(**GRAPHIC/VIDEO:** Animated graphic of manometer column at 110 mm)

Text:

SELECT the valve, listen to the heart sounds, watch the mercury, and read Colette's blood pressure. SELECT O.K. when you have it. O.K.

(**AUDIO:** (SFX: 7-year-old heart sounds.) **NARRATOR (VO):** SELECT the valve, listen to the heart sounds, watch the mercury and read Colette's blood pressure. SELECT O.K. when you've got it.

Feedback:

Branching:

ul.4.15p

Special Instructions

Unit: ul
Lesson: Blood Pressure
Topic:
Title:

Screen: u1.4.15p
Type:
Graphic File:

(**GRAPHIC/VIDEO:** Animated graphic of manometer column at 110 mm)

Text:
What is Colette's blood pressure?

94/68
92/66
92/68

(AUDIO: NARRATOR VO): What is Colette's blood pressure—94/68, 92/66, or 92/68? SELECT your answer now.

Feedback: (AUDIO + Text)

NARRATOR (VO):
94/68 = That's not right. Try again.
92/66 = That's not right. Try again.
92/68 = That's right (SELECT "GO AHEAD" to continue.)

Branching:

u1.4.14 (Orthostatic)

Special Instructions:

Analysis of Practice

This piece allows you as the student to practice what you've just learned by choosing the right approach to the child. It makes you aware of the feelings of the patient and helps you to see her as a human being and not just part of the job. It also lets you actually "take" her blood pressure with an ingenious, interactive animation. If you get the pressure wrong, you can try again.

Case Study Experience

The case studies present the information in yet another way. This time the student watches videos of a medical assistant taking the vital signs. The challenge is to catch the medical assistant's errors.

Case Studies Script Sample

Unit: u2
Lesson: Case History—Pediatric
Topic:
Title:

Screen: u2.4.1
Type:
Graphic File:

(**GRAPHIC/VIDEO:** CLOSE UP SHOWS RUTH PROPERLY FEELING FOR PULSE AND FINDING IT. 1) DISSOLVE TO MEDIUM SHOT OF RUTH. SHE NOTES HER WATCH, THEN LOOKS AWAY, CONCENTRATING ON THE HEARTBEAT. 2) DISSOLVE TO MEDIUM SHOT. SILENTLY, SHE BEGINS TO CONCENTRATE ON THE RISE AND FALL OF COLETTE'S CHEST. 3) CAMERA CUTS TO COLETTE'S CHEST. 4) DISSOLVE TO CLOSE-UP OF RUTH'S HAND AS SHE WRITES PULSE AND RESPIRATION ON ENCOUNTER FORM. DISSOLVE TO SHOT OF RUTH REACHING FOR MANOMETER CUFF.)

Text:

(AFTER RUTH FASTENS CUFF. ACTION FREEZE.)
Error

(**AUDIO:** (SFX: NORMAL, REGULAR CHILD'S HEARTBEAT OVER PULSE. NORMAL, REGULAR CHILD'S BREATHING MATCHES RISE AND FALL OF COLETTE'S CHEST. RUTH SPEAKS AS SHE TRIES TO WRAP TOO LARGE A CUFF AROUND COLETTE'S ARM, FINALLY FASTENING IT LOOSE, AND REACHING ALMOST TO THE CHILD'S ARMPIT. **RUTH (ON CAMERA)**: I'm going to take you're blood pressure now, Colette. What's going to happen is, I'll put this cuff around your arm, and pump it up. You'll feel a little squeezing, like when your mommie gives you a big hug. Just nod if you're ready. (COLETTE NODS "YES." RUTH PLACES CUFF ON ARM AND FASTENS.)

Feedback:
[Selection before Ruth fastens cuff] **NARRATOR (VO):** (Track 2) Sorry, no error yet—but stay alert. (SELECT "GO AHEAD" to continue.)

(Selection when Ruth fastens cuff) **NARRATOR (VO):** (Track 2) Good work. You've helped Ruth become a better medical assistant. (SELECT "GO AHEAD" to continue.)
[MISS] **NARRATOR (VO):** (Track 2) You missed an error. We've stopped the time so that you can step in and help Ruth. If you think you know what that error is, you can choose to continue. If you'd like to see it again, choose replay.
Branching:
HIT, OR CONTINUE = u2.4.1q
REPLAY = u2.41
Special Instructions:

Unit: u2
Lesson: Case History—Pediatric
Topic:
Title:

Screen: u2.4.1q
Type:
Graphic File:

(**GRAPHIC/VIDEO:** FREEZE FRAME OF ERROR)
Text:
What error did you spot?
Using wrong size blood pressure cuff
Unprofessional attitude
Failure to tell patient she's counting respiration

AUDIO:

Feedback:
Unprofessional, or Failure = Not correct. Try again.
Using = That's right. What would you do to correct this error?

Note on Encounter form that cuff is wrong size.
Get proper size cuff.
Wait until it's time to remove thermometer, then get proper cuff.

Note, or wait = Not quite. Try again.
Get = That's right.

Branching: u2.4.2

Special Instructions:

Unit: u2
Lesson: Case History—Pediatric
Topic:
Title:

Screen: u2.4.2
Type:
Graphic File:

(**GRAPHIC/VIDEO:** HOLD FROZEN ACTION)

Text:

Using wrong size blood pressure cuff. Ruth has applied a cuff that's too wide and too long. This will lower the patient's blood pressure. SELECT "GO AHEAD" to help her get it right.

(**AUDIO:**)

Feedback:

Branching: u2.5.1
Special Instructions:

Unit: u2
Lesson: Case History—Pediatric
Topic:
Title:

Screen: u2.5.1
Type:
Graphic File:

GRAPHIC/VIDEO: REPEAT ACTION AS RUTH TRIES CUFF.

Text:

(WHEN RUTH PLACES CUFF ON ARM. FREEZE ACTION)
ERROR

(**AUDIO:** Just nod if you're ready. (COLETTE NODS "YES." RUTH TRIES CUFF, REALIZES IT'S TOO BIG.) Colette, somebody must have been taking the blood pressure of a giant—look how big this is. I'm going to get a nice new cuff for you—one that fits. I'll be right back. (DISSOLVE or WIPE TO RUTH RETURNING WITH PROPER CUFF, PLACING IT ON COLETTE'S ARM.) That's better.

Feedback:

[Selection before Ruth places cuff on arm] **NARRATOR (VO):** (Track 2) Sorry, no error yet—but stay alert. (SELECT "GO AHEAD" to continue.)
[Selection when Ruth places cuff on arm] **NARRATOR (VO):** (Track 2) Good work. You've helped Ruth become a better medical assistant. (SELECT "GO AHEAD" to continue.) [MISS] **NARRATOR (VO):** (Track 2) You missed an error. We've stopped the time so that you can step in and help Ruth. If you think you know what that error is, you can choose to continue. If you'd like to see it again, choose replay.

Branching:

HIT, OR CONTINUE = u2.5.1q
REPLAY = u2.5.1

Analysis of Case Study

This section has a number of branching possibilities, which increase student involvement, but perhaps the best feature is that the students have the power to stop the disc and replay it. The chance to replay the material helps the students focus on the material and provides a sense of accomplishment when they finally find the error. Without the possibility to replay the material, the students would simply miss the information and experience failure. This approach is mirrored in the feedback answers that suggest "try again" or "choose replay." This section of the program also continues the emotional quality of the previous segment by using the same little girl as a patient.

Posttest

The program ends with a multiple-choice posttest. This is the same test students took as a pretest, but the questions are rearranged. Like the pretest, the posttest is not numerically graded in order to reduce test anxiety and increase learning. Instead of grades, the subjects are again listed with a bright bulb or dim bulb next to the topic, depending on how well the students knew that specific material. This device makes them aware of their strengths and weaknesses and gives them a chance to return to specific topics for additional study. The supervisors can, however, get a numerical grade for their workers if they want. Final certification of this skill, however, must occur in practice.

CONCLUSION: RESPONSE TO THE PROJECT

This program is too new to have a formal evaluation of its effectiveness, but written and verbal responses from the medical assistants who have used it are very positive. They like going though it at their own pace. They like the privacy. Students who speak English as a second language enjoy the opportunity to replay difficult sections. Other students said that the interactive visualization helped them learn the material. Based on this initial response, the program has been made available in all of HCHP's facilities, and additional multimedia training programs are in the works.

REFERENCES

Bauer, Fred. Telephone interview with the author, November 1995.

Cosner, John. Telephone interviews with the author, November 1995.

"Multimedia Sights and Sounds Bombard Banks." *Bank Technology News* 7 (February 1994).

Williams, Comma. Telephone interview with author. November 1995.

10

ONLINE ADVERTISING CASE STUDY: ZD NET PERSONAL VIEW CAMPAIGN

Summary

Name of production: ZD Net Personal View Online Ad Campaign
Writers: Matt Lindley, Kevin Wells
Developer: Ziff-Davis Interactive Media & Development
Subject: ZD Net Personal View: A Free Customized News Service
Audience: World Wide Web Users of Lycos Search Service
Medium: World Wide Web
Presentation location: Where Web is viewed: Home, office, schools
Goals: Persuade, inform
Structure: Branching, hierarchical branching

PROGRAM DESCRIPTION AND BACKGROUND

Program Description

ZD Net is the online network of Ziff-Davis, a major publisher of computer magazines, such as *PCWeek, MacWeek, Computer Shopper*, and more than a dozen others. Personal View is a free, customizable news service that is available on ZD Net. With Personal View, a user can enter key words, and Personal View will compile a daily update of articles and other information related to the key words.

Personal View benefits ZD Net in a couple of ways. Its major function is to lure more users to ZD Net and the services and advertisements offered there. In addition, when users register their name and address for a Personal View account, they identify themselves as customers of Ziff-Davis products. To make more people aware of Personal View, ZD Net decided to advertise Personal View.

Online Advertising

Online advertisements can be placed on the World Wide Web and on commercial online services, such as CompuServe, America Online, and Prodigy. ZD Net decided to place the ad shown in Figure 10–1 on the World Wide Web. An online ad occurs in three stages: a banner, a middle page, and a Web Site.

The Banner A banner is small image and text composition that looks like a billboard or a banner. (See the top part of Figure 10–1 or see the Additional Material, Chapter 10 of the CD-ROM for color images.) The goal of the ban-

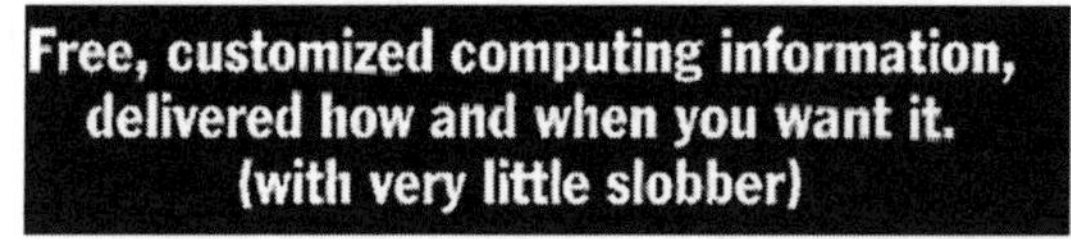

ZDNet
'Personal View'

Personal View Banner (top) Leads to Mid-Page (below)

Figure 10–1 Top: ZD Net Personal View banner. The actual ad has the dog in color and the ZD in a red box. Bottom: ZD Net Personal View middle page. The middle page has the dog in color, the ZDs in red boxes, and the buttons circled in red.

ner is to persuade the user to click and go to the middle page (the bottom part of the figure). This banner is placed on a popular Web site whose users have some connection to the subject matter being advertised. In this case, ZD Net was advertising a customized search service, so they decided to place the banner on Lycos, a Web search site.

Search pages, such as Lycos, Yahoo, and InfoSeek, are good locations to place ads for two reasons:

1. Heavy traffic. Most people get onto the Internet to find information, and a search tool is a frequent first stop.
2. Audience focus. Search tool pages are also able to focus the audience for a product in ways that are impossible for any other type of advertisement. A different ad will appear on the search page, depending on what a user is searching. For example, if the user types "hard drive," an ad for a hard drive manufacturer or a computer shopper magazine will appear on the screen, along with a list of Web sites on the topic. If the user typed in a different word to search, such as "music," he or she might see an ad for an online music store or a new CD. Load a search page, such as Lycos or Infoseek, and try it out on a sophisticated browser, such as Netscape Navigator. Type different search words and see what ads appear. Of course what ads can appear are limited to the paying ads currently running on a particular search service. Not all browsers and search services function this way, so try a few until you find one that works. (See the Chapter 10 section of the CD-ROM for links to search sites.)

The Middle Page The middle page is usually more detailed than the banner. The main reason is that the advertiser has the user's interest because he or she clicked on the banner.

Nevertheless, it is still highly possible to lose a customer on the middle page. Usually the middle page is quite simple but lures the viewer further with a clear explanation of the product or some other incentive. Clicking on the middle page leads to the advertiser's Web site, which can be quite extensive, displaying information on the product and links to related information on other sites. In this case the final Web site is the actual product: Personal View.

The Evolution of Online Advertising

Online ads are a type of interactive advertising or "intermercial." Many of the techniques used in online advertising are also used in other interactive advertising forms. Emerging technological advances, such as real-time audio, animation, and video, have spurred extensive innovation and growth in this field. These advances will allow online sites to present audio and video just as television and radio do. It will no longer be necessary to wait for big media files to download to the computer's hard drive before you can view them.

Advances such as these are fostering changes in the design of the ads themselves. Online advertising is a relatively new phenomenon, and as with any other new medium, it takes time to discover what works and what does not. Matt Lindley, the Creative Director of Advertising for Ziff-Davis Interactive Media & Development, breaks the evolution of online advertisement into three stages.

1. Logos. Initially clients placed their logos on screen, thinking that the logos would attract buyers. But experience quickly showed that a company name alone does not necessarily cause a user to click for more information.
2. Repurposed print ads. Next, many advertisers tried to scan a big print ad and put it online, but with the current slow modem speed, users are unlikely to wait several minutes to download a big ad.
3. Online ads. The emerging trend today by forward-thinking advertisers is to design an ad with online in mind from the beginning. This means designing it within the technical limitations of today's online technology. It also means drawing from the persuasive techniques of modern advertising to create an ad that will appeal to the online audience.

The Personal View ad fits the third category. Other interesting ad examples can be seen on the Web sites for the advertising agencies Modem Media and Poppe Tyson (links on the CD-ROM). Modem Media's campaign for Zima clear malt beverage is particularly interesting. It sets a very hip tone with a final Web site containing offbeat stories about Zima Drinker Duncan and a refrigerator full of downloadable files, such as stereograms, music, and games. Users can also fill out a form, join the Z generation, and get plenty of free prizes.

The audience for interactive ads is growing explosively. The majority of upper income American homes are currently online. (Barkow) With the rapid increase in CD-ROM users, direct mail CDs will compete with print catalogs and other advertising. Finally, interactive television will add millions more to the interactive audience.

Advantages of Online Advertising

Online advertising would not be growing so rapidly if it were not an effective way of selling products. It has numerous advantages over print and broadcast, among them the following:

- Measurability. Every time a user clicks on an online ad, the click is recorded. This makes it possible for advertisers to know exactly how many people are viewing their ads and how many people are following these ads from the middle page to the home page. It also tells them when interest in an ad is beginning to fade.
- Rotation. If an ad is beginning to fade, the advertiser can pull it immediately. Or the advertiser can choose to rotate new ads into the slot.

Advertisers can also adjust the portions of an ad that are not getting attention. This is usually not possible in print or broadcast ads, which are scheduled weeks or months in advance.
- Direct contact with customers. By simply clicking a button on an ad or an advertiser's Web site, a customer can e-mail the advertiser, download product information or a sample, or even order a complete product.
- Interactivity. There are myriad possibilities here. For example, a car buyer could click on different colors for a car he or she is interested in, or link from the ad to an online auto magazine that has reviews on a certain model.
- Cost. It is much cheaper to let the customer find information on a Web site than it is to hire a salesperson. A downloaded or viewable sample costs the advertiser nothing (beyond the basic cost of the Web site). Compare this to the cost of an expensive mailing.
- Unlimited space. Once an advertiser can get a user to a Web site, then the advertiser can use as much space as needed to present the products. A site can have links to dozens of pages and images within the advertiser's site and links to related sites that might help the user understand the product. This is a far cry from the severe space limitations of a broadcast or print ad.

Limitations

Of course, it is not a completely rosy picture. Online technology is rapidly changing, but the slow modem speeds of most users make it difficult to transmit online large files, such as video, sound, and large pictures. This means that to work effectively, files must be kept to a minimum size. The smaller they are, the faster they will appear on the user's screen and the happier the user will be. If users have to wait too long for a screen to load, they will cancel the operation and click elsewhere. Notice the small size of the images in Figure 10–1.

Another major problem is getting people to click on an ad. Unlike a TV ad, which will run whether viewers do anything or not, an online middle page and Web site will not be seen at all unless the user clicks on the banner. Getting users to click will be dealt with in more detail in the analysis of the Personal View advertising campaign below.

Production Background

Ziff-Davis Interactive Media repurposes print material from Ziff-Davis Publishing's computer magazines and creates original content about buying and using computers. This content is distributed via the online service ZD Net and through most of the other major commercial online services and the World Wide Web.

The ad campaign for Personal View was created in-house at Ziff-Davis Interactive by Matt Lindley, Creative Director of Advertising, and Kevin

Wells, Creative Director. The purpose of this ad was to draw additional traffic to Personal View and thus to ZD Net. Ziff-Davis Interactive also produces advertisements for clients ranging from Apple, to Lotus, to Epson. These ads appear in the online versions of Ziff-Davis magazines and other locations.

The development process for this ad is typical of many other online ads:

1. Needs meeting. The creative team meets with the client to identify the client's needs.
2. Creative platform. This is the creative team's basic strategy session when they decide what they are trying to say, identify who the audience is, and come up with possible approaches to present the message.
3. First-round creative. This is the first attempt at creating the ads. The ads are posted on a server. With an online connection, clients can look at them at their own desk anywhere in the world and give their comments.
4. Second-round creative. Based on in-house reaction and client comments on the first-round creative, a second series of ads is created.
5. Third-round creative. This is usually the finished product, although with online ads, second round is often the final.

This process is similar to what happens in print and broadcast advertising, but in online the entire process can take place in two days or less. The major reasons for this compressed time frame follow:

- Client comments can be instantaneous. As soon as the first round of ads is put on the server, the clients can see them and comment on them. There is no need to gather everyone together for a meeting.
- The ad copy and images can be quickly revised because they are created in digital media.
- Ads can be distributed on the Web instantaneously. There are no magazines to be printed or TV show schedules to deal with. An ad is placed on a server, and it is immediately available to the consumer.

CHALLENGES IN WRITING THE ZD NET PERSONAL VIEW ONLINE AD CAMPAIGN

The goal of this ad campaign was to get Web users to click their way from the banner to the middle page and finally to Personal View on ZD Net. Each stage of this process had its own challenges.

Banner

The banner functions a bit like an attract program in a museum setting because it is the first aspect of the advertising campaign that the viewer will see. The banner's job is to lure the viewer into clicking and moving on to the middle page. This challenge is made more difficult by the small size of the banner. An additional challenge is the complexity of the Personal View product. Because this was the first service of its type on the Web, most people would not even know what a customized computer news service was.

A number of things can be tried in the banner to catch the viewer's eye and get the person to click. One common approach is the value-added banner, which offers free items, such as downloads of software, or a chance to try a product for free. Another tactic is a teaser: an intriguing line that creates more questions than answers and makes the viewer want more information. The teaser should, however, have some connection to the product. It is generally not a good idea to lure the viewer in with a false teaser, such as saying, "Sex, Sex, Sex," on the banner and then try to pitch computer printers on the middle page. Most users get angry and just click off.

The banners for the Personal View ad campaign were developed in three stages: first-round creative, second-round creative, and third-round creative. The first and second rounds presented a number of options for the final banner, which evolved by the third round.

First-Round Creative Banners

Figure 10–2 illustrates the eight possibilities for the banner that were presented in the first-round creative, when the first drafts of the advertisement were presented. Only one banner would be used in the final campaign. As the banners illustrate, one challenge for an online copywriter is that he or she must do more than write. ZD Net's Matt Lindley, for example, works with Photoshop, Illustrator, and Infiniti 3-D to create his images as well as his text.

Both the teaser and the free gift approach were tried in the first-round creative. The first two banners are teasers that offer little information about the product but try to lure users on with catchy questions and an incomplete sentence that users will want answered.

The third banner tries to explain the product with a metaphor related to food. "A la carte" is a concept most people understand. The metaphor is further explained in small print, and the ZD Net logo is included.

The two options near the bottom—"The search is over" and "Looking for Something"—try to focus the ad tightly on the audience. Remember that the location of this banner is on the Lycos search page. Lycos is a Web search tool, so people who are on this page are looking for information of some kind.

The last banner on this list abandons the food metaphor and focuses on a metaphor closer to news: a paperboy.

All of these ads were ultimately rejected. Some of the reasons included lack of catchy graphics, a need to be clearer about the product and its capabilities, and a desire to form a stronger link with ZD Net.

Second-Round Creative Banner

The clients did like various elements of the first-round creative ads:

- "News a la carte" in script (from banner 4).
- "Computer news" (from the next to the last banner).

When was the last time you got exactly what you asked for?

IF NEWS WAS FOOD, THIS IS A BUFFET...

NEWS A LA CARTE

ZDNet introduces 'Personal Page.' It's News how, and when, you want to see it.

News a la carte

Where Buck Rogers gets his news.

The search is over. ZD Net Personal Page.

LOOKING FOR SOMETHING?

How about your own, customized computer news delivered free every day? ZDNet

FIRE THE PAPERBOY!

ZDNet introduces 'Personal View.' News how and when you want to see it.

Figure 10–2 The eight options for the final banner presented at the first-round creative.

- "News how and when you want it" (from the last ad).
- The ZD Net logo (from the last ad).

These elements were combined with a stronger graphic of serving dishes and a slightly larger logo to create the second-round creative banner (see the top part of Figure 10–3). This banner too was finally rejected because the "A la carte" metaphor seemed too distant from news, and the graphics were not catchy enough.

Third-Round Creative Banner

For the third-round creative, the writers tried to tie the metaphor closer to the news and come up with a catchier graphic. The last attempt in first-round creative mentioned a paperboy, but another way to get the news is to have it retrieved by a favorite lovable pup. A dog image is eye-catching and unusual on the Web. A bit of humor was also added ("with very little slobber").

Final Banner

The final banner develops the third-round creative concept further by using black and white to make a more striking image and emphasize the dog. The placement of the dog graphic is also changed to act as punctuation to set off the ZD Net logo and "Personal View." The ZD Net logo itself was enlarged. (See Figure 10–1, page 146, for the final banner.)

Middle Page

Advertisers have more space on the middle page because they are no longer paying a high premium to have a banner on someone else's site. Nevertheless, it is still important to keep the digital size of the image small. If it takes viewers too long too download, they will skip it.

Working within this constraint, the goal of the middle page is usually to lure viewers on to the advertiser's Web site and the final destination. The exceptions are advertisers that do not have Web sites. In these cases, the middle page is the final destination. But generally, getting to the advertiser's Web site is the goal. There are a number of ways to do this, including:

- Product descriptions, explaining what this product will do for the user and how it works.
- Free stuff, such as a free demonstration download of the product or a free utility, such as a screen saver.

Second Round Creative Banner

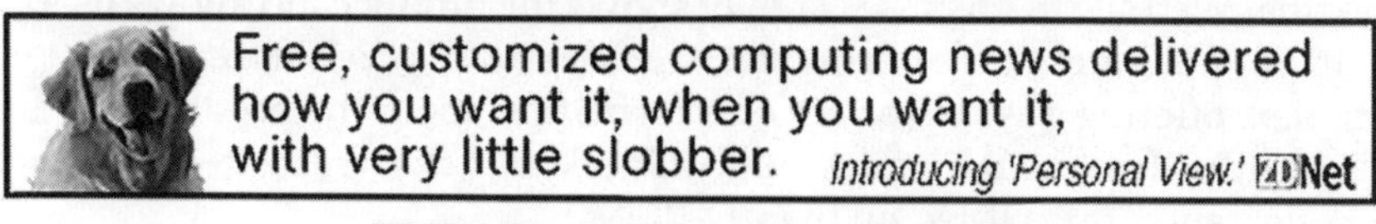

Third Round Creative Banner

Figure 10–3 Top: Second-round creative banner. Bottom: Third-round creative banner.

- Pricing deals, such as low-cost introductory offers or discount coupons that can be printed and given to retailers

A middle page can include a number of these options, allowing the user to click on the one of most interest. This leads the viewer directly to the section of the Web site that has the information that he or she is seeking. This is a type of hierarchical branching.

First-Round Creative Middle Page

The first attempt at the Personal View middle page used both product description and a chance to try the product for free. (See the top part of Figure 10–4.) The dog graphic and ZD Net logo were carried over from the banner. Users were given three options:

1. Try Personal View.
2. Go to the ZD Net Home Page.
3. Go to Barbados (an in-house joke).

Second-Round Creative Middle Page

The second-round creative made a number of changes. (See the bottom part of Figure 10–4.) The description is clearer and more formal. Slang such as "hottest computing news" is dropped in favor of "the latest high-tech developments." This new wording also broadens the content of Personal View beyond computers. The sources of the information are also added. The text layout is different, making it smaller and directly under the dog, which tends to lead users' eyes down the page instead of to the right, as in the first draft. The text next to the buttons is made larger than the descriptive text up top. This makes sense because the goal is to get the user to push that button. To increase the motivation, the button the advertisers don't want users to push is made smaller.

Final Middle Page

The final middle page is the simplest yet. The list of sources was dropped to simplify the page. The other button was also eliminated. The viewers are given one choice: try Personal View. (See Figure 10–1, page 146, for the final middle page.)

Web Site

The final Web site in this case actually shows the product and allows users to try it. For a different type of product, the advertiser's Web site could be very complex, offering a wide variety of information about the product, tours of the facility, free items, and so on. (Check out the Web sites for Zima, Chrysler, and others listed on the CD-ROM.)

The Full Personal View page carries banners for other advertisements, which will in turn lead to middle pages and their Web sites, which will have ad banners that lead to other middle pages and Web sites that also have ads. Do you begin to see why it is called the World Wide Web?

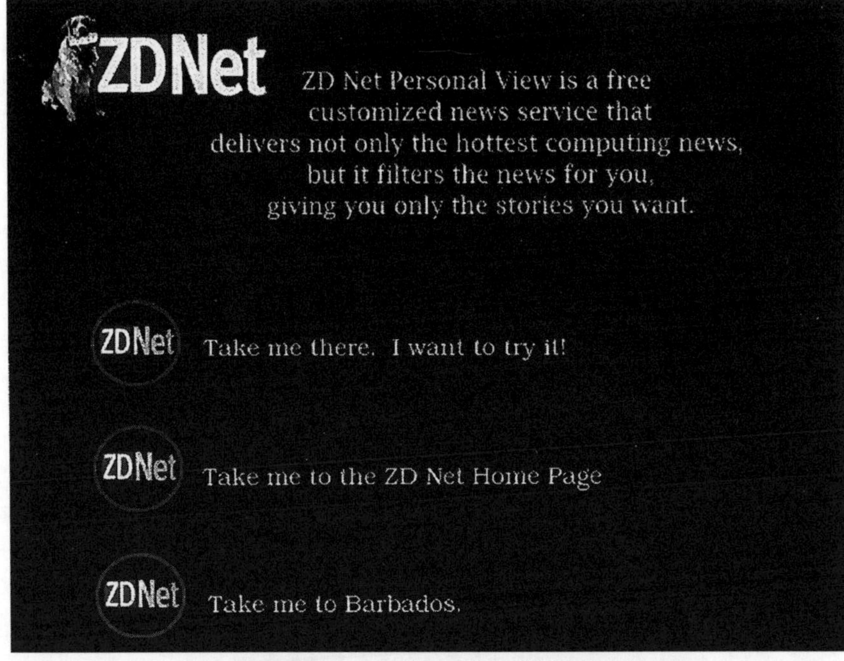

First Round Creative Middle Page

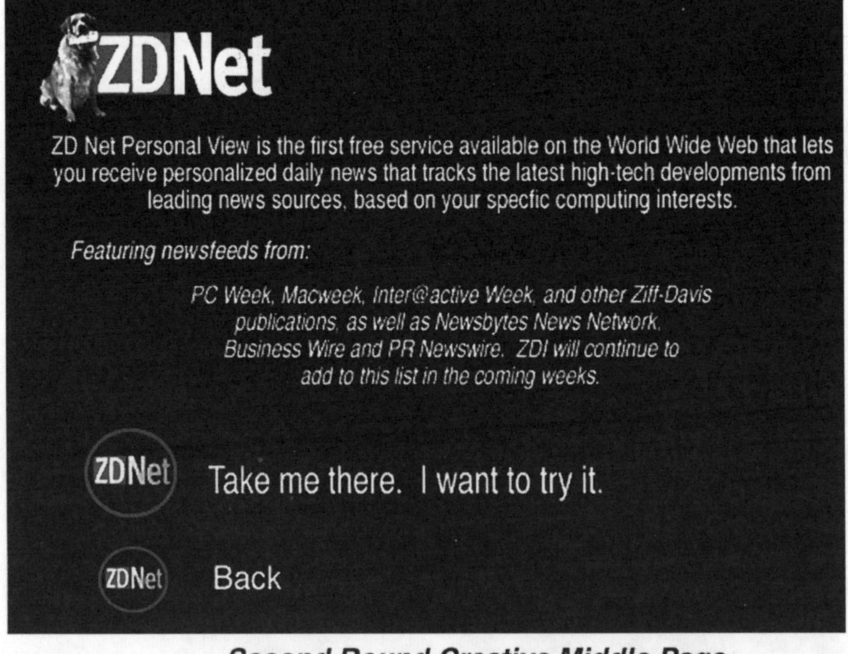

Second Round Creative Middle Page

Figure 10–4 Top: First-round creative middle page. Bottom: Second-round creative middle page.

ZD Net Personal View is a free customized news service that delivers not only the hottest computing news from major news sources, but it filters the news for you, giving you only the stories you want to follow (view sample page). Be kept up-to-the minute on information that interests you most!

To get your own *Personal View*, click below to fill out the registration form and your personal news profile. The next time you log on to the ZD Net home page, click the "Personal View" button, enter your password, and access your very own *Personal View*.

Interested? Register Now (required for *Personal View*)

Figure 10–5 Personal View Web site.

CONCLUSION: RESPONSE TO THE PROJECT

ZD Net has recently been rated the number one online advertising location in terms of the number of users. Initial response to the Personal View ad campaign has been strong, but the ad is ongoing so final numbers are not yet in.

REFERENCES

Advertising on ZD Net. World Wide Web Publication. Ziff-Davis Interactive. http://www.zdnet.com/~zdi/pview/cgi

Barkow, Tim, editor. "Raw Data." *Wired*, 4.07 (July 1996).

Lindley, Matthew. Interview with the author. Cambridge, MA, November 1995.

Location Location Location. Brochure. Ziff-Davis Interactive, 1995.

11

WORLD WIDE WEB SITE CASE STUDY: T. ROWE PRICE WEB SITE

Summary

Name of production: T. Rowe Price Web Site
Writers: Peter Adams, Ken Godfrey, Matt Freeman
Developer: poppe.com, a division of Poppe Tyson Advertising
Subject: Mutual funds, investment, and retirement planning
Audience: Seasoned investors, first-time investors, anyone interested in mutual funds
Medium: World Wide Web, America Online
Presentation location: Where Web is viewed
Goals: Inform, teach
Structure: Branching, hierarchical branching

PROGRAM DESCRIPTION AND BACKGROUND

Program Description

The T. Rowe Price Web Site is the online home of T. Rowe Price Services. This site offers extensive information to help investors learn about and invest in mutual funds. The Home Page (Figure 11–1) shows a number of clickable icons and pictures that lead to the various sections of the Web site: What's News, Mutual Fund Information, Retirement Planning, About T. Rowe Price, FYI, and Discount Brokerage.

Part of the information in these sections is static; it is the same for each viewer and changes infrequently. This includes basic information on mutual

Figure 11–1 Home page for the T. Rowe Price Web Site (see the CD-ROM for the color image).

funds, investment planning, T. Rowe Price itself, and a library collection of articles on different aspects of investing.

The strength of this site is that most of the information is dynamic; the information is either updated frequently or can be personalized for each user.

Some sections are updated monthly, such as Spotlight on Investing and the Topical Features section. Other areas are updated much more frequently. It is possible to get a weekly international market summary, daily prices on mutual funds, and even real-time stock market prices through Market Watch.

Other sections of the site can be personalized to the individual investor's needs. These include the mutual fund Watch List, which reports only the funds the user chooses, and the Online Investment Strategy Planner, a tutorial that helps establish the user's approach to investing.

The site also provides tools in the form of calculators, guides, and applications that help investors make informed investment decisions. (See the Chapter 11 section of the CD-ROM for a link to the T. Rowe Price site and other sites mentioned in this chapter.)

T. Rowe Price and the Commercial Web Site

There are four basic categories of Web sites:

1. Personal. Created by individuals to provide information about themselves or their interests.
2. Educational. Created by schools, museums, and other educational institutions to provide information.
3. Governmental. Created by government agencies or elected officials as a service to their constituents.
4. Commercial. Created by companies. The T. Rowe Price site falls into this category.

Types of Commercial Web Sites

According to poppe.com's Peter Adams, companies create sites for various purposes:

- Transactional site. The primary purpose is to perform transactions, such as ordering merchandise. All the content in the site revolves around setting up that function. Examples are Wells Fargo Online Bank, Virtual Vineyards, and Ticket Master.
- Consumer site. This type of site is promotional. It's fun and highly visible but does not usually offer much information. An example is Zima.Com.
- Marcom site (marketing communications). This approach has lots of information about the company, including material on the company's products and how to contact the company. The Chrysler Technology Center is an example.
- Content site. The T. Rowe Price site is a content site. There is limited information about the company, T. Rowe Price. Its primary goal is to provide content (investment information) to audiences. A content site differs from a Marcom site in that a content site is much bigger, has much more content offered to users, and there is less emphasis on mar-

keting and more on information. This is not to say it can't be used for marketing purposes. It is also possible to transform a content site into a transactional site, such as buying or selling mutual funds, but much of the information would have to be repositioned and redesigned. A content site is financially supported by transforming part of it into a transactional site or through online advertising. (Adams)

Production Background

T. Rowe Price commissioned the Poppe Tyson agency to create its Web presence through the online subsidiary poppe.com. The site was created in-house at poppe.com under creative director Peter Adams. Adams, Ken Godfrey, and Matt Freeman wrote the material for it.

Preproduction Process

The process of writing and designing the T. Rowe Price site followed the standard approach that poppe.com uses for developing content sites. A key part of the approach is to work from the beginning with the entire production team: writers, programmers, art directors, and designers. At poppe.com, developing a Web site is a collaborative process with several stages:

1. Gather content. The team engages in lengthy talks with clients to understand their business and digest existing material on the subject. The goal of this first stage is to understand and identify all the content that will be involved in the site.
2. Define categories and placement of content. The gathered content is spread out on a table before the entire production team, who ask a variety of questions: How would users make sense of all this content? What do they need to know when they get to the Home Page? What general category of information does this site offer? What is the main focus within this category? (The T. Rowe Price site category is mutual fund investing with a focus on investment planning and retirement.)

   Once the above questions are answered, then the team needs to:

   - Group content into categories
   - Determine the importance of each category
   - Decide on accessibility of categories. How quick do users need to get this information? Should it be on the Home Page?
   - What information is going to change regularly and what is going to remain static?

3. Organize information below the main categories and decide on the interactive structure. For example, how will categories and

subcategories be linked? The team evaluates whether a tree structure, branching, or dynamic flow will be best, and then they flowchart this interactive structure. They start at the Home Page, then the level 2 pages, then the level 3 pages, and continue to the bottom level. The final form at this stage is flowchart boxes with legends indicating the type of content and whether it is dynamic or static. This flowchart is attached to a marketing creative brief that explains the goal of the site in detail.

4. Writing the content. When the flowchart is approved, the team writes and designs the actual pages, starting from the top down and building section by section.

CHALLENGES OF WRITING AND DEVELOPING THE T. ROWE PRICE WEB SITE

The main challenge with this site was to write and organize it intelligently from the user's perspective so that it would be easy to navigate and understand. This was not an easy task because of the breadth and difficulty of the content.

A second challenge was determining how to manage so much dynamic content on a large site. How can the information be updated without keeping a whole team of HTML writers on the project and costing the client a fortune?

MEETING THE CHALLENGES

Dynamic Flow

Dynamic flow of information is the major technique that the poppe.com team used to make the program easy to navigate and understand. Dynamic flow means letting the users choose paths through the information, based on interactive questions. This lets users develop content around their interests. It is, however, hard to write and design, and users need to be instructed how to interact, but it ultimately creates a far more interesting and valuable site. (See the Additional Material section in Chapter 11 of the CD-ROM for illustrations of the following examples.)

Dynamic Flow Example #1 User-Designed Information—Watch List
The Watch List is a dynamic flow that helps users navigate mutual fund price and performance information quickly and easily. The Watch List is prominently featured on the Home Page in the first text below the welcome (see Figure 11–1, page 158):

> For up-to-date customized T. Rowe Price fund information, *register* now and create your own Watch List. Registration is free! Your personal Watch List will be updated daily and available 24 hours a day.

Clicking the underlined word "register" links to the Watch List Registration page, where the user types in his or her name, e-mail address, and password, and chooses a mutual fund from the following:

- Money Funds
- Taxable Bond Funds
- Tax-Free Bond Funds
- Domestic Stock Funds
- International Stock Funds

If the user chooses the last item, International Stock Funds, then he or she jumps to another list of choices:

- Emerging Markets Stock Fund
- European Stock Fund
- Global Stock
- International Discovery Fund
- Japan Fund
- Latin America Fund
- New Asia Fund

A user who chooses the Japan Fund and Emerging Markets Stock Fund finds that the next screen shows these two funds, with their current prices and their price changes.

Once a user has established a Watch List, every time this person logs on, he or she will be able to access the information for these two funds instantly instead of having to search a long list of mutual funds. Of course, a Watch List can be altered at any time.

This approach can be called user-designed information. The users designs how the Web page will present the information.

Dynamic Flow Example #2 The Interactive Tutorial: Online Investment Strategy Planner

A different approach to structuring information through dynamic flow is the interactive tutorial. This approach uses some of the training techniques discussed in the previous case study. This section of the site is reached from the Home Page by clicking either an image or text that reads "Mutual Fund Information." From the Mutual Fund Information page, the user can choose the Online Investment Strategy Planner. This leads to a page of text with an image of the T. Rowe Price chairman, who explains how the tutorial works and gives the user the choice of continuing with the tutorial by choosing: "Step One: Define your financial goals and time horizons."

The next few pages explain some of the concepts of investing in a non-interactive fashion. The Step One page introduces an image of another T. Rowe Price executive, a text explanation of possible financial goals, and the option to move to "Step Two: Understand risk and your risk tolerance." This page has another executive and an explanation of the material, and it leads to "Step Three: Finding funds to match your objectives."

After the basic information in these pages, the program becomes interactive, and the user is allowed to select the time horizon for his or her goal:

- 3–5 years
- 6–10 years
- 11+ Years

The user next selects the level of risk: Low, Moderate, or High.

The final result is a suggested investment strategy showing a mix of stocks and bonds, and with one more click, the user can choose the T. Rowe Price mutual funds geared to implementing this strategy.

Flowcharting the Dynamic Flow

Flowcharting a dynamic flow site can be difficult. It is done by starting with the main path on the flowchart and then doing separate flowcharts for each approach, for example, the low-, moderate-, and high-risk choices. The writer needs to anticipate the paths users will take but does not have to go to the last events (the last sections of information) for every chart variation. These sections might stay the same for several charts.

Managing Content on a Content Site

One of the challenges is figuring out how to update a site with lots of dynamic content without the cost of having a whole team of HTML writers on staff. Poppe.com solved this problem by creating content interfaces that allow the user to change the content without programming. For example, anyone can add new press releases to the site simply by cutting and pasting copy. An old release can also be put into an accessible archive for future use.

Other Techniques

There are a number of other ways that poppe.com made this complex information clear and easy to navigate. One was simple, precise writing, using all the tools of the print journalist that were discussed in Part I of this book.

There were several attempts to personalize this site, such as the pictures of the different executives that accompany the text in the Investment Tutorial. The goal was to give the impression that these individuals were giving the advice. This gave a human face to the narrator.

There was a consistent use of images throughout the site, which helped link the different sections to the Home Page. For example, the What's News Home Page image of a woman reading the paper is repeated in the What's News sections.

CONCLUSION: RESPONSE TO THE PROJECT

The site has been very popular. Over 10,000 users registered in the first few months. Peter Adams estimated this saved T. Rowe Price tens of thousands of dollars over traditional ways of presenting the information (direct mail, salespeople, etc.). This Web site also creates unmeasurable value, such as developing awareness of the T. Rowe Price brand.

REFERENCES

Adams, Peter. Telephone interview with the author, March 1996.
T. Rowe Price Web Site. http://www.troweprice.com

12

KEY POINTS FROM PART II: HOW TO WRITE NONNARRATIVE INFORMATIONAL MULTIMEDIA

GATHERING INFORMATION

As in any other information-based program, the first thing to do in informational multimedia is to gather as much information as possible on the subject and the audience. Study that information, and let your approach emerge from the material. If you are writing for a client, you also need to learn as much as you can about their expectations of the project.

CLARIFYING THE GOAL OF THE PROJECT

Be clear what the program is trying to achieve. Most programs have a combination of goals, but be sure your primary goal is clearly defined. Possible goals include to entertain, to teach a specific topic, or to inform about a broad topic, allowing the users to take what information they need.

DISCOVERING AN APPROACH

Simulation (Chapter 7)

If your information is focused on a process, consider a simulation, such as *The Nauticus Shipbuilding Company*. In a simulation, you first assign a role and a task to the user, such as a naval architect building ships. You then define all the elements of the task and describe the attributes and behaviors of each element. For example, the elements of the shipbuilding process include choosing hulls, propulsion systems, and superstructures. An attribute of an air cushion hull is that it is has shallow draft; a behavior is that it will sink in rough seas. Once the attributes and behaviors are defined, the user can perform the simulated task and receive realistic feedback.

Database (Chapter 8)

If your information is on a broad, loosely related subject, such as flight and space exploration as in *Sky High*, the key concern is organizing information into discreet units or categories and making this information accessible to the user. One way to do this is to organize the information around a concept map, such as the journey through time in *Sky High*. Another way is to use a guide or agent to lead the user through the material. It also helps the user's comprehension to present information with a variety of media (video, text, graphics, audio) and in a variety of ways, such as games, quizzes, and explorable spaces.

Training (Chapter 9)

If the information is narrowly focused and is on a subject the audience needs to learn precisely, consider a training model, such as that demonstrated in *Vital Signs*. A classic approach to training is to present the material in a variety of ways, starting at the simple and moving to the complex. This is the structure of *Vital Signs*. Its sequences are (1) Registration, (2) Pretest, (3) Humorous Introduction, (4) Overview, (5) Basic Terms, (6) Detailed Instruction, (7) Practice, (8) Case Study Experience, and (9) Posttest. You also need to present information in a variety of ways to accommodate each user's learning pattern.

It might serve students well to make the multimedia education process resemble the interpersonal education process by giving your program attributes, such as immediacy of response, nonsequential access of information, adaptability, feedback, options, and interruptibility (Chapter 6).

Web Site (Chapter 11)

If your information is fluid and needs to be constantly updated, consider going online, such as the *T. Rowe Price Web Site*, which offers daily updates on stock information and other financial news. Attempt to present your information dynamically, allowing the user to personalize the presentation of information. For example, instead of offering a general list of stocks, the T. Rowe Price site allows users to customize the information they receive by choosing the degree of investment risks and the number of years that they want to invest.

Online Advertising (Chapter 10)

If the primary purpose is to present information to customers and get them interested in your product, consider online advertising. In this case be aware of the standard structure of banner, middle page, and Web site. Try to use the many advantages of online advertising to present your information in the best way possible. These advantages include measurability, rotation, direct contact with customers, interactivity, reduced cost, and unlimited space.

LINKS AND STRUCTURE (CHAPTER 6)

Once your basic approach is determined, then you need to decide what type of structure will work best for your material. Several different types of structure and links are often combined in one piece. Possible structures include linear, linear with scene branching, hierarchical branching, single-level linking, worlds structure, and simulation. Links can be direct, indirect, and intelligent.

WRITING THE PROGRAM (CHAPTERS 4 AND 7)

The writing formats for information programs vary, but a fairly standard approach is that demonstrated in *The Nauticus Shipbuilding Company*. After an initial proposal is approved, writers produce a design document. This document often includes the design objective, creative treatment, project schedule, and a navigation/program flowchart. The final stage is usually a complete script, which includes all the dialogue, narration, and descriptions of the images and actions. There are a number of script format options (Chapter 4), depending on the type of project and degree of interactivity.

MECHANICS OF WRITING (PART 1)

There are many organizational devices that help in the planning of informational presentation, such as flowcharting and databases (Chapter 3). You also have to keep in mind the basic techniques of the print, radio, and script writer, such as keeping sentences short, using active voice, and writing visually (Chapter 2).

PART III

WRITING NARRATIVE MULTIMEDIA

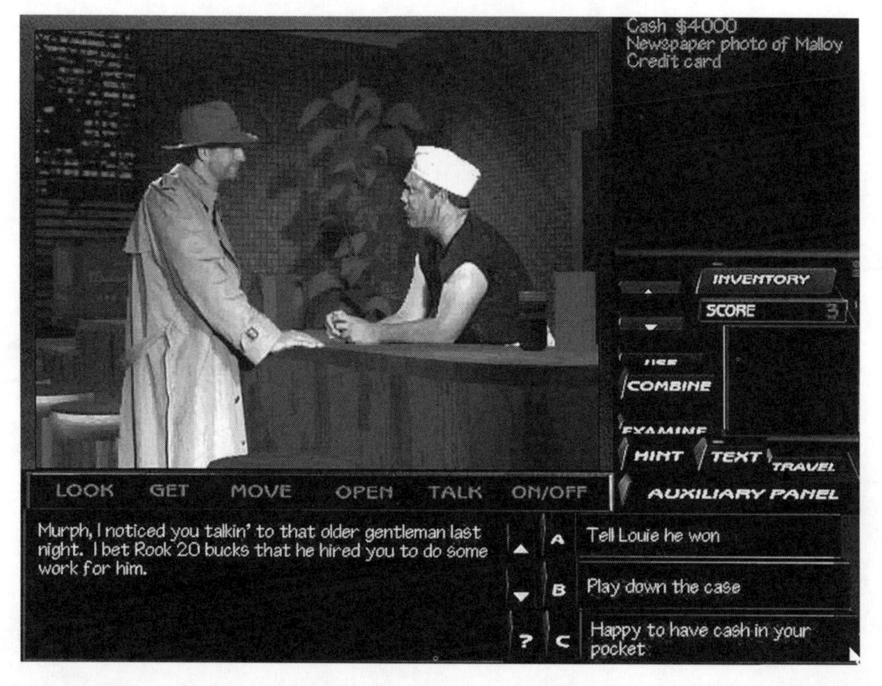

An interactive dialogue scene from *The Pandora Directive*. Courtesy of Access Software, Inc. © 1996 Access Software, Inc.

13

INTRODUCTION TO NARRATIVE MULTIMEDIA

A narrative is what we commonly refer to as a story, but "narrative" can be a complex critical term about which entire books have been written. Briefly, a narrative is a series of events that are linked together in a number of ways, including cause and effect, time, and place. Something that happens in the first event causes the action in the second event, and so on, usually moving forward in time.

Narrative multimedia involves telling a story using all the multimedia elements we've discussed in previous chapters, including the use of many media and interactivity. In narrative multimedia the player explores a story in the same way the user explored information in the programs discussed in the previous chapter. Often the player is one of the characters in the story and sees action from that character's point of view. But even if he or she is not a character, the player still has some control over what the characters will do and how the story will turn out. Interactive narratives can be used for pure entertainment or to present information in an experiential way.

NARRATIVES, SIMULATIONS, AND WORLDS

As David Riordan, the designer of *Voyeur*, points out, an interactive narrative, a simulation, and a worlds structure are three distinct forms.

In a virtual world program, such as *Myst*, the player explores an environment. The designers of a virtual world create a physical space, such as a mysterious island, where the player has the freedom to move about and interact with various elements, such as opening doors, examining objects, and even talking to people if any are present.

In a simulation, such as *The Nauticus Shipbuilding Company* (Chapter 7), a player explores all the different possibilities in an activity, such as building a ship or flying an aircraft. Simulations are not narratives. Even if they have a

Portions of this chapter originally appeared in the *Journal of Film and Video*.

script attached to them, if the elements in the program come up in a random pattern, they do not comprise a narrative.

In an interactive narrative, a player explores a story. Interactive narratives have beginnings, middles, and ends, even though each user may experience these elements differently. There is nothing unplanned in an interactive narrative. Someone who plays the program long enough, will eventually see all the material the writer created. An interactive narrative essentially allows each player to discover the story in a different way.

Simulations, worlds, and narratives can, of course, be combined. *Dust: A Tale of the Wired West*, profiled in Chapter 18, integrates a narrative into a virtual world. And *Wing Commander 3* gives players just enough narrative to engage them in the fantasy before going into a flight simulation.

CLASSICAL LINEAR NARRATIVE DEFINED

There are many different types of narratives, such as realist and modernist, but this chapter focuses on classical narrative. This is the type of narrative that dominates linear film, video, and interactive media. Before diving into the intricacies of interactive narrative, we'll begin with a quick review of the basics of classical linear narrative in film and TV.

Character

Classical linear narrative film and video are character driven. It is the character who grabs our attention and whose situation we are drawn into. Most successful film and video today clearly define their characters early in the piece. Who are the characters? Where are they from? What do they want or need, and why do they want it? What the character wants usually provides the action story of the film or video; why they want it provides the motivation for the actions and the underlying emotional story.

As an example, the pilot for the *Murphy Brown* television show establishes her character as a hard-driven, hard-headed, Motown-loving, liberal, successful TV reporter and a recovering alcoholic who is just returning from the Betty Ford Clinic. We learn all this information about Murphy through the items in her office, her colleagues' comments, her clothes, and her interactions with others. What Murphy wants (her action need) is to get an interview with the man who may have had an affair with the vice president of the United States. Why Murphy wants this interview is to prove that she is still a top reporter—her emotional need. If we are going to care about the story, it is important that we identify with this character and her needs. Identification can be achieved in a number of ways, including casting an appealing actor, creating sympathy for an underdog, and having the character do positive things. The best way to achieve identification, however, is to develop the character so that the audience clearly understands the character's needs.

Structure

Once the character's needs are established, then the writer can begin to structure the script. The key elements of classical narrative structure are exposition, conflict, climax, and resolution. Figure 13–1 lays out the basic structure of the vast majority of films and TV shows produced today.

Exposition or Setup

The beginning of the story must set up the lead character, the setting, and what the character wants—the goal to be achieved or the problem to be solved. Current films and videos tend to limit pure expositional sequences at the beginning and jump right into the story, integrating the story with the exposition. Some pieces open with an action scene and then slow down the pace in the next scene for exposition. However it is done, near the beginning of a script, the audience must learn who the character is, where he or she is, and what he or she wants.

Conflict

Once the writer knows the lead character and his or her goal, then he or she can start the character on the way to achieving that goal. Of course, if the character achieves the goal in the first scene, it will be a very short story. To avoid this happening, the writer introduces conflicts or obstacles. There are three basic types of conflict:

1. Person versus person.
2. Person versus the environment.
3. Person versus self.

In the *Murphy Brown* example, the people who oppose her goal of getting an honest interview with the vice-president's lover include Murphy's boss,

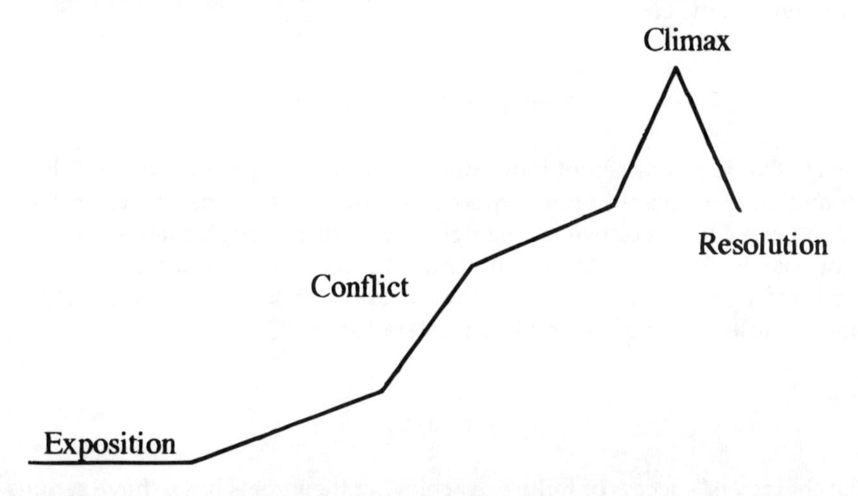

Figure 13–1 Classicial linear structure.

her colleagues, and the interview subject himself. The environmental obstacles include the frantic pace of the newsroom and the high pressure of the TV ratings game. Action stories are built around environmental obstacles where the hero has to climb mountains, ford rivers, and battle the elements. The last type of conflict, person versus self, is a way of adding considerable depth to a piece. In the case of Murphy, she has inner doubts as to whether she is still the hot reporter she was before dealing with her alcoholism.

A number of writing critics, particularly Syd Field in *Screenplay*, point to a key plot point or event in the exposition that shoves the character out of the exposition and into the conflict. In Murphy's case, it is when her boss sets up a meeting with the potential interviewee. Once the conflicts begin, then each conflict or obstacle should be more challenging than the last obstacle so that the story rises in intensity.

Climax

Finally the story nears the peak of intensity, and a final event jacks it up to the climax, which is where the character either achieves the goal or not. In Murphy's case, the climax takes place at the actual interview in the TV studio. Murphy asks the questions she wants and gets the honest interview, achieving her action goal and her emotional goal: to prove to herself that she still has it as a reporter.

Resolution

The resolution wraps up the story after the climax. The resolution of *Murphy Brown* involves a talk with her boss and, more important, a talk with her painter back at her house, where we learn that she achieved her emotional goal and is once again confident of her skills as a reporter. In most stories, the character changes or travels a character arc, as did Murphy; she changed from unsure about her abilities as a reporter at the beginning to renewed confidence at the end.

Scenes and Sequences

A narrative is comprised of individual scenes and sequences. A scene is an action that takes place in one location. A sequence is a series of scenes built around one concept or event. In a tightly structured script, each scene has a mini-goal or plot point that sets up and leads us into the next scene, eventually building the sequence. Some scenes and most sequences have a beginning, middle, and end, much like the overall story.

Jeopardy

The characters' success or failure in achieving their goals has to have serious consequences for them. It is easy for the writer to set up jeopardy if it is a life-and-death situation, such as escaping a murderer or blowing up a death star. It is harder to create this sense of importance with more mundane events. This is accomplished through properly developing the character. As in the Murphy Brown example, we care about her getting the interview because her emotional need for getting the interview is great. In a well-written script, if something is important to the character, it will be important to the audience.

Point of View

Point of view defines from whose perspective the story is told. The most common point of view or POV is third person or omniscient (all knowing). In this case the audience is a fly on the wall and can flit from one location to another, seeing events from many characters' points of view or from the point of view of the writer of the script.

The other major type of point of view is first-person or subjective point of view. In this case, the entire story is told from one character's perspective. The audience sees everything through his or her eyes. The audience can experience only what the character experiences. Used exclusively, this type of point of view has numerous practical problems. The primary one is that we never get to see the lead character's expressions except in the mirror. Because of this, stories that are told in subjective point-of-view narrative are sometimes told in third-person point of view in terms of the camera. This allows us to see the lead character. Voice-over narration is often used with subjective point of view.

Pace

Pace is the audience's experience of how quickly the events of the narrative seem to move. Many short sequences, scenes, and bits of dialogue tend to make the pace move quickly; longer elements slow it down. Numerous fast-moving events in a scene also quicken pace. Writers tend to accelerate pace near a climax and slow it down for expositional and romantic scenes. A built-in time limit accelerates pace and increases jeopardy by requiring the protagonist to accomplish his or her task in a certain time frame. For example, Murphy Brown had to decide what to do before the live broadcast of the interview that night.

Conclusion

The above has only scratched the surface of a complex topic, but it should be an adequate foundation for the multimedia narrative discussion that follows.

A key issue we will be looking at is how the writing of multimedia narrative differs from writing linear narrative.

THE ELEMENTS OF INTERACTIVE MULTIMEDIA NARRATIVE

They key difference between linear narrative and interactive narrative is the interactivity. Amy Bruckman of the MIT Media Lab writes, "In making a story non-linear, the story teller relinquishes the power to control the flow of information to the viewer. . . . A balance must be struck between giving the viewer freedom and maintaining narrative coherence" (Bruckman 12). Finding this balance—giving the player some control over the narrative, while allowing the writer to perform the necessary functions of the classical storyteller, including establishing characters and an engaging story structure—is the key challenge for the writer of interactive narrative.

Character and the Role of the Player

Character is as important in an interactive piece as in a linear piece, but characterization is vastly more complex because of the role of the player. Lena Maria Pousette, the writer of *Voyeur*, identified the key questions the writer must begin with: "What is the [game's] objective? Who is the player? And what does the player get to do?" (Willis 9) In an interactive piece, the player expects to be one of the characters in the story or at least have significant control over the characters.

Player Control

The degree of the player's control over the characters is one of the first decisions in writing a program. The basic types of control the player is allowed are choice of: scenes, the character's actions, or all the character's behavior.

Scenes

In this approach, the player can decide which path of the story the characters will choose, but once launched on that path, the characters function independently until the next branching point. *Boy Scout Patrol Theater* (Chapter 14) is a good example. The Boy Scouts in the story must decide whether to search the farm, the neighborhood, or the school. Once the player makes the choice to search the school, the characters function on their own until the next interactive point. The characters are usually seen in third person. (See example on page 177.)

Boy Scout Patrol Theater

SCENE 2
TROOP HQ

2—1. WS GROUP

ALEX
Okay. We all know why we're here.

CU GRAPHIC HIGHLIGHTING THE THREE AREAS BRENDAN IS TALKING ABOUT: ONE IS THE SCHOOL, TWO IS THE FARM, THREE IS THE NEIGHBORHOOD.

BRENDAN
Here's a map of the area we're covering. Let's divide it up into parts and cover each one. This is where she was last seen—the school. Here's where she lives. Between the two is the old Wilson Farm.

WHICH PART DO YOU WANT TO SEARCH? [IF A. THE SCHOOL]

SCENE 2A
2A—1. CU ALEX

ALEX
Chas and Don, you guys go see if she's not still hanging around the school.

M—1.
TRANSITION MONTAGE TO SCHOOL
1. POV HALLWAY
2. POV SCIENCE ROOM
3. POV POOL
4. POV STAIRS

SCENE 3
3—1. 2 SHOT BOYS enter a classroom.

Actions

In some programs, the player can control the actions of the characters. *Kings Quest VII: The Princeless Bride* functions this way. The player sees the Princess and her mother in third person. If the player clicks on another person in the scene, the Princess will talk to the new character, but the player has no control over what the characters say. If the viewer moves the on-screen arrow to the edge of the screen, the Princess or her mother will walk in that direction. The scene tends to be seen in long or medium shots so that the player can direct the action.

All Behavior

This is the highest degree of interactivity. In this mode, the player chooses what the character does and says. In *Dust: A Tale of the Wired West* (Chapter 18), the interactivity is almost always done in first person, which allows the player to become the character. In the shot from *Dust* shown in Figure 13–2, the player is talking to a gambler and must respond by choosing one of the tough guy lines on the bottom of the screen.

Combinations

Few programs function purely in one of the approaches above. Some programs, such as *Burn: Cycle,* a futuristic adventure game, very effectively combine approaches. This program appears very cinematic. Sometimes the character functions on his own, and other times the player controls the hero's actions, such as where he will run and whom he will shoot at.

Figure 13–2 Player controlling all behavior. © 1995 CyberFlix Inc.

Variable Control

In some programs, players can decide on how much control they want. In *Voyeur* the player watches the events in the mansion across the street, sees the news on television, and receives telephone calls. If the player just sits and watches, the corrupt politician is the protagonist of the story. If the player decides to try to stop the corrupt politician, the player can have a major effect on the plot.

Impact of Player Options

The degree of player control, player point of view, and the type of character played in a first-person point-of-view story all have significant impact on the story.

Player As Protagonist

To maximize player interactivity and immersion in the story, the best option is to allow the player to become the protagonist of the story by controlling all the character's behavior and seeing the action in first-person point of view. There are, however, drawbacks to this approach. One is that it is difficult to portray certain types of action in first-person point of view. For example, how do you show someone kissing the protagonist? The player also never gets to see the protagonist's expressions and actions, which are the main ways character is revealed. Because of this, first-person point-of-view, interactive stories tend to rely heavily on dialogue. Gender issues are also raised with first-person point-of-view interactive. Is the character male or female? If the character is assigned one gender, as in *Dust*, are there character identification problems for the player? If no gender is assigned, how do the other characters address the player/protagonist?

If the player is the protagonist, it is also difficult for the writer to develop him or her as a complex character. If the writer does develop the protagonist, as in the case of Tex Murphy in *The Pandora Directive*, you/the player are left with "a fictitious version of yourself who isn't like you at all and who does things you have never done in a world you have never visited." (Platt 147) The writer will also have to hope that the goal of the protagonist is something the player can identify with.

The alternative approach for the protagonist, as practiced in *Dust*, is to have a very general character, in this case, the Stranger. The player knows nothing about him, and so can perhaps more comfortably become him. But will the player be able to understand and empathize with the action and emotional needs of this sketchily drawn character?

Player Determining the Character

A way around the quandary of either defining a character that the player cannot fit into or leaving the character vague is to give the player a role in determining the character. Both *Dust* and *The Pandora Directive* do this to some degree. In both cases, depending on what dialogue the player chooses for the protagonist, he becomes nasty or nice. His change in behavior affects how the story progresses.

Some programs give the player even more power to create the characters. In *Caesar's World of Boxing*, the player gets to "interview" potential managers and trainers and choose one. The player also can define the physical appearance and fighting style of the boxers by entering information and adjusting the sliders on a game panel. This approach may not work for every story, but making the player an active part of the characterization process allows character development, while maintaining the interactivity of the narrative.

Player As Minor Character

Instead of being a major character, the player can be a minor character, as in *Voyeur*. The player may not seem so central to the action, but the advantage is that the portrayal of the minor character is not as crucial. If the minor character is only sketchily drawn, it will not have as much of an impact on the story as a poorly developed main character. It is also much easier to show the main action of the story in third person. For certain types of training and education programs, this type of third-person portrayal is essential. *A la rencontre de Philippe* is an interactive language program in which the player takes on the role of helping Parisian friends find an apartment. This allows the player to watch the native speakers interact in French, which was one of the goals of the program and which would have been more difficult if the player was a first-person protagonist.

Character Setup and Relationships

The player is only one of the characters in a program. Many others must be set up, but the demands of the interactive narrative do not make it easy to bring them to life. Space is always at a premium, scenes tend to be short, and character setup tends not to be interactive and thus is kept to a minimum.

An interactive writer needs to be able to introduce the characters quickly and simply. And once the characters are established, the writer also has to keep track of the different relationships of all the characters in all the possible versions of the story. Some writers develop a character matrix, so that they clearly know how all the characters fit together. (See the *Voyeur* case study in Chapter 16, page 252 for an example of a matrix.)

Overall Structure

Just as in a linear piece, in an interactive narrative, once the character and his or her goal are established, then the basic structure of the story needs to be developed. In interactive writing, however, this is far more complex than the simple linear structure illustrated in Figure 13–1 at the beginning of this chapter.

Linear Structure

Defined: Linear structure has no branching choices for the user.

Use: Linear structure is frequently used in narrative multimedia to set up the story. All of the narratives profiled in this book open with linear sequences before user interaction is possible. Linear video is also played during an interactive piece for additional background and to tie interactive scenes together.

Linear Structure with Scene Branching

Defined: This structure allows the user to choose alternative scenes, but after these alternative scenes are played out, the user is always routed back to the same main story line.

Use: This is a common structure in training and educational narratives. In *Patrol Theater* the basic structure is a linear story about trying to find a lost girl. At various decision points, however, the players get to make a choice, such as choosing to search the farm, the school, or the neighborhood. If they choose the farm, then they detour momentarily from the main story and search the farm, but eventually return to the main story. (See Figure 13–3.)

Hierarchical Branching

Defined: This structure involves taking the story in a completely different direction based on the viewer's choice at a preset decision point.

Use: Complete Story: Using hierarchical branching to take the complete story into different directions has limited options. For example, as illustrated in Figure 13–4, the character comes to a point where she can choose one of three options: marry Alan, marry Bob, or marry Carl. After that choice is played out, then the character can choose to be faithful, have an affair, or get divorced. The problem here is obvious: The number of choices increase exponentially. Adding one more set of choices to this chart would mean an addi-

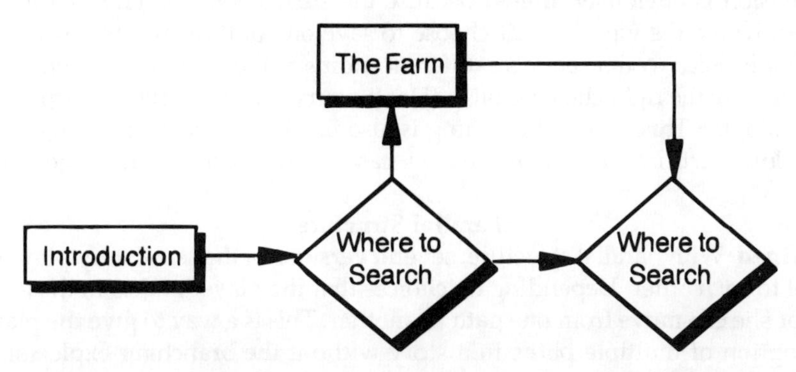

Figure 13–3 Linear structure with scene branching in *Patrol Theater*.

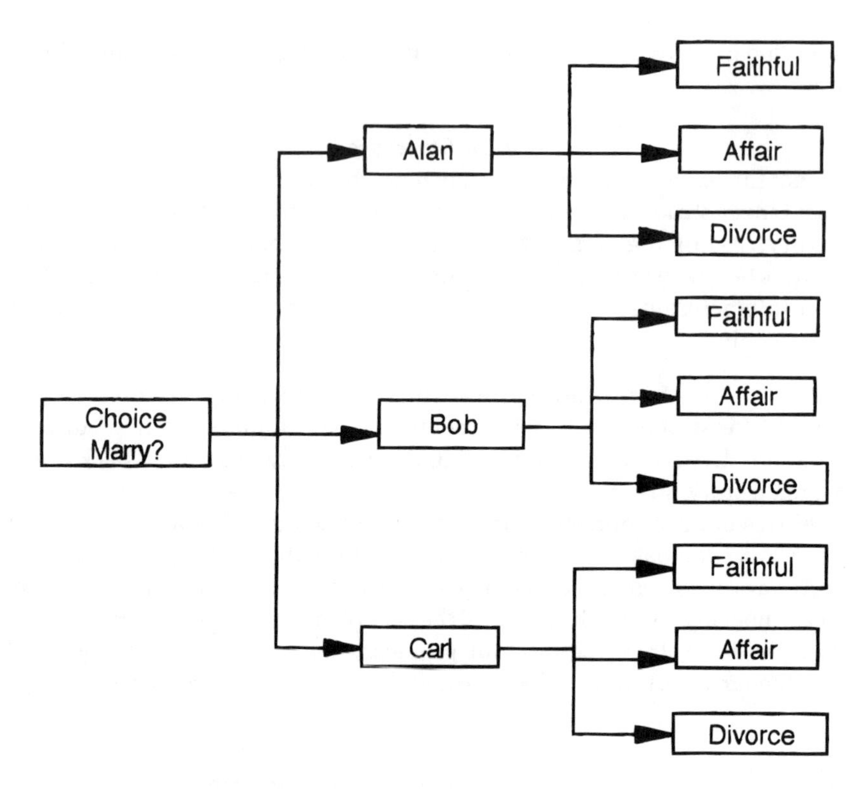

Figure 13–4 Hierarchical branching explosion.

tional 27 scenes, the next level would be 81 additional scenes, and the one after that 243 scenes! This is clearly too much material for a writer to present or a viewer to access.

Endings: Although it is rare for an entire story to be completed with hierarchical branching, it is commonly used for the ending of programs. This device gives the viewer a feeling of greater control over the narrative, and branching explosion is obviously limited because the story ends. The end of *The 11th Hour*, where the viewer must choose to save one of three women, is a good example. Each woman equals a different ending to the story. The wrong choice is oblivion; the right choice is bliss. (Don't worry; I won't blow the surprise.)

Dialogue: This type of branching is also used in interactive dialogue. See the flowcharts in *The Pandora Directive* case study in Chapter 17, page 274.

Parallel Structure

Defined: With parallel structure, several versions of the same story play parallel to each other. Depending on choices that the player makes in the story, he or she can move from one path to another. This is a way to give the player an option of multiple paths in a story without the branching explosion of hierarchical branching.

Use: *The Pandora Directive* (Figure 13–5) uses parallel structure. After a linear introduction, the player enters an interactive scene. Depending on the choices that he or she makes, the player can move up to: the A path, which is a Hollywood-type version of the story where the hero wins true love; the C path, a bleak, film noir experience of the story where everything goes wrong; or the B path, which is a middle ground. Each new interactive scene gives the player options to move back and forth between paths depending on the choices they make.

String of Pearls Structure

Defined: This structure moves away from simple branching. A string of pearls structure is a linked series of worlds structures connected by plot points or tasks that the player must accomplish to move forward in the narrative. As defined earlier, a worlds structure lets the user explore a location. By itself, a worlds structure cannot form a coherent narrative, but combined with other forms it can.

Use: *Dust: A Tale of the Wired West* uses the string of pearls structure. When the player/stranger first comes to town in the middle of the night, he is free to roam the town of Diamondback for as long as he wants. There are poker games to be played, hookers to talk to, and mysterious buildings to explore. This is a clear worlds structure—interesting, but by itself there is no story.

To move to the next day and advance the narrative, the player must find a place to sleep. He can either stay at the hotel or get one of the town's citizens to take him in. There are a number of ways to accomplish this goal. To stay at the hotel, he needs money. He can get cash at the saloon if he is lucky at blackjack, poker, or the slot machine. If he is nosy, he might also find the four bucks that somebody lost in the hotel couch. But when he does get the

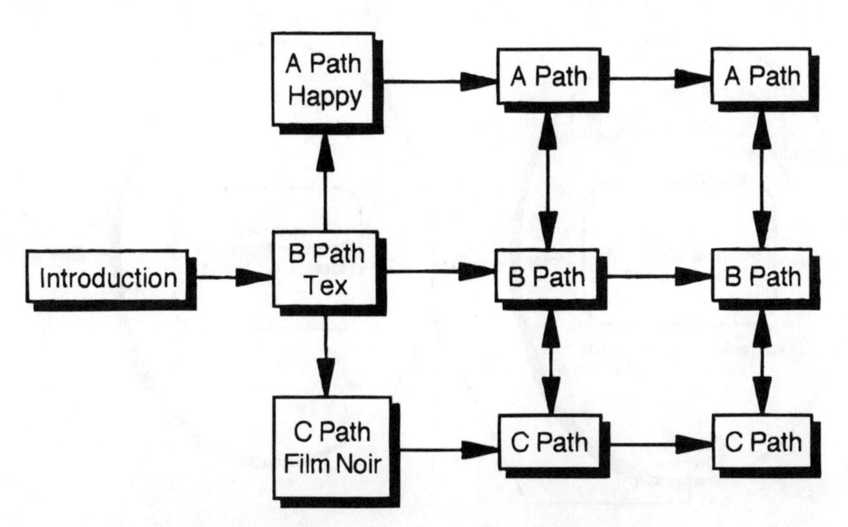

Figure 13–5 Parallel structure in *The Pandora Directive.*

money, the hotel owner says there are no vacancies. To get a room, it helps to meet Raddison, another character who lives there and who will introduce the Stranger (the player) to the owner. In order to get a citizen to take him home, he needs to sweet-talk the abrasive Mrs. Macintosh.

The player can perform all of these actions in any order desired, but eventually he or she has to find the right combination of actions to get a place to sleep and thus exit from the first night of the story and begin the next day/pearl on the string. In the second pearl, the next day's action, the player must get boots, guns, and bullets before moving on to the third pearl. (See Figure 13–6.) All of the player's accomplishments move the story forward to the final shootout and solving the mystery in one of six possible endings.

Variable State Environment and Types of Links

Defined: The most sophisticated interactive narratives today, which include *Dust* and *The Pandora Directive*, have moved beyond direct links and simple branching to something that Dave Riordan, the designer of *Voyeur*, calls a variable state environment. With the help of software and sophisticated design that responds in a sensitive way to the player's actions, there are multiple outcomes to scenes, depending on where the player has been and to whom he or she has talked. In short, the environment responds to the player, much as it does in real life.

A variable state environment can take into account hundreds of actions as opposed to just the A or B choices in branching. And each interaction played differently will yield different responses. Different combinations of different interactions will also yield different responses.

Use: In *The Pandora Directive*, if you as the player are tactless with your girlfriend, you will get into a fight. This causes you to get drunk and because

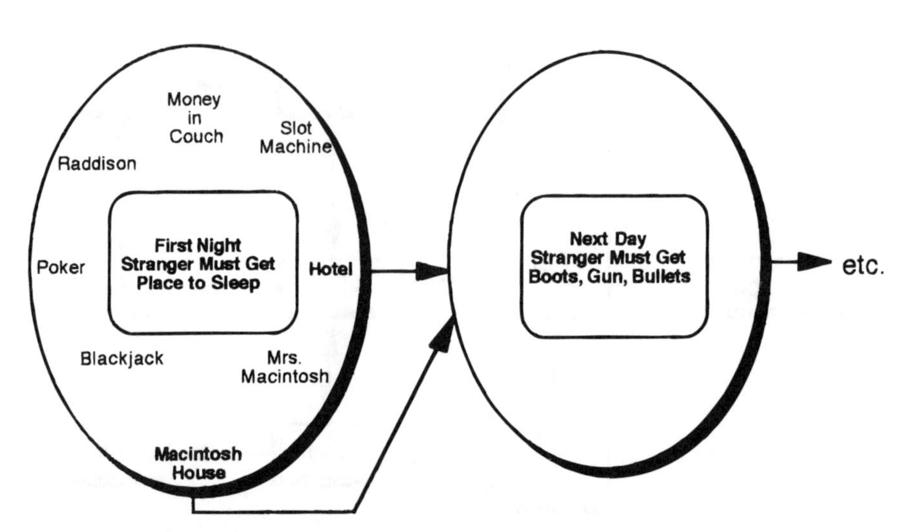

Figure 13–6 String of pearls structure in *Dust: A Tale of the Wired West.*

you are drunk, you are unable to save a nightclub singer's life. In *Dust: A Tale of the Wired West*, if you are rude to the mayor, his daughter will like you and later help you solve the mystery. This type of convoluted reactions to the player's actions is far more like real life than the direct reaction to a player's choices in the earlier generation of video games.

Exposition or Setup

Exposition is another issue that presents special challenges for the interactive writer. "If you spend time introducing the characters, the viewer is not being asked to do anything. In interactive that is death. Instead you need to discover the back story more as you go." (Riordan)

Tony Sherman said that one reason *Dracula Unleashed* works is that it has a built-in back story. Most people already know the basic story and characters of the original Dracula, and his production can build on that.

If a writer is not dealing with a known story, however, solving exposition problems can be a bit more complex. In the detective story *Under a Killing Moon*, Aaron Conners uses a number of expositional devices that are already established in this genre, but a key difference is that he gives his player the option of choosing them or not. A major device is that of voice-over. By clicking the mouse, a player can get the detective's thoughts on other characters, situations, and even objects. Players can also get background through video flashbacks. For example, as a result of clicking on the portrait of the detective's ex-wife, a short scene appears explaining her relationship with the detective.

Sets and Props As Expositional Devices

In interactive, special attention is also paid to sets and props to give exposition. *Voyeur* makes extensive use of these. They can be subtle props, such as a gun in a suitcase, or more overt props, such as a letter the player is allowed to read, or even active props, such as a television set that gives background information on the characters. The use of props in interactive multimedia differs from their use in linear video because in multimedia, the player gets to choose which props to examine, has far more props to choose from, and can do things that would be impossible in linear, such as move closer to a letter to read it.

Guaranteeing That Essential Exposition Is Seen

The danger of players' choosing what exposition they'll examine is that it is difficult to guarantee that essential exposition will be seen. One solution is to provide exciting linear exposition scenes for the first viewing that can be skipped on later plays of the game. Another approach is to separate the back story from the multimedia program. In *Gabriel Knight*, exposition is presented in a comic book that comes with the game. In other productions, it is the function of the design to lure the player into choosing the essential exposition, often with clever interactive devices.

Demonstrating How the Program Works

Players must be told how to interact with a program. What can they do? How do they move? Can they pick things up? How does the interactive dialogue work? The best programs integrate this information into the exposition and do not make the users read vast amounts of instructions before they can play.

One way to do this is to set up a simple situation at the beginning of the program that shows how the game works. For example, in *Dust*, the player is confronted with a nasty dog as soon as he enters the town. To get by this dog, the player must pick up objects, talk to characters, access help, and move about. A less integrated approach is to have a tutorial that plays a scene for the user and shows what to do.

Plot Points

Plot points or beats are story information that moves the plot forward. For example, in *Voyeur*, a key plot point is that Zack is angry at his father because his father fired him from an important research project. In an interactive story, making essential plot points is as difficult as presenting exposition. Because the user can choose which scenes to view, there is no guarantee that the user will choose a specific scene with a certain key plot point.

One solution to this problem is "to put two or three beats in a scene." (Pousette) This way if the user selects a scene, multiple plot points will be established. Another approach is to have the same information appear in a number of different scenes. The difficulty here is that the information can't be presented in exactly the same way or players will get bored if they select several of these scenes. The solution is to feed the essential information into multiple scenes but do it differently each time.

In a narrative that includes multiple story variations, such as *Voyeur* or *The Pandora Directive*, establishing plot points is even more complex than setting up exposition. Often much of the exposition will be the same for all possible stories. For example, in *Voyeur*, the back story on the corrupt politician and his desire to be president does not change from story to story. Plot points are, however, usually different in each story variation. This means that essential plot points have to be established for each story. It also means that scenes that are common to all variations cannot include plot points which contradict the plot in a specific story variation. Some writers use plot points or beats charts to keep all of these elements clear. (See the *Voyeur* case study, Chapter 16, page 262 for an example.)

Scenes

As the two above examples suggest, strong scene writing is important to the interactive writer. Writer Maria O'Meara believes "crafting a scene well is the most valuable technique of the interactive writer. Every experience in an interactive ought to be a tiny story or scene. Even if it's short, it still needs to have a beginning, middle and end." (O'Meara 3) Pam Beason of Microsoft agrees: "Every scene must contain a complete thought. An idea cannot be split over two scenes." (Beason) Jane Jensen, writer-designer of the *Gabriel Knight* series, says other characteristics of the interactive scene are that "scenes are smaller and there are vastly greater amounts of them. You have to think nonlinearly. As you approach a given location, think what will occur there." (Jensen)

The interactive writer, in other words, must write vertically as well as horizontally. He or she cannot be concerned only with what scene follows another. The writer also has to be aware of what other scenes in other possible stories might be connected to this one. Some interactive writers script ten or fifteen related scenes at the same time in order to keep tabs on all the connections. And rewriting can be ghastly. Change one element in one of fifteen connected scenes, and all the other scenes need to be rewritten.

Stephan Fitch sums it up: "Interactive writing is more like 3-D writing. The writer has to see the layers and move through the layers of the script, keeping track of parallel actions in a scene." (Willis 8)

Pace and Time

Interactive multimedia has no set running time. It depends on how the player plays the game. The challenge here for the writer is to create a consistent sense of time in the piece when a player might spend twenty minutes in a scene or might skip it altogether. Because time is also an important factor in pace, how does the writer deal with the way this variability of time affects pacing?

Player Creates the Pace

Gabriel Knight's Jane Jensen says that there is no way to have the kind of pacing in interactive that there is in linear, in which a writer can carefully create and sequence a number of scenes to create a faster or slower pace. In interactive, the player creates the pace. For example, a player goes into a haunted house and has to find a way out. The writer's job is to make sure that the scenes are dramatic in themselves and that the player is surprised when things happen. The player may think a certain room is safe from the last time he or she played, but this time it might contain a monster. (Jensen) How the player interacts with this environment creates the pace of the sequence, but that interaction is affected by the kinds of elements the writer-designer gives the player to interact with.

Multimedia Pace—Mini-Series Pace

The combined running times of multiple plays of an interactive movie is much longer than the running time of a two-hour feature movie. An interactive movie can be thought of more like a mini-series or a serial. For example, the writer can deal with much of the exposition the first time the game is played, which allows pace to be increased in later plays.

Manipulating Time to Affect Pace

Other writers and designers have actively manipulated time to affect the pace of the story. In Tony Sherman's *Dracula Unleashed*, the player has four days to solve the crime. A clock in the game keeps track of the time. In real time, going to a library and talking to someone may only take thirty seconds, but in game time the player may be deducted an hour. And while he or she is at one location, other scenes happen whether the player sees them or not, just as they would in real life. If the player is knocked out, he or she will miss several scenes and be docked eighty minutes on the clock. Sherman feels that although this time manipulation can add a sense of urgency to the game, the players do set pace. The story material stays the same; it is how it is played that affects the overall pacing.

Dave Riordan designed a similar use of time in *Voyeur*. Players have a weekend to solve or prevent the crime. To do this, they can choose which room to explore in the politician's mansion, but while in one room, events continue to happen in other rooms, unseen by the player.

An even more interesting use of time is in Riordan's *Thunder in Paradise*. In this program, the time spent in one scene affects what happens in later scenes. For example, in one scene the heroes have to battle the villains surrounding an island to save the heroine who is held there. If the heroes take a long time to defeat these villains, the other villains on the island itself have more time to prepare for them, and the heroes' difficulties are increased when they finally land. This use of time is an important step in making games reflect how time is experienced in real life. It can also give the designer more control over pacing. For example, if the player spends a long time on one scene, the next scene could automatically be altered to increase the pace of the sequence.

Dialogue and Other Sound

One of the difficulties of characterization in interactive media is the limited dialogue that is allowed because many scenes are less than a minute, and it usually takes longer to develop a dialogue scene. Shannon Gilligan, writer of *Who Killed Sam Rupert*? and several other titles in the *Who Killed* . . . series, compares dialogue writing in interactive media to "writing a symphony of snippets." She claims that it is how the writer relates these snippets together through the design that makes a successful sequence. (Gilligan)

The potential use of other sounds, particularly nonsynchronous sounds, is much greater than that of dialogue. Sound takes much less storage space on the disc than video. To take advantage of this, *Voyeur* has about thirty audio-only scenes that the voyeur can eavesdrop on. *Under a Killing Moon* uses the tradition of the ironic voice-over in the detective story and includes over five hours of voice-over that gives the player information about characters, objects, and situations.

NARRATIVE MULTIMEDIA GENRES

Currently action adventures and mysteries dominate interactive narrative. *Where in the World Is Carmen Sandiego?*, perhaps the most popular narrative multimedia educational series, is a mystery. Even the "first interactive horror movie," *Dracula Unleashed*, has a mystery plot, with the lead character trying to solve a murder. The appeal of the mystery and adventure story is clearly that they are strongly goal oriented. The player has something to aim for, obstacles are easy to establish, and jeopardy is built into the genre.

Are other genres also possible? *Caesar's World of Boxing* explores the boxing story. Much of the time in this program is spent preparing the boxer for the final challenge. Other genres, such as the caper film, also follow this character preparation approach and might be worth exploring. Jane Jensen and Maria O'Meara think romance would be a possibility if the writer could find something to drive the story forward. (O'Meara; Jensen) Tony Sherman, however, cautions that it will be difficult to expand interactive genres unless the audience changes. (Sherman) The primary audience for video games is young males. At present, the video game player makes up the bulk of the audience for the interactive video narrative. They are not likely to view a romance video.

Comedy

A genre that is particularly problematical in interactive is comedy. Surprise is such a major part of humor. Will a joke be funny if the player sees it more than once? How would humor, such as the topper, that requires precise sequencing work? Could a video have a running gag without guaranteeing that all the gag scenes would be accessed or without writing vast amounts of gag scenes to have different ones presented each time?

Shannon Gilligan thinks that the solution is to use interactive humor in nontraditional ways. She says, "Humor is set up in the space between the interactive elements . . . for example by contrasting characters and information between scenes." (Gilligan) In the *Magic Death*, which she wrote, there is an eccentric movie director character who is programmed to appear at the wrong place at the wrong time. The contrast between him and the serious scenes creates the humor. Aaron Conners takes a similar approach in *Under a Killing Moon* but instead concentrates on contrasting picture and sound. His character constantly makes wisecracks about the things that the player is seeing.

Nontraditional Genres

Traditional story genres, such as comedy and romance, may not be the only way to develop interactive narratives. Stephan Fitch suggests that viewers might simply like to browse a story to get more information. For example, in a true story, they may want to access background interviews and additional information. Another motivator might be artistic curiosity. Some people might like to watch different versions of the same story to understand various nuances, in the same way audiences watch a complex linear film several times to comprehend it fully.

A third option that Fitch suggests involves the Internet. Videos could be placed online. Anyone on the network could alter these videos, by reediting, adding new sound tracks, and so forth. Their version of the video could be reposted on the Net, and anyone accessing their version would have to pay them a small fee. (Fitch 63) At present, however, it is the goal-oriented story model that dominates the interactive movie.

INTRODUCTION TO NARRATIVE MULTIMEDIA CASE STUDIES

The case studies in this part of the book will demonstrate how various goals were achieved and challenges met in specific multimedia narrative programs. The following programs are examined:

- *Boy Scout Patrol Theater*, an interactive video disc and projection TV program located at the National Scouting Museum.
- *The 11th Hour: The Sequel to The 7th Guest*, a puzzle-based, psychological horror video game on CD-ROM.
- *Voyeur*, a political thriller on CD-I and CD-ROM.
- *Dust: A Tale of the Wired West*, a Western on CD-ROM.
- *The Pandora Directive*, the CD-ROM sequel to the sci-fi, detective mystery, *Under a Killing Moon*.

An understanding of how these writers dealt with narrative issues will provide the insight to deal with similar issues when they arise in your work. Each case study answers the following questions:

- Program Description and Background. Is the program a typical example of its genre or is it unusual? Who commissioned, developed, and wrote the program? What was the preproduction process?
- Goals. What were the writers' and designers' goals in creating this project? What information or experience were they trying to communicate?
- Challenges. Which goals were particularly difficult to achieve? What approaches were successful in achieving these goals and which were discarded?

- Response to the Project. Did the program achieve its goals? Was it a critical and/or commercial success?

The case studies are documented with script examples, screen shots, and flowcharts. Additional script samples and other material, including color screen shots and working demos, are available for many of the programs on the CD-ROM.

REFERENCES

Beason, Pam. Telephone interview with the author, July 1994.

Bruckman, Amy. "The Combinatorics of Storytelling: Mystery Train Interactive." MIT Media Lab, April 1990.

Conners, Aaron. Telephone interviews with the author, July 1994, August 1995, December 1995.

Fitch, Stephan. "Cinema Server = s/t (story over time)." Master's thesis, Massachusetts Institute of Technology, 1993.

Gilligan, Shannon. Telephone interview with the author, July 1994.

Halliday, Mark. "Digital Cinema an Environment for Multi-threaded Stories." Master's thesis, Massachusetts Institute of Technology, 1993.

Jensen, Jane. Telephone interview with the author, July 1994.

O'Meara, Maria. Letter to the author, June 1994.

O'Meara, Maria. Interviews with the author. Brookline, MA, July 1994, October 1995, December 1995.

Platt, Charles. "Interactive Entertainment: Who Writes It? Who Reads It? Who Needs It?" *Wired* 3 (September 1995): 145–197.

Pousette, Lena Marie. Telephone interview with the author, December 1995.

Riordan, David. Telephone interviews with the author, June 1994, October 1995, December 1995.

Sherman, Tony. Telephone interviews with the author, July 1994, September 1995.

Stalter, Katharine. "*Voyeur*. A Look into the Creative Process Behind the CD-I Game from POV Entertainment Group." *Film and Video* (April 1994): 64–120.

Willis, Holly. "Let the Games Begin." *Hollywood Reporter* (October 1993): S-1–S-32.

14

MULTIPLAYER NARRATIVE CASE STUDY: *BOY SCOUT PATROL THEATER*

Summary

Name of production: *Boy Scout Patrol Theater*
Writer: Maria O'Meara
Developers: Sand Inc.; Butler, Raila, & Company; Telematic Systems
Audience: Visitors to the National Scouting Museum
Medium: Interactive video disc and projection TV
Presentation location: National Scouting Museum, Murray State University, Murray, Kentucky
Subject: Search and rescue skills and other content from *The Boy Scout Handbook*
Goals: Entertainment, training
Structures: Linear, hierarchical branching

PROGRAM DESCRIPTION AND BACKGROUND

Boy Scout Patrol Theater is an interactive video that is projected on a large screen and played by a team of eight, the number of Boy Scouts in a patrol. The eight players must help a patrol in the video find a lost girl. In their search for the girl, the players must solve numerous problems, dealing with such topics as electricity, fire, and shock. The problems' solutions are drawn from the *Boy Scout Handbook*.

The hardware setup for this interactive piece is elaborate. The eight players sit at a table, which has a nameplate for each of the video's characters and a keypad in front of each player for answering questions. When a player sits in a certain character's seat, the player assumes that character's role in the video. (See Figure 14–1.)

Points are achieved by correctly answering the questions in the game. The nameplates light up when it is that person's turn to answer a question. Sometimes questions must be answered by the patrol leader, sometimes by the entire patrol, and sometimes by just two characters. This setup simulates the decision-making processes that occur in a Boy Scout patrol.

Sensors in the seat let the computer know what seats are occupied. If fewer than eight people are playing the game, the questions for absent characters/players are reassigned to those who are present.

The *Boy Scout Patrol Theater* has audience space for thirty people. There are several variations on the same questions so that members of the audience can watch a game being played and then play their own game with fresh material.

Museum Multimedia and Multiplayer Narrative

This is an unusual, interactive, multimedia museum program. Most museum multimedia is nonnarrative and played by one or two users. The *Boy Scout*

Figure 14–1 *Patrol Theater,* National Scouting Museum.

Patrol Theater has a story and is played by a large group. (See *The Nauticus Shipbuilding Company* case study in Chapter 7 for a more detailed discussion of multimedia in museums.)

Multiplayer, multimedia narrative is rare and restricted to museums or similar settings. Multiplayer hypertext narratives, however, have been popular on the Internet for years. (Hypertext is limited to text; there are no images.) A number of companies are currently developing multiplayer online games that include on-screen images or avatars that represent each player. At this point, these games are closer to glorified chat rooms than true narrative, but multiplayer online narrative is an area that should see some interesting developments in the near future. (See the Chapter 14 section of the CD-ROM for hot links to multiplayer online narratives.)

Production Background

The Boy Scouts of America commissioned Michael Sand of Sand Inc. to develop the exhibits for the museum. Sand hired Madeline Butler and Paul Raila of Butler, Raila & Company and Fred Raab of Telematic Systems to develop the interactive media. For the *Boy Scout Patrol Theater* project, Butler, Raila & Company hired Moeller Inc. for the electronic hardware and Mystic River Productions to produce the video. Mystic River hired the writer Maria O'Meara.

The developers first decided what all the exhibits would be. Once they determined that they were going to have a patrol theater, the developers and the client came up with the rough structure of a Boy Scout patrol solving a mystery. Madeline Butler developed an outline and flowchart. Maria O'Meara wrote the script.

CHALLENGES AND SOLUTIONS IN WRITING *BOY SCOUT PATROL THEATER*

The Audience and the Story

Because the primary audience of this museum is Boy Scouts, former Boy Scouts, and their families, there were a number of restrictions on developing the story: the content had to be drawn from the *Boy Scouts Handbook*, there had to be eight characters and eight players to simulate a real eight-member Boy Scout patrol, and all the main characters had to be boys.

An early decision was that the basic story would be a mystery with humor. Because of this, there couldn't be anything too gruesome in the mystery or it wouldn't be funny for this audience. The mystery, however, had to be important enough to engage the audience. It couldn't be something as trivial as a lost purse. The missing person scenario fulfilled all the story requirements.

Turnaround Time

Patrol Theater is the only exhibit of its kind at the Scouting Museum. In order to allow the maximum number of museum visitors to play the game, it is essential to move each set of players quickly through the exhibit. One of the ways the writers dealt with this challenge was through limiting interactivity. Frequent linear scenes keep the story moving forward, and if players choose a dead-end interactive branch, such as searching the school a second time, they are quickly turned back—in this case with a shot of the school and a caption that reads SCHOOL'S OUT. Even the interactive questions are timed; players must answer them before the music stops or lose points.

The need for a quick turnaround also had an impact on character development, which in this case was particularly complex because the Boy Scout patrol consisted of eight main characters. The writer did not have the time for complex character development so instead opted for using easily recognizable types and taking a moment at the beginning to introduce them to the audience.

Presenting *Boy Scout Handbook* Information

It was important to integrate the *Boy Scout Handbook* information in a series of problems that would be engaging. This was achieved primarily through use of humor and diversity of presentations.

Humor

Humor was integrated into the information through funny graphics and silly sound effects that were elicited by wrong answers to test questions. Humor also serves as a memory aid. Once seeing the trench and water solution lampooned in the example that follows, it's unlikely a player would choose it again.

WHAT IS A GOOD WAY TO PUT OUT THE FIRE?

a. Bring water
b. Stomp on it
c. Dig a trench around it

[a. Hal looking through bottomless bucket—BACK IN AN HOUR!!]
[c. Hal peeking over top of trench—DEEP TROUBLE!!]

Diversity of Presentation

Another way to keep the *Handbook* material interesting was to present the material in a variety of ways, through questions, memory games, and role playing.

Questions Various types of questions had to be answered by the players to earn game points and advance the story, such as the one that follows about insects.

4-3. 3 SHOT MR. QUINCY, HAL, GREG

MR. QUINCY
You *may* ask me something, boys, but first you must tell me what kind of insect this is. You know how important it is to recognize the plants and animals of your own region.

GREG
But Mr. Quincy, this is important.

MR. QUINCY
Of course it's important. It's our planet, the planet earth.

SCENE 4A

4A-1. CU INSECT #1

HAL
(voice-over)
Let's just answer the question.

WHAT KIND OF INSECT DOES MR. QUINCY HAVE?

a. a bee
b. a hornet
c. a wasp

Memory Games According to the writer, Maria O'Meara, memory games were included because they are particularly popular with Boy Scouts. For example, scout troops often play a version of the Kim Game, a memory game from Rudyard Kipling's *Kim*. In the script sample that follows, the scouts are shown a picture of the lost girl and are later quizzed on what she was wearing in the picture.

SCENE 5

LANZ LIVING ROOM

5-1. CU ELEANOR'S PHOTO

MARIE (voice-over)
This was taken only a couple of weeks ago. In fact she's wearing the same outfit she was this morning.

5-2. 3 SHOT MARIE, ED AND FRED

MOM (from off camera)
Marie. Bring that picture out here for the police to study.

Marie runs off and the kids are left with no photo.

ED
Hey Fred. She took the picture.

FRED
Ed, we need a complete description. Let's try to remember everything we can.

WHAT WAS SHE WEARING?

a. A red sweatsuit
b. A red dress
c. A red bathrobe

Role Playing Other information from the *Handbook* was integrated more directly into the story, as in the following longer script sample, where players must successfully perform a variety of tasks, such as treating a shock victim, putting out a fire, and searching an abandoned house. (The complete script is on the CD-ROM.)

Boy Scout Patrol Theater Script Sample

VOICE-OVER SCRIPT FOR INTRODUCTION TO PATROL THEATER

Welcome to Patrol Theater, a game of skill and chance . . .
Where your team must play against the clock
To get hidden clues and find the missing child.

At certain points in the story, a question will appear on the screen. Try to answer the question before the music stops. See if your patrol can beat the all-time high score.

Sometimes the whole team votes on the answer.
Sometimes two people vote as partners.
But you're all working as a team, so help each other get the right answer.

You'll know it's your turn when your name-plate lights up. Vote for the right answer by pushing A, B, or C on your keypad. Let's give it a try now.

(All players' lights go on.)

(menu screen)

DO YOU WANT TO MEET THE PATROL?

A. YES

B. NO

C. MAYBE

[If A. or B.]

Graphic: A SCOUT IS FRIENDLY. VOTE AGAIN.

SHOOTING SCRIPT

LIVE ACTION

Alex—Patrol Leader
Bob—Assistant Leader

Chas—young, easily impressed, Don's translator
Don—smart, uses bigger than average words

Ed—good with people, likes little kids
Fred—Ed's twin

Greg—itching for action, doesn't like a lot of gabbing

Hal—Mr. Practical—to the point

SCENE 1
THE ALERT
1-1. CU SENIOR PATROL LEADER on phone

SENIOR PATROL LEADER
Alex, there's a child missing. Her name is Eleanor Lanz. She's five years old and our troop has been asked to help find her. She was last seen at the Benson School playground at noon.

1-2. CU ALEX on phone

ALEX

Well, we'd better put our camping trip on hold and put the patrol mobilization plan into effect. Where should we search?

SENIOR PATROL LEADER

I want you guys to take west of the railroad. I'll contact the other patrols. You get started right away.

1-3. CU Bob on phone

Bob

Right, Alex. I'll be right there. I've got the maps.

1-4. CU CHAS on phone

CHAS

At your father's workshop? Fine.

1-5. CU DON on phone

DON

Glad to pitch in. Glad to pitch in. I'll bring the first aid kits.

1-6. 2 SHOT ED on phone, FRED listening next to him

ED (to Fred)

We've got to find a missing kid.

FRED

Our bikes are out front.

1-7. CU GREG on phone

ALEX (voice-over)

We're going to need to communicate with each other when we're out on the field.

GREG

I've got the walkie talkies right here. Had them ready for the camping trip.

1-8. CU HAL on phone

HAL

Be there as fast as my feet will carry me.

SCENE 2
TROOP HQ

2-1. WS GROUP

ALEX

Okay. We all know why we're here. Bob has divided the map up into areas. We're going to use the buddy system to cover each one.

BOB

Here's a map of the area we're searching.

2-2. MAP GRAPHIC

BOB (voice-over)

This is where she was last seen—the school. Here's where she lives. Between the two is the old Wilson Farm.

WHICH PART DO YOU WANT TO SEARCH?
A. THE SCHOOL
B. THE FARM
C. THE GIRL'S NEIGHBORHOOD

IF A. THE SCHOOL
SCENE 2A
2A-1. CU ALEX

ALEX

Chas and Don, you guys go see if she's not still hanging around the school.

M-1.

TRANSITION MONTAGE TO SCHOOL
1. POV HALLWAY
2. POV SCIENCE ROOM
3. POV POOL
4. POV STAIRS

SCENE 3
3-1. 2 SHOT BOYS enter a class room.

CHAS
We've been everywhere.

DON
Yeah. If she's not here, she's not in the school . . .
Look, that man . . .

3-2. MS Janitor on ground holding a wire

SCENE 3A
WHAT SHOULD THEY DO?
(Test Question)

a. Turn off the lights
b. Use a dry cloth to pull the wire away
c. Pull him away from the wire

[a. evil-looking electric wire assaulting the two boys
CAN'T GET RID OF ME THAT EASILY]
[c. janitor looking up BE CAREFUL, BOYS!]

SCENE 3
3-3. 3 SHOT CHAS, DON using neckerchief to pull wire out of JANITOR'S hand. The janitor moans. He is clearly still breathing.

CHAS
I'll go call an ambulance.

DON
I'll stay here with him.

SCENE 3B
WHAT SHOULD DON DO?
a. perform CPR
b. cool him off
c. raise his feet and keep him warm

[a. Janitor I'M STILL AWAKE!]
[b. blue Janitor surrounded by icicles BRRRRR!!]

CARD: LATER
SCENE 3
3-4. 2 SHOT DON & JANITOR. Don raises Janitor's legs.
3-5. 3 SHOT DON, CHAS, JANITOR—PARAMEDIC enters.

CHAS (to janitor)
Listen, we're looking for a little kid. Eleanor Lanz. You know her?

JANITOR
What are ya? A couple of boy scouts?

DON
As a matter of fact, we are.

JANITOR
Oh, well I haven't seen her, and I've been around all day.

CHAS
Okay, thanks.

WHICH PART DO YOU WANT TO SEARCH?
A. THE SCHOOL
B. THE FARM
C. THE GIRL'S NEIGHBORHOOD

[IF B. THE FARM]

2B-1. 2 SHOT ALEX AND BOB

ALEX
Greg and Hal—search the farm.

(Scenes have been deleted. In those scenes, the boys search the farm and the neighborhood, but don't find the little girl. They regroup at headquarters, where they must decide where to search again.)

(Graphic Decision Point)
WHERE DO YOU WANT TO SEARCH AGAIN?
A. THE SCHOOL
B. THE FARM
C. HER NEIGHBORHOOD

[a. Shot of School, caption reads SCHOOL'S OUT]
[c. Shot of house, NICE HOUSE, NOBODY HOME]

[IF B. THE FARM]

[After plotting the best way to get to the farm and putting out a brush fire along the way, they arrive at the farmhouse.]

SCENE 11
THE FARM
11-1. WS FARM buildings—barn and farmhouse
11-2. WS with group

ALEX (counting heads)
Well, we're all here . . .

GREG
No one else has found her?

BOB
No, as far as we know, this is the last place she could be.

ALEX
Bob, Ed, Fred and Hal. You guys search the barn. The rest of us will search the house.

Graphic Decision Point
WHERE IS ELEANOR?
a. The Barn
b. The House

[If b.]
SCENE 12
HOUSE
12-1. 2 SHOT ALEX AND DON

DON
This place is a wreck!

12-2. POV wrecked room

ALEX
Hope she's okay.

BOYS
Eleanor? Eleanor? Are you in here?

SCENE 12 A
WHEN SEARCHING AN ABANDONED BUILDING, WHAT SHOULD YOU DO?
a. Crawl across the floor
b. Stay close to the walls
c. Hold hands and walk in a line

[a. Don crawling on floor—Balloon reads YOWEE ZOWEE! BROKEN GLASS!]
[c. Alex at one end of frame—Don at the other. They are looking down a huge hole WHERE DID EVERYBODY GO?]

SCENE 12B
WHEN SEARCHING AN ABANDONED BUILDING, YOU SHOULD NEVER . . .
a. Go in after dark
b. Start at the top [High angle. Boys peering out]
c. Go near the walls [Boys plastered against wall]

12-3. MS OF BOYS walking along wall

DON
This place could be structurally unsound. The floors could collapse at any moment. I think it's safest for everyone to stay near the walls.

GREG
I sure hope we find her before it gets dark.

HAL
If we don't, she could spend the night in here alone.

SCENE 13 {if a.}
BARN
13-1. WS BOB, ED, FRED, HAL opening door and going in.

BOYS
Eleanor, are you in here?

HAL
How could she be in here if the door is closed?

BOB
Maybe she crawled in through a hole. Look, over here—sweatsuit fuzz!

ED
This is a big place for a little girl.

FRED
Yeah, there's two floors. Maybe three.

13A
WHERE SHOULD THEY START LOOKING?

a. In the basement
b. In the back rooms
c. On the top floor

[a. a balloon coming out of darkness THAT LAST STEP IS A LU LU]
[b. empty room, balloon reads NOBODY HERE BUT US GHOSTS]

13B
WHERE WOULD A FRIGHTENED CHILD MOST LIKELY BE?
a. In a corner
b. In the middle of a large room
c. On the stairs

[b. Close-up of Eleanor—balloon reads NO WAY]
[c. Close-up of Eleanor—balloon reads TOO SCARY]

13-2. CU HAL

HAL

Let's start at the top. That way it'll be impossible to miss her.

13-3. 2 SHOT ED AND FRED

ED

I'll bet she's hiding in a tiny space like a corner . . .

FRED

Or under some bales of hay.

BOB

What makes you say that?

ED

Our little sister . . .

FRED

Amelia . . .

ED

Got lost once, and we found her in a closet.

FRED

I guess she felt safe in there.

A whimpering sound.

13-4. MS from top of stairs looking down at group.

BOB

That's her. She must be upstairs. (on walkie talkie) You guys, get out of the house, we know she's in the barn.

13-5. POV going up the stairs.

ED

I heard her again.

HAL

You're right. She's up there somewhere.

13-6. WS GROUP
They approach the girl's hiding place. Of course it is very scary, with cobwebs and maybe a falling rake or two to add suspense and tension. She is hiding in a tiny nook.

GREG
There you are, you little potato.

13-7. CU ELEANOR

BOB
Come on out.

The girl won't come.

ED
Eleanor. Your mom is waiting for you.

FRED
It's time to go home.

She comes out.

13-8. WS Group

ALEX
Bob, call in and explain exactly where we are.

ELEANOR
Can I go home soon?

ALEX
That's what we're here for. To take you home.

SCENE 14
14-1. NEWS REPORTER GIVING REPORT

REPORTER
And we have good news tonight. Little Eleanor Lanz took the wrong way home from school today. She was lost for several hours before she was found by Scout Troop 34 in an abandoned barn. Good work, guys.

GRAPHIC—The End

[The final screen gives the players their score.]

Analysis of Script Sample

This program is a good introduction to interactive narrative. It demonstrates basic scene and action branching in a way that is easy to understand. This narrative has hierarchical scene branching, when the boys choose which of three places to search for the missing girl. There is also hierarchical branching at an action level, such as in the electrocution rescue, where the players can choose from a variety of possible actions.

Nevertheless, the interactivity in the overall plot is limited compared to some of the other case studies in this part of the book, such as *Dust: A Tale of the Wired West* and *The Pandora Directive*. This is because the interface designer (Madeline Butler) and the writer (Maria O'Meara) of *Patrol Theater* felt they could better maintain the suspense of finding the girl in a linear story, while reserving the primary interactivity for the questions and games.

In addition to having less complex interactivity, *Boy Scout Patrol Theater* is different from the other narrative case studies in that it is not designed primarily for home entertainment. Interactive narrative has many uses beyond video games. It is used in many genres, including training, education, and marketing. Its use in these genres is often similar to what we see in *Boy Scout Patrol Theater*. Users play roles in an interactive narrative where they can explore the consequences of different decisions, thus learning to make the correct choices.

This piece also demonstrates that complex interactivity in and of itself is not necessarily a positive thing. The interactivity in *Patrol Theater* is relatively simple, yet it achieves its purpose well. A writer should not be afraid to use limited interactivity if it will accomplish the goal of the program.

CONCLUSION: RESPONSE TO THE PROJECT

Boy Scout Patrol Theater was one of the original programs installed when the museum opened, and it remains one of the most popular programs there. No formal evaluation of attendance per exhibit has been done, but this program frequently draws large, enthusiastic audiences and a steady stream of players.

REFERENCES

O'Meara, Maria. Telephone interview with the author, November 1995.
Butler, Madeline. Telephone interview with the author, November 1995.

15

PUZZLE-BASED GAME CASE STUDY: *THE 11TH HOUR: THE SEQUEL TO THE 7TH GUEST*

Summary

Name of production: *The 11th Hour: The Sequel to The 7th Guest*
Writer: Story and screenplay by Matthew Costello, revisions by David Wheeler
Developer: Trilobyte, Inc.
Audience: Rated for teenagers (ages 13+ and up)
Medium: 4 CD-ROMs, includes The Making of *The 11th Hour*
Presentation location: Home
Subject: Psychological horror story
Goal: Entertain
Structures: Linear, string of pearls

PROGRAM DESCRIPTION AND BACKGROUND

The 11th Hour: The Sequel to The 7th Guest is a psychological horror video game. As stated in the title, it is the sequel to *The 7th Guest,* one of the most popular computer games ever created. *The 11th Hour* uses the same haunted house and many of the same characters as the first game, which was set in the 1920s, but the new game places the action in the present, where a series of mysterious murders and disappearances plagues the towns surrounding the house.

One of the people who disappears is Robin Morales, a successful TV producer. Carl Denning, her ex-lover and the star of her show, goes to the haunted house to find her. (See Figure 15–1.) The player assumes the role of Denning, directing his search of the house. The point of view alternates

Figure 15–1 Foyer of the Stauf mansion.

between seeing Denning from a third-person point of view, as in a traditional movie, and seeing through Denning's eyes in first-person point of view. The player/Denning is helped in the search by a personal digital assistant (PDA), which mysteriously appears at his home. The PDA includes a video screen, VCR-type controls for rewind and playback, a keyboard, an electronic map of the house, and a help button.

This PDA game book plays segments of video about Robin's investigation of the haunted house. To earn these snippets of video, the player/Denning has to solve dozens of puzzles created by Henry Stauf, an evil toymaker and master of the mansion. A successful player of the game gradually pieces together the video, which shows what happened to Robin. The program ends with a final deadly game between Denning and Stauf.

The 11th Hour: The Sequel to The 7th Guest and the Video Game

Unlike some of the narratives described in later chapters, both *The 7th Guest* and *The 11th Hour* are puzzle-based games, which have a strong appeal to a major portion of the gaming audience. The puzzles include word puzzles, board games, and even artificial intelligence games. Most of the puzzles have a limited connection to the story.

Writer Matthew Costello said that what set *The 7th Guest* apart from other video games of this type was that it was one of the first games that actually tried to scare computer game players. *The 11th Hour* continues in this horror tradition but moves from the Gothic horror of the first game to psychological horror.

Production Background

Matthew Costello wrote the story and script for *The 11th Hour*. This script was revised by the video director David Wheeler. The project was developed by Trilobyte Inc., whose head designers, Graeme Devine and Rob Landeros, had major input into the script, particularly how it would be used in the overall game. Trilobyte, located in Medford, Oregon, is a major developer of video games. *The 11th Hour* was distributed by Virgin Games, Inc.

GOALS AND CHALLENGES IN WRITING *THE 11TH HOUR: THE SEQUEL TO THE 7TH GUEST*

The challenge in writing and designing *The 11th Hour* was to tell a compelling, interactive horror story without abandoning the puzzle-based game format that had been so successful in *The 7th Guest*. The developers wanted the story to be interactive, but they did not want to hand over complete control of the story to the user. As designer Graeme Devine said in a recent interview: "I've learned perhaps most of all that I want to be, need to be, a storyteller, and that means that I want it to be my story—have my start, my middle, my end—rather than allow the stories to be so interactive that there's a zillion endings, a billion middles, and a hundred beginnings." (Demaria, 284)

MEETING THE CHALLENGE

The Interactive Story, the PDA Game Book, and Puzzles

The primary way the writers and designers met the challenge was through the use of the PDA game book. The story of Robin Morales's disappearance was originally written as a linear video, but instead of playing it as a linear video, the user can access only bits and pieces of it on the game book. These intriguing bits and pieces lead the user forward in the search for Robin. The player can also play back the video snippets and gradually assemble them into the complete story. The player eventually learns that the game book and its images are an attempt by Samantha, an earlier victim of the house, to help Denning save Robin.

The player needs to understand what happened to Robin in order to make the right choice at the end of the game. This process is not unlike the traditional mystery in which the investigator gradually puts together the story of what happened by piecing together bits of information. (See *The Pandora Directive* case study in Chapter 17.) One difference here is that the game book actually delivers video images as opposed to just getting information about the past through dialogue.

The second major difference in *The 11th Hour* is that the video snippets are not discovered through carefully putting together the evidence and clues related to the event. Instead the video is earned by solving puzzles in the Stauf Mansion that are unrelated to the Robin Morales story. Many of the puzzles involve a treasure hunt in which investigator Denning must win games and interpret clues to find certain objects, such as a champagne bottle. When he finds that bottle and pops the cork, he is rewarded with a video scene.

Although nothing the player does will alter the Robin Morales story in the game book's video, the player does have the choice of where to explore in the house and which games to play and which games to skip. In order to nudge the narrative forward, however, not all puzzles and not all rooms are open to the player at one time. This is illustrated on the game book map, which indicates which rooms are open at a certain time and place in the game. What video the player can access is also limited by where the player is in the game.

Linear Narrative and Introduction of the PDA Game Book

The game book is introduced in the linear beginning of the story when a package arrives at the home of Carl Denning. Before the package arrives, Denning is watching a TV show that is discussing the disappearance of his producer and lover, Robin Morales.

INTRO-1 INT/DENNING'S COUNTRY HOME—AFTERNOON

A UPS truck is pulling away and a package is on the doorstep. Denning crouches down and picks it up and goes back inside. He returns to his chair and opens the package, revealing a small, portable computer of some kind. He switches it on, and a game flickers to life on the machine . . . "Funhouse From Hell"—Cartoony images of mayhem, monsters . . .

Slowly, the computer game changes to an image of Robin looking frightened in the basement of an old house. She speaks to him from the small screen.

ROBIN

Carl. . . help me . . . please! . . . I can't get out . . .I. . .

The image of Robin fades away and the video screen goes blank as if the game has shut itself off. Denning shakes the box and clicks it on and off but it seems to have died.

DENNING

What is this!?

He sets the game computer on the arm of the chair, gets to his feet and begins to pace. The game starts beeping.

He grabs it and switches it on. An image of the Stauf Mansion appears briefly and fades away and the game shuts down again.

DENNING

Damn!

Then the screen comes alive for another brief moment: An image of Robin appears. She mouths the word "Help," but there is no sound and the picture quickly fades. Denning pulls on a leather windbreaker and stuffs the game in his pocket as he crosses the room and leaves in a rush.

[The remainder of the introduction is also linear until Denning actually enters the Stauf Haunted House]

Interactive Narrative and the Puzzles

Once Denning enters the house, the remaining video has to be earned by solving puzzles and finding objects in a treasure hunt. These puzzles are justified narratively because the evil master of the house, Henry Stauf, is a toymaker and game designer who likes to torture his guests with difficult and deadly puzzles.

One of the first puzzles occurs when Denning enters the house. The game book beeps, and a creepy male voice (Stauf) says, "Winter coat worn for a mixer?" The words also appear on the game book screen. By touching the help button, the player/Denning gets this clue from a mysterious female voice: "Be warned that 'worn' means *destroyed*." (The player can, of course, make the puzzle more challenging by not pressing the help button.) A second try with the help button elicits, "Mixer might not be a party. What if it's a beverage?" The following hints include: "Something's mixed up here" and "A beverage might be found in the library."

With the help of the map in the game book, the player can find the library but still might need a couple more clues to discover the object of his search. The help button offers: "Winter coat is an anagram" and "Winter coat is an anagram of 'Tonic Water.' " The player/Denning now knows he is looking for tonic water. But before being allowed to find the tonic water, the player first has to solve a puzzle that involves putting all of the same color of books together in a limited number of moves. If he succeeds at this, he is finally allowed to get his hands on the bottle of tonic water. The reward is a video clip about Robin played on the game book (in boldface type in the script that follows).

Interactive Video Script Sample

Although the video about Robin is presented interactively to the gamer, it was written and shot as a linear story. In the script sample that follows, the sections in boldface type are examples of video fragments that are triggered by Denning's solving puzzles and finding various items. The script sections that are not in boldface type are not initially revealed to Denning, but the player/Denning eventually gets to see all the scenes.

MODULE I SCENES: HARLEY-ON-HUDSON

I-1 EXT/COFFEE SHOP ON MAIN STREET—DAY

There is a line of pick-up trucks parked outside a coffee shop in "downtown" Harley. Like the rest of the town, the coffee shop seems frozen in time—somewhere in the late fifties when the freeway went in and traffic (and life in general) began to pass Harley by. Like a flash to the present, a convertible driven by a young, beautiful woman in dark glasses motors down Main Street and pulls into a parking spot between two beat-up pick-ups in front of the coffee shop. The coffee shop is filled with breakfast customers and all eyes are on the convertible. The woman gets out and she's dressed in a fashionable short skirt, heels and a tailored jacket—all in black—looking as if she'd be more at home in a Manhattan design studio than the sleepy town of Harley. It's Robin. She walks up to the front door of the coffee shop and goes in.

[The following boldface segment is revealed to Denning on the PDA when he touches the tonic water bottle in the haunted house.]

1-2 INT / COFFEE SHOP—DAY

Robin enters the coffee shop and stands just inside the door next to the cash register, keeping her dark glasses on. All motion has come to a complete stop and everyone is looking at her. Finally a waitress speaks up. She's a truck-stop woman—kind of voluptuous, a little rough-edged and attractive in an earthy sort of way. She has a prosthetic hand protruding from the sleeve of her sweater. Her name is Eileen Wiley.

EILEEN
Just sit anywhere, honey. Menus are on the table.

ROBIN
Thanks. Is there a non-smoking section?

There is a slight rumble of laughter. Virtually everyone including the cook is smoking. Eileen grins and shakes her head.

Robin walks toward a booth by the window. The only sound is the clicking of her heels and the slight rustle of her clothing. She sits down, takes off her dark glasses and inspects the menu. Slowly, everyone goes back to their business and the sound level raises back up to that of a normal coffee shop environment. Eileen comes over to Robin's table.

EILEEN
What can I get for you this morning?

ROBIN
Do you have oat-bran muffins.

EILEEN
This isn't an oat-bran kind of place, honey.
We're big on chocolate donuts here.

ROBIN
I don't suppose you have any Perrier water.

EILEEN
Let me check . . . Hey Slim, we got any
Perrier?

Slim is the cook. He sticks his head out from the kitchen.

SLIM
Fresh out of Perrier, Eileen. Had a big run
on it this morning.

Everyone in the restaurant laughs.

EILEEN
Sorry, honey. How about a San Pellegrino?

ROBIN
Oh? That would be fine.

EILEEN
I'm kidding, hon. The only water we got
comes out of the tap.

ROBIN

Just bring me a donut and a coffee.

EILEEN

Now you're talkin'. Shall I make that a cappuccino?

ROBIN

Enough with the jokes, okay?

EILEEN

No, I'm serious. As unlikely as it seems, we actually have an espresso machine.

Robin smiles and shrugs.

ROBIN

Okay.

EILEEN

Be right back.

She leaves and Robin takes out a small palm-size computer and begins to type.

Eileen returns with the donut.

EILEEN

Here you go. Be right back with the coffee.

ROBIN

You're Eileen Wiley, aren't you?

EILEEN

Who wants to know?

ROBIN

I'm Robin Morales. I'm a producer with *Case Unsolved*—the TV show.

EILEEN

Is that the one with Carl Denning?

ROBIN

Uh-huh.

EILEEN

Ooh I like him . . . Wouldn't mind serving him up a couple of specials.

She laughs and Robin smiles.

EILEEN (CONT'D)

What's he like?

ROBIN

He's . . . uh . . . he's a man.

EILEEN

You mean he's a man like you can't live with him or a man like you can't live without him?

Robin thinks about it a moment, then grins.

ROBIN

He's both.

EILEEN

Aren't they all?

They both laugh and Eileen sits down.

EILEEN (CONT'D)

So what are you doing in Harley?

[The following segment is revealed to Denning on the PDA when he takes a cork from a champagne bottle in the haunted house.]

ROBIN

I'm researching a story on the Stauf Mansion.

Eileen's mood changes in an instant.

EILEEN

I can't help you.

ROBIN

You're the only person who's survived an encounter with the mansion.

EILEEN

Who told you that?

ROBIN

Everyone else has either disappeared or died.

EILEEN

It's all just stories.

ROBIN

What happened to you there?

EILEEN

You know so much already, why do you need me to tell you.

ROBIN

The newspaper said a guard dog tore your hand off. What really happened?

Eileen's eyes are flooded with tears. She gets up out of the booth.

EILEEN

I gotta get back to work.

ROBIN

I'm sorry I upset you.

Eileen tries to laugh it off.

EILEEN

Not me. Be right back with that coffee.

She leaves. Robin glances around the restaurant. Once again everyone is looking at her . . . But now there is a touch of anger in their eyes. Robin puts on her dark glasses as if to hide behind them and looks out the window.

1-4 INT/MOTEL OFFICE—DAY

A desk clerk is struggling with a crossword puzzle in the office of THE HARLEY INN, a dingy, run-down, 1950's motel. He looks up as the door opens and smiles leeringly.

[The following segment is revealed to Denning on the PDA when he touches a satyr in a painting.]

CLERK

Hello, Marie.

An eighteen year old girl moves with a slow sensual saunter toward the desk. She has a look of petulant sexuality, dressed in a short denim skirt, white high heels and a white T-shirt.

MARIE

Where's Chuck?

CLERK

I thought maybe you were here to see me.

MARIE

You wish . . . Is he in his office?

The clerk checks his watch.

CLERK

He's got a meeting in five minutes. He hasn't got time for you today, Marie.

She smirks.

MARIE

Just tell 'im I'm here.

He picks up the telephone and punches a button.

CLERK

Chuck, Marie Wiley's here to see you . . . But you got a meeting at eight . . . Okay, okay.

He hangs up and reaches behind him for a room key and hands it to Marie.

CLERK

Lucky number 7 . . . Have fun.

She takes the key and turns and leaves without another word. The clerk watches Marie's hips move under her tight-fitting skirt as she goes out the door.

[This scene continues, and there are several more scenes in the first module, which is shown during the "Seven O'Clock" section of the game.]

Multiple Endings

Although the player/Denning accesses the video about Robin in bits and pieces, the order in which he accesses the video has no affect on the Robin Morales story. Piecing together Robin's story and properly understanding it does, however, help the player make the right choice at the end of the game, where Denning faces three possibilities. Unlike the earlier puzzles, which weren't directly related to the story, this final choice is "a real dramatic choice which goes to the player's values and interests." (Costello) Following are the multiple endings of *The 11th Hour.*

V-8 INT. TEMPLE'S BEDROOM—NIGHT [REAL TIME]

Denning rushes in, hearing the screams of Robin.

ROBIN(OS)

Oh, God—help. Please, no more—no.

DENNING

Robin!

But he enters the room, and there's no one there. Nothing. The door slams behind him. There is a rumble, the sound of the house fully alive, a deep bass note that swells. Denning slowly turns.

And as he turns we see three doors . . . and each door begins to open . . . slowly . . . End of Module V.

ENDGAME

The opening sequence of the Endgame is triggered after all scenes of Module Five have been witnessed. Then the final choices are presented . . .

E-1 INT. THE STAUF MANSION—NIGHT [11:00]

DENNING stands facing the three doors. Stauf materializes in front of the doors.

STAUF

Hello, Carl Denning and welcome to "LET'S MAKE A REAL DEAL"!

DENNING

Who the hell are you?

STAUF

Why, I'm Monty Stauf, your host on LET'S MAKE A REAL DEAL and have I got a real deal for you . . . I wonder what this is in my pocket . . . (He reaches into his pocket and pulls out a wad of money) . . . Six, count 'em, six hundred dollars!

He peels off six bills and hands them to Denning.

STAUF (cont'd)

Now, Carl, here's the deal: You can keep the six hundred dollars but you must choose a door, be it door number 1, 2 or 3 . . . OR you can pay me two hundred dollars and see what's behind the door of your choice. What'll it be, Carl?

DENNING

I'll pay.

He gives Stauf two hundred.

STAUF

Thank you. Now which door?

DENNING

The one in the middle.

STAUF

Okay! Let's see what's behind door number two!

The door opens to reveal a large television set.

STAUF

A big screen TV! Isn't this fun, Carl? . . . Now, let's make another deal. You can keep the TV AND the four hundred dollars you have left or you can pay me two hundred dollars to see what's behind another door.

Denning gives Stauf another two hundred.

DENNING

Let's see what's behind number one.

STAUF

All right! What a player! . . . Door number one!

The door opens to reveal Marie. She's sitting on a chair dressed in a black bra and panties, garter belt, stockings and high heels.

STAUF

It's sweet Marie! She can be absolutely yours anytime, night or day!

MARIE

Anytime.

STAUF

Imagine the hours of fun and enjoyment you'll have with Marie! A lot more exciting than watching TV.

MARIE

You can watch me if you like.

She places her hands on her knees and trails her fingers up the inside of her thighs. She licks her lips and smiles. Suddenly the big screen TV flickers to life, and Samantha [an earlier victim of the house, who has been helping Denning] appears on the screen.

SAMANTHA

Be strong, Carl Denning. Don't give in to temptation.

STAUF

Damn it! I thought that TV was unplugged!

SAMANTHA

Choose me.

STAUF

What a choice! Marie—sweet, sensuous, sexy Marie—or Samantha in a wheelchair! Hah!

DENNING

What's behind door number three?

Stauf extends his arm and rubs his fingers together.

STAUF

Pay up.

Denning gives him the last two hundred dollars.

STAUF (CONT'D)

Door number three!

The third door opens and Robin is there.

ROBIN

Carl, I've been so frightened. Please, choose me. Save me. I love you.

MARIE

I'll give you anything you want . . .
Anything and everything.

SAMANTHA

Don't listen to them. You'll be lost forever.

STAUF

Shut up, Samantha!

SAMANTHA

He's afraid of you, Carl. Choose me. Destroy the power of this hellish house.

ROBIN

Carl, you have to choose me. After all we've been through . . . I need you, Carl.

MARIE

Anytime . . . anyplace . . . any way you want me.

Stauf confronts the player.

STAUF

Well, what'll it be, sport? The choice is yours . . .

CUT TO: THE DOORS.

E-2 INT. TEMPLE'S ROOM—NIGHT

(Triggered by choosing Robin)

Note: All choices should be made real choices—all saved positions from Mod Five on will be erased after choosing. The Player is told this. They can eventually see all three endings—but not before re-experiencing the last part of the game . . .

Denning chooses Robin's door. He enters and they embrace. There are tears in her eyes.

ROBIN

Thank God.

DENNING

Let's go home.

E-3 INT/DENNING'S COUNTRY HOME—DAY

Robin is in Denning's living room watching a newscast on TV. A woman anchor person is reading the news.

ANCHOR

The body of TV reporter Carl Denning was found floating in the Hudson river today. Denning disappeared during his honeymoon in Harley-on-Hudson after his celebrated marriage to Robin Morales, newly appointed president of the Stauf Broadcasting System.

Robin watches without emotion. She clicks a button on a remote control and the picture fades to black.

E-4 INT. TEMPLE'S ROOM—NIGHT

(Triggered by choosing Marie)

Denning moves toward Marie's door. She gets up from her chair and walks away into the darkness beyond, looking over her shoulder with a seductive smile. Denning enters the door and follows her.

E-5 INT/BEDROOM—NIGHT

Denning enters a bedroom. Marie is on the bed, lounging back, inviting. Denning gets on the foot of the bed and crawls up on top of her. He kisses her and she responds passionately which unleashes a hunger in him. She rolls him over so that she is straddling him. She kisses his neck and chest and unbuttons his shirt as she works her way down. Denning looks down at the mane of hair cascading over his stomach. She looks up at him—but it isn't Marie. It's Stauf in a wig!

STAUF

What a deal!

Denning screams.—THE REST OF THE SCENE IS PLAYED INTO THE CAMERA AS PLAYER'S POV. Stauf rolls off the bed and grabs a barbecued rib from a plate on a dresser. He tosses the wig onto the bed.

STAUF

I'll let you in on a secret—'cause you're so special. (smacks his lips) Mmmm . . . these are good . . .

He laughs. He offers up a rib.

STAUF (CONT'D)

Like a bite? . . . Some choice you made, huh? Oh, don't look so sad. I'm not so bad . . . See . . .?

Stauf metamorphoses back into Marie, still eating the rib, red sauce dripping off her chin onto her chest. More lip-smacking.

She holds out the rib, nearly finished.

MARIE/STAUF

Sure you wouldn't like a bite . . .? After all—(she laughs) . . . It's you!

Marie laughs uproariously and the laughing voice begins to sound like Stauf's, then she metamorphoses back into Stauf, laughing, doubling over. He begins to cough and it becomes a disgusting, choking sound. As he chokes, he begins to change into his native form—the alien creature that's been behind this all along. It looks up, jaws open, salivating—as it leaps, devouring the player into blackness.

***E-5-PG INT/BEDROOM—NIGHT [PG VERSION]

Marie leads Denning into a bedroom holding his hand. When they reach the bed, she pulls him close and they tumble to the mattress. He kisses her and she responds passionately. She rolls him over so that she is on top. She kisses his neck and chest and unbuttons his shirt as she works her way down. Denning looks down at the mane of hair cascading over his stomach. She looks up at him—but it isn't Marie. . . . etc.

E-6 INT. TEMPLE'S ROOM—NIGHT (Triggered by choosing Sam)

Denning moves toward the middle door containing the TV with Samantha's image. He reaches to touch the screen and there is an explosion of white light.

E-7 INT/SAMANTHA FORD'S STUDIO—DAY

Denning finds himself in Samantha's studio. Samantha looks up at him, sitting in her wheelchair next to one of her monitors. She looks more relaxed than anytime before. She smiles.

SAMANTHA

Welcome, Carl Denning. You made the right choice.

DENNING

It wasn't easy.

SAMANTHA

No.

DENNING

I hated leaving Robin behind.

SAMANTHA

I know. You risked your life for her . . . But it was too late to save her.

DENNING

So what happens now?

She extends her hand.

SAMANTHA

Come and see.

He takes her hand and stands behind her as they both look at the monitor. On the screen, the Stauf Mansion is engulfed in flames.

SAMANTHA

You won, Carl.

DENNING

What about Robin?

Samantha shakes her head.

SAMANTHA

She was lost the moment she said yes to Stauf.

They watch the monitor as the house burns. There are tears in Denning's eyes. Samantha looks content, virtually radiating an inner peace. It's been a long battle for her. On the monitor, there is nothing left but blackness.

THE END

Horror and Humor

Another element that the writer Matthew Costello thinks makes this game successful is its blending of humor and horror, because "part of horror is to laugh and be scared." (Costello) If a horror viewer has no release from fearful tension, he or she can overload and turn off to the material.

The following example occurs towards the end of the game when the murderer, Chuck, is himself destroyed by the house.

IV-8 EXT/MANSION—DAY

Chuck struggles with his heavy burden in the overgrown field approaching the mansion.

IV-9 EXT/MANSION PORCH—DAY

Chuck drops his bloody bundle on the porch and knocks on the door. This time when he pushes the bundle in, Chuck gets pulled in with it.

IV-10 INT.—INSIDE THE STAUF MANSION—NIGHT

Chuck finds himself in the kitchen.

JULIA HEINE is at the table cutting something with a cleaver. She is dressed as she was in *THE 7TH GUEST*, except the dress is faded, tattered and stained. She whacks at whatever she's cutting . . . She looks up at Chuck.

JULIA

Are you ready?

CHUCK

For what?

JULIA

Soup's on.

Stauf suddenly appears.

STAUF

Soup's on!

A head emerges from the soup pot.

HEAD

Soup's on!

The kitchen starts to change, the walls turning a deep red, shiny, dripping. And in the cascade of red blood streaming off the walls, onto the floor, there are faces, screaming faces in the wall, looking out, begging. Chuck begins to scream. Julia comes towards Chuck, her meat cleaver dripping blood.

JULIA

How 'bout a Chuck roast?

Stauf laughs.

STAUF

Chuck steak!

HEAD

Chuck him into the soup!

The cleaver comes down.

The Writing Process

The writing process for *The 7th Guest* and *The 11th Hour* was similar even though the story structure was different. The scenes in the first game were designed to be self-contained scenes. In the second game, however, the scenes were meant to be combined to form a complete linear story.

For *The 7th Guest,* the developers had the basic idea about a haunted house game and an evil toymaker. They contacted Matthew Costello, a horror novelist, to develop the story. He created a novella and broke it into scenes connecting them to each room.

The 11th Hour followed the same writing process, but the story grew out of the Stauf files, which were background material for *The 7th Guest.* Costello wrote a novella based on this material and sent it to the designers, Graeme Devine and Rob Landeros, who critiqued it. Then Costello wrote a script using film script format, with the difference that each segment is numbered and tied to a certain room in the mansion and eventually to the prop in the treasure hunt that triggers it. This device broke up the linearity of the story and organized the narrative by the physical environment and by the way that the user interacts with that environment. This script received further comments and revisions by designers Devine and Landeros and video director David Wheeler.

CONCLUSION: RESPONSE TO THE PROJECT

Critical response to the project was strong. It received raves in most of the major gaming magazines, won a Critic's Choice Award from *CD-Rom Today* and an Invision Award from *New Media,* and it topped many best-seller lists.

REFERENCES

Demaria, Rusel, and Alex Uttermann. *The 11th Hour: The Sequel to the 7th Guest—The Official Strategy Guide*. Rocklin, CA: Prima Publishing, 1996.

Costello, Matthew. Telephone interview with the author, December 1995.

16

CINEMATIC NARRATIVE CASE STUDY: *VOYEUR*

Summary

Name of production: *Voyeur*
Writers: Lena Marie Pousette, Jay Richardson, and Michael Halperin
Developer: Philips POV Entertainment Group
Audience: Mature
Medium: CDI, CD-ROM
Presentation location: Home
Subject: Political thriller
Goal: Entertain
Structures: Linear, branching

PROGRAM DESCRIPTION AND BACKGROUND

Program Description

Voyeur opens with a special TV bulletin:

NEWSCASTER
Will he or won't he? This is Tish VanAlden and that's the hot question on everybody's lips during this primary season.
Billionaire bachelor and business genius Reed Hawke has yet to commit himself to the race for the Oval Office. Well, hang on to your hats, folks,

because he's gathering his flock this weekend to "help him reach a decision" and when the Hawkes get together, the feathers are bound to fly.

The feathers are bound to fly because Reed Hawke's children, Jessica and Zack, his niece Chloe, and his sister Margaret all have enough dirt to bring him down if they decide to use it. Reed has gathered his family at his mansion to clear the air one way or the other before announcing for the presidency.

The player/voyeur lives in an apartment opposite the Hawke estate and with a powerful video camera can see and hear what goes on in any room of the mansion. When the user pans the "camera" over one of the mansion's windows and the cursor changes to an eye icon, it indicates that the room holds a video scene, an ear icon indicates an audio scene, and a magnifying glass indicates evidence. The top image in Figure 16–1 shows the view of Reed's mansion through the video camera. The eye icon appears over the foyer. Clicking brings up the foyer video scene in the bottom image.

The goal of *Voyeur* is to figure out which of Reed's family members are going to expose him and then stop Reed before he kills that person for endangering his grab for the presidency. If the player collects enough evidence with the camera, he or she can warn the family member by sending the tape or by contacting the police. If, however, the player contacts the police with inadequate evidence, he or she might be thrown in jail as a peeping Tom. If the player contacts the wrong family member, he or she might tell Reed, and the player could get a visit from Reed's assassin.

Complicating the search for Reed's accuser/victim is that there can be up to six scenes happening at one time in different rooms, so a player watching what is happening in one room will miss what is going on in the others.

Adding to the fun and the replay value of *Voyeur* are the four variations on the main plot, which are loaded randomly each time the game is played. In each variation, a different member of Reed's family attempts to expose him.

Voyeur and the Interactive Narrative

Voyeur was a major step toward moving multimedia entertainment away from video games for kids and into interactive narratives for adults. It was one of the first programs to use adult themes and subject matter, star actors, and a sophisticated, literate script.

Production Background

Voyeur was written by Lena Marie Pousette, Jay Richardson, and Michael Halperin. It was designed by David Riordan. Philips POV Entertainment Group developed all elements of the project, except for managing the actual

Figure 16–1 Top: The game interface and the voyeur's view of the Hawke Mansion. Bottom: The view of the foyer seen through the voyeur's video camera.

video production and hiring the video production crew, which was handled by Propaganda Films. The program was first released on CD-I, an interactive disc format that is used with a special player connected to a regular TV. *Voyeur* was later released on CD-ROM for both Mac and PC.

GOALS AND CHALLENGES IN WRITING *VOYEUR*

Goals

The creators of *Voyeur* wanted to develop a narrative, interactive multimedia program that had a sophisticated cinematic quality and to move away from the arcade-type action adventure game. The goal was to create a story that users can step into and understand who they are in relation to the other characters and what their purpose is in the story, not just an exploratory environment like *Myst*. Through this more sophisticated narrative, *Voyeur* attempted to reach out to the larger audience that watches movies and television.

Challenges

Creating this sense of reality and cinematic quality in an interactive, multimedia narrative presented a number of challenges:

- Overcoming technical limitations.
- Creating a sense of cinematic story complexity and pace, while still allowing repeat play, a key concern for the multimedia audience.
- Giving the program a "real-life" feel.
- Achieving all of the above without losing interactivity.
- Maintaining interactivity while performing necessary story functions, such as setting plot points, characterization, and establishing jeopardy.

MEETING THE CHALLENGES IN WRITING *VOYEUR*

Overcoming Technical Limitations

Voyeur had a number of technical limitations that were the result of executive decisions and the sophistication of the current technology. Because of limited disc storage space and access speed, the video of the actors could occupy only one-quarter of the screen area. The rest of the image (sets, props, etc.) had to be computer-generated because computer-generated images take much less disc space than video or photographs do.

This meant that the actors would have to be shot against a blue screen so the computer-generated backgrounds could be later keyed in. Figure 16–2 shows the actors being filmed against blue screen. The video monitor in

Figure 16–2 Actors shot against blue screen.

Figure 16–2 shows the same image combined with a computer-generated background as it appears in *Voyeur*. This also meant that characters would have to be seen primarily in medium shots and full shots, because close-ups occupy too much screen space.

The writers and designers had to come up with a concept that would turn the technical disadvantages to advantages. Thus the voyeur concept was born. If everything is shot from the point of view of the player, who is a voyeur peering into a building across the street, then it makes sense that the other characters would be seen primarily in medium shot or full shot. (See Figure 16–1.)

The voyeur idea solved the major problem, but another idea to conserve disc space was to put curtains on all the windows. When they are completely closed, the voyeur can still hear what is going on in the room, as in the following audio-only script example. This device saved disc space because sound occupies much less room than video. However, an audio-only scene requires the writer to use the skills of a radio dramatist to spark the user's imagination and create the images in the user's mind.

```
(No Video—Audio only)
E1/210/200 Chantal and Frank in passion.
A symphony of excited sounds.
```

CHANTAL
You like it when I use my tongue, don't you?

FRANK
(moaning)
Yeah, mmmmm. . . . Ahhh.

CHANTAL
Give me your full attention.

FRANK
(sucking in breath)
Ooohh.

CHANTAL
(teasing laugh)
You call that "full attention"? Let's see if this gets your attention.

FRANK
What's that? . . . You're not gonna use that?
(freaking out)
Chantal . . . you're not serious? I don't think—

There's a gasp, heavy breathing and lots of moans.

FRANK
Yeahhhhh

CHANTAL
That's a good boy. Say thank you.

FRANK
(melting)
Mm . . . hmmm. Thank you. Oh, thank you.

CHANTAL
Shut up, Frank.

FRANK
Okay . . . Shut up . . . I'll be quiet.

Creating a Complex Cinematic Story and Pacing

With a workable solution for the major technical limitations in place, the writers and designers still had to come up with a way to give *Voyeur* a complex cinematic story and pacing. One of the problems with many interactive titles is that the story stops while the user makes an interactive choice. This interruption kills the pace of the story and destroys any illusion that these are real people on screen living out their lives—the kind of illusion that linear movies create so successfully.

Simultaneously Playing Multiple Scenes in Real Time

Voyeur achieves cinematic pace and the illusion of real life by playing multiple scenes simultaneously in real time. This means that up to six different scenes can be playing in the various rooms of the Hawke mansion at any one time. The player/voyeur chooses which room to peer into, but while the voyeur is looking at that room, the other five scenes continue on. Each day of the weekend is broken up into several time zones, such as "Saturday 8:00 A.M." (See Figure 16–1.) The player has a limited amount of time to explore each time zone before that time zone cuts to black and the next time zone, such as "Saturday 2:00 P.M.," begins with a title card. A voyeur who spends too much time in one scene will miss other scenes altogether. If the voyeur misses key information, he or she will not be able to catch Reed and save the threatened family member.

An added advantage of multiple scenes' playing at once was to increase replay value. Because users could not see everything the first time through, they wanted to play the game again to see what was in the other rooms. This is an important consideration if the price of a multimedia program is going to be several times the price of a videotape or a music CD.

Following is an outline of the first three time zones, showing all the scenes that would play simultaneously. The numbers refer to the single time zone in which scenes were played simultaneously. For example, in the first time zone, only one scene was played; in the fourth time zone, there were three scenes. Some of the time zones later in the program (not shown here) have as many as six scenes playing at the same time.

SCENE OUTLINE

ACT ONE:

1a INT. SECURITY ROOM:

FRANK and CHANTAL have a secret relationship. Chantal is in the shower when someone creeps into her room. However, it is she who pulls out a gun and directs Frank to the bed. In the midst of this game, the phone rings. REED is on his way home. CHANTAL leaves FRANK tied to the bed.

2a EXT. HAWKE MANOR:

As he makes his way up the front steps, REED is quizzed by the media about his plans for the presidency. It is clear that he has been called to run for the presidency by the people of this country. Still, he claims reluctance to commit himself as a candidate until he is sure his family supports this motion.

3a EXT. ROSE GARDEN/FOUNTAIN:

REED enters the house and makes his way out to the garden where MARGARET is collecting roses for display in the house. MARGARET fusses over REED, affectionately placing a rose in his lapel and expressing displeasure in his choice of ties. CHANTAL clashes with MARGARET, explaining that REED's image will be monitored to fit the presidential image. REED agrees, telling MARGARET that things have changed.

4a INT. MARGARET'S ROOM:

MARGARET stands in front of her mirror modeling outfits and judging whether they fit the "First Lady" image to her satisfaction. All the while she is barking out orders over the phone directing household matters that must be taken care of for the weekend.

4b INT. HALLWAY:

ZACK and LARA arrive in the midst of an argument. LARA does not want to be here, but ZACK says this weekend is very important to him. While LARA goes off to their room, ZACK tries to go up in the elevator to see REED. It is locked. FRANK (over loud speaker) tells ZACK to speak with CHANTAL.

4c CHANTAL'S ROOM:

CHANTAL working out.

5a INT. SOMEWHERE:

ZACK learns (from LARA) that his room has been taken over by FRANK and his security division and that he and LARA have to stay in guest quarters. As ZACK is obsessed with being CEO, he is convinced that this rooming situation has something to do with his position. It is clear that LARA is unhappy with the marriage.

5b EXT. GARDEN PATIO:

JESSICA and MASA arrive together and meet MARGARET on the patio. MARGARET maintains her air of control by ignoring MASA. Suddenly, a figure dressed in motorcycle garb bursts through the door. FRANK wrestles the figure to the ground, only to find it is CHLOE. Despite this case of mistaken identity, it appears that FRANK is uncomfortable about the family gathering. As soon as CHLOE's identity is revealed, CHANTAL speaks into her phone: "She's here, Mr. Hawke."

Master Story and Four Variations

In addition to playing multiple scenes at one time as in the above example, *Voyeur* also has four story variations. Each time the user starts a new game, a different linear story variation loads. The master story of all the characters' coming to the house is the same for all variations, but in each variation, a different character decides to take on Reed and gets killed, unless the voyeur intervenes.

The effect of these multiple story lines is to make the game more of a challenge to discover which family member is in danger because on each playing of the game, it is a different character. It is also intriguing to see the subtle variations in plotting that will push first one character and then another over the edge.

The following script samples illustrate how a variation is developed out of the main story line. Each character has essentially two story lines: one in which they make a deal with Reed and one in which they try to expose him. The game is programmed so that every time a new game is started, a different character will try to expose Reed, while the other three characters will make a deal.

The following example illustrates part of the two variations of Reed's daughter, Jessica's story. The "100" at the end of the number code at the top of the page indicates that this is the main story line in which Jessica sells out to Reed. The "520" at the end of the number code indicates that this is the alternate scene that could be played, Jessica's variation on the main story in which she tries to expose Reed. These are not the only scenes that run during this part of the program. Other characters also have scenes, but they are not shown here for the sake of clarity. In the actual script, each new scene starts on a new page. They are divided here by a line.

(MAIN STORY)

START: 02:00:10:00 END: 02:00:43:20

P1/325/100—Jessica takes Reed up on his proposition for the foundation.

REED'S OFFICE—NIGHT—DAY 2

REED and JESSICA enter the room. He gestures for her to sit down as he positions himself in his swivel chair.

JESSICA
(terse, business-like)
I've decided to take your offer on the condition that you use your power to clear Masa of all charges against him. He's innocent.

REED
He may not be guilty. But, I can assure you, my dear, that your friend Masa is far from innocent.

JESSICA'S about to protest—

REED
However . . . I agree to your terms. So, I'll draw up the papers and put money into escrow.

JESSICA
Look . . . Dad. I'm, uh, sorry that—

REED
Never apologize, Jessica. Sign of weakness.

JESSICA turns and exists. Reed exits camera right.

(JESSICA'S VARIATION)

START: 02:01:39:01   END: 02:02:01:20

P1/325/520—Reed listens to a recording of Jessica's call to the press. (Taped scene/Jessica)

REED'S OFFICE—NIGHT—DAY 2

REED steps into frame with a SMALL TAPE RECORDER and places it on the desk. He inserts a TAPE and pushes PLAY. We hear:

JESSICA'S VOICE
Hello, Mr. Greenblat.

GREENBLAT'S VOICE
Greenblat here.

JESSICA'S VOICE
Jessica Hawke.

GREENBLAT'S VOICE
Do you have it?

JESSICA'S VOICE
Yes, I have that material we talked about.

GREENBLAT'S VOICE
It's your father, right?

JESSICA'S VOICE
Yes, yes, it clearly implicates my father.

GREENBLAT'S VOICE
Well, listen. Meet me at seven.

JESSICA'S VOICE
7 A.M.?

GREENBLAT'S VOICE
Seven.

JESSICA'S VOICE
Fine.

REED turns off the player, touches the intercom button on the speaker phone.

CHANTAL (OS)
Yes sir.

REED
I need you.

Reed exits.

(MAIN STORY)

START: 02:06:18:23 END: 02:06:44:05

Q1/260/100—Jessica and Masa make love in celebration of the deal with Reed.

JESSICA'S BEDROOM—NIGHT—DAY 2

JESSICA comes out of the bathroom dressed in Japanese silk robe. Room is lit in CANDLES, INCENSE is burning. MASA is kneeling on the BED engaged in deep breathing exercises. His hands at his sides. Jessica without a word straddles his lap, pulling his robe open and then her own. She takes oil from a SMALL JAR and anoints MASA's brain chakra, heart chakra and then her own. They look deeply into each other's eyes.

MASA

You are my love. You have freed me from my past life.

JESSICA

And you mine.

Their lips meet.

(JESSICA'S VARIATION)

START: 02:06:56:12 END: 02:07:06:01

Q1/260/520—Lead in to Jessica & Masa's Murder Scene

JESSICA'S BEDROOM—NIGHT—DAY 2

JESSICA and MASA are lying together on the bed. Masa starts to rise and Jessica makes a complaining noise. Masa kisses her and finishes rising, walks to bathroom dressed in pajama bottoms. Jessica curls up around his PILLOW.

FREEZE SCENE.

(JESSICA'S VARIATION)

START: 02:06:56:12 END: 02:07:06:01

Q1/260/720—Jessica's MURDER SCENE—Continuation of Q1/260/520

JESSICA'S BEDROOM—NIGHT—DAY 2

JESSICA uncurls herself from MASA'S PILLOW, stretching.

JESSICA
(calls off to bathroom)
So . . . the foundation's going to need a name. We could name it in honor of your village. The Sangatsu Foundation . . .

REED steps in. JESSICA is startled.

JESSICA
Dad

CHANTAL stands framed in the doorway. She reaches up to whisk the hair out of her eyes and we see the BLOOD-SOAKED HARA-KIRI KNIFE in her hand.

JESSICA starts to scream as REED puts his hands around her neck. Chantal closes the blinds.

(JESSICA'S VARIATION)

START: 02:12:26:29 END: 02:13:25:25

Z1/110/520—Reed announces. Jessica's dead.

EXTERIOR HAWKE MANOR—APPEARS ON PLAYER'S TELEVISION SCREEN

Graphic SPECIAL BULLETIN appears on the T.V. screen

CLOSE on Reed

REED
Ladies and gentlemen. I only have . . . a brief statement to make. My daughter Jessica and I used to spend many happy hours together talking about the future of this grand and glorious country.

Fight down the emotions.

REED

. . . excuse me . . . We are tempered in our lives by hardships. As you all know, last night my daughter's life was cut short by the hand of a suicidal terrorist . . . So many times she said to me, "Daddy . . . you must listen to the voice of the American people."

Composes himself.

Therefore, I have decided to run for the office of President of the United States. Jessica, I know you're listening . . . this one's for you.

[If Jessica followed the main story—her "100" scenes—and sold out to Reed, then one of the other characters, such as Reed's son Zack, would have tried to expose him and ended up dead, and the scene that follows would end the program instead of Jessica's scene above.]

START: 02:13:40:23 END: 02:14:33:12

Z1/110/530—Reed announces. Zack's dead.

EXTERIOR HAWKE MANOR—APPEARS ON PLAYER'S TELEVISION SCREEN

Graphic SPECIAL BULLETIN appears on the T.V. screen

CLOSE on Reed

REED

As some of you may know, my son Zack was killed last night. We had been working around the clock to put the finishing touches on Hawke Industries Missile Defense Systems. He must have taken his computer into the bathroom; apparently it slipped.

He composes himself.

REED

There is nothing I can do for my son now but his selfless commitment to the security of this country has made me realize that I must follow my

REED(*cont.*)
commitment to the welfare of its people. Therefore I have decided to formally announce that I am a candidate for the Presidency of the United States. I only wish my son could be here to see his work completed. Thank you. Thank you.

Maintaining Interactivity within a Complex Cinematic Story: The Voyeur Character

The multiple story lines and the simultaneous playing of scenes in real time give *Voyeur* a cinematic story and pacing. Interactivity is maintained through the character of the voyeur. The voyeur sees the activities at the mansion through first-person point of view so the player becomes the voyeur.

First-person point of view is fairly common in interactive narratives (see *The Pandora Directive* and *Dust: A Tale of the Wired West* case studies in Chapters 17 and 18), but what is unusual here is that the player/voyeur is a minor character as opposed to being the protagonist. The advantage of the player's being a minor character is that it is possible to see the main action of the game in third person, as a viewer normally would on a cinema screen. What is lost is that the player is not central to the action. Both approaches have validity, depending on the goal of the program.

The voyeur/player can videotape what he or she sees in Reed's mansion. The voyeur can also hear what goes on there and read letters and examine props. The voyeur can do several things with the information gathered. Adding to the tension is the real-time pacing of the game in which the voyeur has only so much time to look for clues before the game moves on to the next part of the day.

The Voyeur Character's Interactive Options

The voyeur has several options, which give this piece a wide range of interactivity and add personal jeopardy for the player/voyeur.

Option #1: Just watch. The voyeur can just watch the action and do nothing; in that case one of the family members is murdered, and Reed announces for the presidency. (See the Jessica and Zack endings in the previous script samples.)

Option #2: Warn a family member. The voyeur can warn the family member that he thinks is threatened by mailing him or her the videotape of evidence collected.

If the voyeur warns the threatened family member, he or she is saved, and Reed is exposed, as in the following variation on the Jessica ending:

Z3/115/520—Jessica exposes Reed

EXT. HAWKE MANOR/ALLEY—NIGHT—APPEARS ON PLAYER'S TV

Graphic SPECIAL BULLETIN appears on the T.V. screen.

Hand-held shaky cam as the reporter and cameraman run to Jessica and Masa.

REPORTER #1
Excuse me, Miss Hawke, why are you leaving . . .

JESSICA
I have material that proves that Hawke Industries, with my father's knowledge, was responsible for poisoning an entire village in Japan.

REPORTER #1
Is this going to affect your father's decision to run for president?

JESSICA
Well, I intend to present this evidence at the highest level in Japan, where I am sure criminal charges will be filed. But that's all I have to say.

REPORTER #1
But what about the reports—

They exit.

THE END

If, however, the player/voyeur mistakenly warns one of Reed's allies, the voyeur could get a visit from Reed's assassin, Chantal:

Z2/320/100—REED LOOKS OUT HIS WINDOW INTO VOYEUR'S APARTMENT

REED'S OFFICE

REED stands looking out his office window—making eye contact with the VOYEUR (player). The sound of the

VOYEUR'S apartment door opening is heard. The VOYEUR turns around to look at the door (animation of his/her POV).

Z2/905/300—CHANTAL KILLS VOYEUR/PLAYER
INT. VOYEUR'S APARTMENT

CHANTAL steps into the doorway.

CHANTAL
You came close, eh?

She pulls out a nasty looking gun and begins screwing on the silencer with a gloved hand.

CHANTAL
Yah, very close.

She smiles enticingly as she raises the gun and aims it at YOU.

CHANTAL
. . . Compliments of Mr. Hawke.

SHE PULLS THE TRIGGER. THE SCREEN GOES BLOOD RED.

THE END

Option #3: Contact the police. The voyeur can also contact the police before or after the murder and give them his evidence. The police may think the voyeur has adequate or inadequate evidence. In the case of inadequate evidence, the voyeur could go to jail. Following is an example of inadequate evidence:

START: 02:20:46:21 END: 02:20:54:18

Z4/915/100—Cop asks to see the tape

VOYEUR'S APARTMENT

Cop appears at player's door.

COP
You the one that called with the stuff on Reed Hawke? So show me the tape.

START: 02:21:09:20 END: 02:21:23:26

Z4/915/200—Cop negatively reacts to player's tape

VOYEUR'S APARTMENT

COP negatively reacting to Player's tape.

COP

This tape doesn't prove anything. I should haul you in, you pervert. I wouldn't be surprised if Mr. Hawke presses charges.

Cop exits.

If the voyeur has enough evidence for the police, Reed is exposed:

START: 02:21:38:24 END: 02:21:50:08

Z4/915/300—Cop positively reacts to player's tape.

VOYEUR'S APARTMENT

COP positively reacting to Player's tape.

COP

I never would have thought Reed Hawke was capable of this, but this tape nails him. We'll take it from here.

Cop exits.

Following is the ending if the voyeur contacts the police after the murder:

START: 02:17:37:06 END: 02:18:16:27

Z3/110/100—Reed responds to the fact that Player has evidence on tape.

EXTERIOR HAWKE MANOR/ALLEY—NIGHT—DAY 2

Reporters' MICROPHONES are thrust into REED's face as he is being hauled away in HANDCUFFS.

REPORTER #1

Mr. Hawke, Mr. Hawke, what is your response to these allegations of murder?

REED

I categorically deny any and all charges brought against me as a result of this so-called eyewitness.

REPORTER #2

But is this going to change your plans to run for President, Sir?

REED

I guarantee you that I will clear my name of any and all charges and be back in the forefront of a new movement to bring the power of government back to the people.

Reed is dragged away.

REPORTER #1

Well, here you have it. Total denial of all charges. However, sources inside the police department say that they have the murder scene on tape. Looks like Reed Hawke is finished. But, stay tuned for further developments.

THE END

Establishing Characters, Plot Points, and Conflicts

In addition to developing multiple story paths and interactive options for the player, the writer of interactive narrative must also perform most of the writing tasks common to linear narrative, such as setting up characters, developing rising conflict, and establishing key plot points. The complex story structure and simultaneous playing of scenes in real time make these tasks much more difficult in *Voyeur*.

Character Consistency

The complexity of four different story lines and a large cast made it essential to find a way to keep track of the various characters' attitudes toward each other. Sometimes characters never meet, but even references in conversation have to be consistent, particularly because the purpose of the game is for the voyeur/player to evaluate the evidence he or she gathers from the scenes.

The following character matrix (just a portion of the entire matrix is shown) helped the writers achieve this consistency. The chart is read from left to right showing what each character feels about the characters listed on top of the chart. For example, Reed thinks of himself as a messiah, his sister Margaret as entrapment, and his daughter Jessica as a thorn in his side.

VOYEUR CHARACTER CHART					
	REED	MARGARET	JESSICA	ZACK	CHLOE
REED	Messiah	Entrapment	Thorn in side	Disdain	Fear of self
MARGARET	Symbiotic	Unheralded	Threatened	Protective	Enabler
JESSICA	Unrequited	Shame	Needful	Rival	Big sister
ZACK	Obsessed	Maternal	Threatened	Deserving	Abscess
CHLOE	Vengeful	Betrayal	Foolish	Clown	Desperate

Repeating Plot Points

With the character matrix to keep the relationships clear, the writers next had to integrate this character material into the script. In interactive narrative, and particularly in *Voyeur*, the writer can never be sure what material the viewer has or has not seen. This constraint required that the same plot points be placed in several scenes, but written in such a way that if the player did see more than one of these scenes, they would not be redundant.

The information about Zack's stormy relationship with his dad, for example, is introduced in at least four scenes. The writers keep the material fresh by changing the locations of the scenes and by making the Zack plot point a minor part of two of the scenes, as the following examples show.

Example 1. This is the first we hear of Zack's problems with dad. It is integrated into a newscast with other family members and accessed by the voyeur/player clicking on his TV set.

START: 02:34:41:23 END: 02:36:19:09

A2/050/100—Gossip about Reed and family.

INT. VOYEUR'S APARTMENT—DAY—DAY 1

ANGLE on Voyeur's T.V. The screen has a SPECIAL BULLETIN graphic on it. Tish VanAlden appears on background shot of Hawke Manor.

TISH

Will he or won't he? This is Tish VanAlden and that's the hot question on everybody's lips during this primary season.

(Snapshot of Reed)

Billionaire bachelor and business genius Reed Hawke has yet to commit himself to

the race for the Oval Office. Well, hang on
to your hats, folks, because he's gathering
his flock this weekend to "help him reach a
decision" and when the Hawkes get
together, the feathers are bound to fly.

(Snapshot of Zack)
I mean, imagine how his son Zachary must
feel after his sudden promotion off the
Missile Defense System project, just in time
for it to propel dear old dad into the White
House. Getting a little chilly in Daddy's
shadow, Zack?

Example 2. The first time we see Zack. He is arguing with his wife about his father.

START: 01:05:16:24 END: 01:06:12:13

C1/220/100—Zack and Lara arrive in the midst of an
argument

FOYER—DAY—DAY 1

ZACK and LARA, carrying OVERNIGHT BAGS, enter the
FOYER and head toward the elevator. ZACHARY HAWKE
is Reed's only son and he's a little too tightly wrapped for
his own good. LARA, his wife, is in her late twenties,
fresh-faced and normally optimistic. But it's clear that
this couple has arrived in the midst of an argument.

LARA
Why do you continue to do this to yourself . . .

ZACK
Look, we're not going into this again. I told
you how important this weekend is to me.
We're staying here and that's it.

Preoccupied, ZACK goes to the elevator and punches the
button. It doesn't respond.

ZACK
(turns and sighs, trying)
Look . . . Lara, please just let me deal with my
father—

FRANK'S VOICE
(over the intercom)
Mr. Hawke. Can I help you?

ZACK's attention shifts back to the elevator.

ZACK
What the hell is with the elevator, Frank?

FRANK'S VOICE
(cordial in an androgynous way)
I'm sorry, Mr. Hawke, your father's orders.

LARA
Come on, Honey, you can see your father later.

ZACK
(agitated)
Look, Lara, will you please just go upstairs and unpack.

He turns back to the elevator. LARA walks off.

ZACK
Open up, Frank.

FRANK'S VOICE
I'm afraid Mr. Hawke doesn't want to be disturbed at the moment. He asked me to have all appointments scheduled through Chantal.

ZACK
Schedule an appointment? That son of a bitch!. . . Lara, wait up.

He storms off.

Example 3. In case the player missed that scene, then the same information is included as the minor part of a scene between two of Reed's staffers. This time Zack is a voice in an audio-only scene:

(No Video—Audio only)

C1/250/100—Frank upset with Chantal.

CHANTAL'S ROOM

FRANK
(angry)
Look Chantal, fun is fun but work is dif . . .

CHANTAL
(interrupting)
—Shut up! Don't you dare talk to me that way.

FRANK
(feebly protesting)
Look I only meant—

CHANTAL
(noise of leather swish)
IS THAT CLEAR!

FRANK
(gasping)
Yes. . .

CHANTAL
(noise of leather swish)
Who's in charge?

FRANK
You are.

CHANTAL
Good . . . now—

Sound of a buzzer, it's Zack and Lara by the elevator.

CHANTAL
Shit, answer that!

FRANK
Yes, ma'am . . . .
(tone change)
Mr. Hawke. Can I help you?

ZACK
(over intercom)
What the hell is with the elevator, Frank?

FRANK
I'm sorry, Mr. Hawke, your father's orders.

LARA
Come on, Honey, you can see your father later.

ZACK
Look, Lara, will you please just go upstairs and unpack . . . Open up, Frank.

FRANK
I'm afraid Mr. Hawke doesn't want to be disturbed at the moment. He asked me to have all appointments scheduled through Chantal.

ZACK
Schedule an appointment? That son of a bitch! . . . Lara, wait up.

CHANTAL
That's a good boy! Now get out. I'll call you when I need you.

FRANK
Yes ma'am.

Example 4. A little later in the script, the same information is presented again, but this time through Zack's wife, Lara, and in a different context. The problem is not getting an appointment with Reed; rather, it is that Zack's room has been given to Reed's personal assistant.

START: 01:09:08:06 END: 01:10:05:18

D1/270/100—Lara tells Zack that they have been moved to the guest room

HALLWAY—MAGIC—DAY 1

LARA and ZACK meet in the hallway. She is still carrying the OVERNIGHT BAGS.

LARA
(breaking it gently)
They've moved us to the guest room.

ZACK

What?

LARA

Your father's assistant has taken over your room.

Zack winds up in rage and raises his arms toward Reed's penthouse suite.

ZACK

Damn you, Dad! This is one of your sick little games. Control, control, control, . . .

A beat.

LARA

Well at least the guest room has a king-sized bed. . .

A beat.

ZACK

MDS was my idea. God, when I think of the setbacks . . . the mountain of problems we had to solve . . . and we get that close to makin' it work . . . and the son of a bitch just takes it . . . everyone thinks he's this big hero . . . Well, I know the truth, and he's not going to get away with it.

ZACK picks up the BAGS and they exit.

Multiple Plot Points in One Scene

Another way to ensure that the player sees key information is to include multiple plot points in one scene, so if the player does access a scene, much key plot information has been established. In order for the scene not to be overly dense with information, however, the writer has to find a number of different ways to present the material.

The following example sets up Jessica's relationship with Margaret, Margaret's relationship with Jessica's fiancé, Chloe's relationship with them both, and Frank and Chantal's relationship with them all. Notice how what is not said is as important as the dialogue. Margaret clearly does not listen to Jessica and completely ignores her fiancé. Chloe's costume and actions set her distinctly apart from the rest. (This scene is illustrated in Figure 16-1 at the beginning of this chapter.)

START:01:07:52:00   END: 01:08:53:06

D1/220/100—Chloe arrives, disturbing gathering of Margaret, Jessica, Masa, & Frank

FOYER—MAGIC—DAY 1

Margaret steps out, followed by Frank who is carrying a BOTTLE OF RED WINE and a TRAY OF WINE GLASSES. He puts the tray of glasses down on an off-screen table.

MARGARET

Put it right there. I want this weekend to be perfect. It's been so long since the family has been together.

A couple steps into the atrium. JESSICA HAWKE is in her mid-thirties and dresses with a style that reflects her self-assured manner. Her companion, MASA, is a tall, attractive Japanese man in his late twenties.

JESSICA

Hello, Margaret.

MARGARET turns, sees Jessica and swoops over to greet her, pulling her from Masa who's left in the background.

MARGARET

Jessica! You're here. You look more mature every time I see you.

JESSICA

Where's Dad?

MARGARET

Reed's upstairs. He'll be joining us later.

MARGARET leans in, kissing the air to the side of her cheeks. She turns her back on JESSICA'S COMPANION and toward the wine tray. JESSICA gestures to him.

JESSICA

You remember Masa.

MARGARET, ignoring MASA, leads JESSICA toward the wine service.

MARGARET
(to Frank off stage)
Frank, do be a dear and take Jessica's bags.

FRANK moves to follow out the order, but MASA intercedes.

MASA
I will get Jessica's bags. And mine.

He exits.

MARGARET
(to Jessica)
It must be miserable for you over there . . .

Off-stage we hear the sound of doors bursting open. A LEATHER-CLAD FIGURE in a hooded sweatshirt, carrying a DUFFEL BAG and a MOTORCYCLE HELMET, enters abruptly. With the reflexes of a pit bull, FRANK attacks the intruder and wrestles him around. As the intruder spins around, the sweatshirt hood falls off, revealing long blonde hair. FRANK sees the intruder's face and his mouth drops open, his hands frozen on the intruder's chest. He's a she.

FRANK
Hey! . . . Chloe?

CHLOE
Frank, I never knew you cared.

Now FRANK sees that his hands are cupped to CHLOE'S breasts. She knees him in the groin. She dusts herself off and picks up her bag as Frank tries to get his wind back. She saunters over to MARGARET, who, for the first time, is speechless. CHLOE grabs the wine bottle out of her hand.

CHLOE
Jessica. Mother . . .

Before MARGARET can regain her composure, CHLOE downs a swig from the bottle and leaves. JESSICA leaves. MARGARET hurries after her. CHANTAL steps into frame speaking into her MOBILE PHONE.

CHANTAL

She's here. Come on, Frank, up we go.

CHANTAL goes to Frank and helps him up off the ground. They walk off, leaving Margaret alone.

MARGARET

(frustrated)

OOOHHHHH!!!

She storms off after Jessica.

Establishing Rising Action in All Four Story Variations

In any story, it is not enough to ensure key plot points; those beats must be carefully orchestrated in rising action that builds to a climax. In *Voyeur* with its four variations, this process became particularly complex. To ensure smoothly rising action in all the story variations, the writers broke the story into five acts and twelve key beats.

ACT 1 INTRODUCTION

Introduction of situation
Development of relationships
Foreshadowing of conflict

ACT 2 RISING ACTION

First action points
Angling for positions
Turning point

ACT 3 CRISIS

Main action point confrontations

ACT 4 TRAGIC FORCE

Repercussions from confrontations
Force of last suspense
Revelations

ACT 5 RESOLUTION

Climax: pay-off, point of highest emotional activity
Conclusion

Once the beats were laid out, the writers developed a chart (see page 262) to make sure that the key beats were developed for each character's story variation. The chart numbers refer to the scenes where the beats are located (see page 263).

Characters, Place, and Time

The challenge of properly developing rising conflict is shared to a large degree with linear scriptwriting. The problem of having the same character in two different places at the same time is, however, unique to interactive, and a particular problem with a piece as interactive as *Voyeur*, which has multiple scenes playing simultaneously. To avoid having the same character in two different places at the same time, the writers developed the following chart (see page 263).

The numbers refer to the time line. In the first time line, there is only the one scene (Chantal and Frank). In the fourth time line, there are three scenes happening at the same time: 4a with Margaret, whose name is at the top of the sheet; 4b with Zack, which also includes Lara; and 4c with Chantal. This was only the first draft of this structure. The final draft was much denser, with as many as six scenes playing in a single time zone. The final script had about 100 scenes. Thirty to forty of these scenes were common to all the scenarios and were always available to be seen. There were ten to fifteen unique scenes for each of the four variations that were played only when that scenario was loaded.

CONCLUSION: RESPONSE TO THE PROJECT

All of the careful planning and skilled writing helped *Voyeur* become a much-honored interactive narrative, winning seven Academy Awards from the Academy of Interactive Arts and Sciences, including awards for best interactive film, best drama, best direction, and best story. It also won a gold medal Invision award and a gold Cindy. This success spawned a sequel *Voyeur II.*

REFERENCES

Pousette, Lena Marie. Telephone interview with the author, December 1995.

Riordan, David. Telephone interviews with the author, June 1994, October 1995, December 1995.

ACT ONE: INTRODUCTORY BEATS			
	INTRODUCTION OF SITUATION	DEVELOPMENT OF RELATIONSHIP	FORESHADOWING CONFLICT
MARGARET	Demonstrates her control over household. 4a	Has a softer side. 3	Some of her powers have been usurped. 3
ZACK	Attempts to wield power he doesn't have. 4b	Has abandoned Lara emotionally. 5a	Obsessed with becoming CEO. 5a
JESSICA	Feels like an outsider. Margaret re-arranged her room. 6a	Masa is her strength and grounding. 6a	Has evidence that threatens Reed. Feels conflicted about using it.
CHLOE	Enjoys being the black sheep. Acts for effect. 5b	Reed is notified of her arrival. 5b	Something about this house causes her tremendous pain. 6b
REED	Will announce presidential candidacy tomorrow morning. 2	Is charismatic and has been called to the presidency. 2	Is concerned about family's reaction to his announcement. 2
FRANK	Is head of security. Has long-standing relationship with Reed. 4b	Has secret relationship with Chantal. 1	Is uncomfortable about this family gathering. 5b
CHANTAL	Controls all access to Reed. Is Reed's personal assistant. 4b	Has secret relationship with Frank. 1	Isn't afraid of confrontations with family members. 3

CHARACTERS & SCENES CHART

MARGARET	JESSICA	ZACK	CHLOE	REED	MASA	LARA	CHANTAL	FRANK
							w/Frank	1a
				2a				
3a				w/Marg			w/Marg	
4a		4b				w/Zack	4c	
w/Chloe	w/Chloe	5a	5b		w/Chloe	w/Zack	w/Chloe	w/Chloe
w/Jessica	6a		6b		w/Jessica			
7a	w/Zack	7b	7c	w/Marg		w/Chloe		
8b		w/Chantal	w/Marg		8c		8a	w/Chantal
10a		10b		w/Frank		w/Zack		9a
11a	w/Chloe		11b	w/Marg				
w/Zack	12b	12a		w/Jessica				
	13a			13b	w/Jessica		w/Reed	
				w/Lara		14a		
			15a	w/Chloe				
		16a		w/Zack				

17

PARALLEL STORIES NARRATIVE CASE STUDY: *THE PANDORA DIRECTIVE*

Summary

Name of production: *The Pandora Directive*
Writer: Aaron Conners
Developer: Access Software Inc.
Audience: General audience
Medium: CD-ROM
Presentation location: Home
Subject: Tex Murphy detective mystery
Goal: Entertain
Structures: Parallel story paths, linear, hierarchical dialogue branching

PROGRAM DESCRIPTION AND BACKGROUND

Program Description

The Pandora Directive is the fourth interactive movie in the Tex Murphy science-fiction mystery series. The program is released on CD-ROM and intended for home use. It is played by one person and is highly interactive. Much of the game is played in first person. Users can choose where Tex goes, what he does, and even what he says. Money is a new feature in this Tex adventure. There are several opportunities for Tex to get money, and he needs it to buy information and other items to solve the mystery. If a player runs out of money, he or she can't finish the game.

At the beginning of *The Pandora Directive,* Tex is hired to find Dr. Thomas Malloy. Tex soon learns that Malloy has secret information that the National Security Agency (NSA) and others are willing to kill for. To safeguard his secrets, Malloy sent out five puzzle boxes, each carrying a component of the Pandora Directive, which will explain his project. Tex's search for Malloy quickly turns into a quest for those boxes, which seem to have a bad habit of getting their owners killed. Romantic complication ensues between Tex and Malloy's daughter, Regan, which doesn't exactly thrill Tex's girlfriend, Chelsee. The climactic ending takes place in a Mayan labyrinth where Malloy's project is hidden. The plot has three basic story paths with seven possible endings, so Tex's success in love and war depends on how you play the game.

The Pandora Directive and the Interactive Movie

Aaron Conners, the writer of *The Pandora Directive,* breaks video games into three basic subgenres:

1. Arcade games, such as *Doom,* which focus primarily on action and require a quick trigger finger to win the day.
2. World games, such as *Myst,* which allow the user to explore a world.
3. Interactive movies, such as *The Pandora Directive* and its predecessor in the Tex Murphy series, *Under a Killing Moon,* which attempt to integrate the best aspects of movies (characters, humor, action, well-developed plots) with the puzzles and interactivity of video games.

Writers of interactive movies are developing the most sophisticated uses of narrative in interactive multimedia, and both *The Pandora Directive* and *Under a Killing Moon* are in the forefront of the interactive movie genre.

Production Background

The Pandora Directive was developed and produced by Access Software Inc. of Salt Lake City. In addition to the Tex Murphy series, Access has a number of other successful adventure games and best-selling golf games: *Microsoft Golf, Links 386,* and *Links 486 CD.* Chris Jones, the cofounder of the company, produces and stars in the Tex Murphy series, which includes *Mean Streets, Martian Memorandum, Under a Killing Moon* (the first collaboration with Aaron Conners), and *The Pandora Directive.* Conners wrote and codesigned the *Pandora Directive* based on his novel of the same name, which was published by Prima Publishing. Chris Jones codesigned the game. The video sequences were directed by Adrian Carr.

GOALS AND CHALLENGES IN WRITING *THE PANDORA DIRECTIVE*

Goals

One of Conners's goals was to present a complex story that combined the best elements of the detective genre with off-beat science-fiction material reminiscent of *The Twilight Zone* and *The Outer Limits*. Some critics have compared the Tex Murphy series with *The X Files*. Conners also wanted to present well-developed characters, particularly in Tex, but also in his love interests, Chelsee and Regan.

So far this sounds like any good movie. But we are talking interactive movie here, and Conners also wanted to allow for maximum interactivity on the part of the user. His goal was interactive choices integrated in a way that disturbs the flow of the narrative as little as possible. He hoped to achieve this by having the choices affect the story in the same way that such choices affect us in real life.

Although not strictly a writing goal, Conners as writer-codesigner and his codesigner, Chris Jones, also wanted this video game to capture the feeling of a theatrical movie. They achieved this through heavy use of close-ups, video, and action sequences. These space-hungry elements required the game to be released on six CDs.

Challenges

The key elements of these goals and the major challenges are:

- Developing a complex interactive story and characters.
- Creating smooth and realistic interactivity at the shot and dialogue level and the scene and sequence level.
- Making the complex story and interactivity work together in an engaging and coherent fashion.

WRITING *THE PANDORA DIRECTIVE*: MEETING THE CHALLENGES

Although this case study will be focused primarily on *The Pandora Directive*, comparisons will occasionally be drawn with the previous Tex Murphy mystery, *Under a Killing Moon*.

Developing a Complex Interactive Story and Characters

The Novel

Writing *The Pandora Directive* novel first, said Conners, gave him a chance to develop the story and characters thoroughly. He started the novel, writing freehand in a smokey Salt Lake City bar with red vinyl seats and sparkly counter tops, the kind of place Tex Murphy might hang out in. Conners first roughly outlined the story, listening to snatches of conversation and sometimes jotting down lines of dialogue.

He also developed the basic characters at this stage. He decided what he wanted them to be like and what their signature character quirks would be, such as using faulty grammar. Finally, he laid out how he wanted the characters to progress and develop in the story. He generated a lot of pages in this preparatory stage.

Once this preliminary work was done, he sat at the computer and used Word 6.0 to develop an extended hierarchical outline broken down by acts and scenes. He determined what would happen in each scene and gradually laid out the story. He wrote the novel based on this outline.

The Script

This is one of the more complex programs on the market, and the writing process reflects this complexity. After Conners completed the novel, his co-designer, Chris Jones, cut key story elements out of the novel to make a rough script, which was just one path of the story and conversation (the B path, the same as the novel). Screenwriter Scott Yeagamn polished this script, and Conners completed it.

The script serves primarily as a reference for people outside of Access Software, such as actors, so they can understand what the program is about. The script includes few interactive elements and comprises only 20 percent of all the material written for the project. A script sample follows.

INT. BREW AND STEW—DAY (Interactive Scene #22)

. . . Tex sidles up to the bar.

LOUIE
Hey, Murph. How goes the battle?

TEX
(a forced grin)
Louie, you wouldn't believe it if I told you.
(Louie doesn't ask)
Say, did Chelsee leave some things of
mine . . .

LOUIE
(retrieves a couple items from under the bar)
You bet . . .
(lays them on bar top)

LOUIE (Cont'd)
Amongst the items . . .
Looks like someone's business card
. . . and your lucky Pez dispenser.

TEX
(Picks things up. Inspects Pez dispenser)
Wondered where that went to. Thanks.

TEX
(on a more serious note)
So how's she doing?

LOUIE
Yuh mean Chelsee?
(weighs it)
She just turned 30. She thinks it's the end of the world.

TEX
I don't understand it.

LOUIE
You're not supposed to. Just accept that she's having a hard go of it and leave it at that. She's looking for something more in her life, that's all.
(beat)
Tell me somethin', Murph? You ever been in love? I'm talking about "True Love."

Tex twists his neck nervously, plays with his Pez dispenser.

TEX
I dunno, Louie. What the hell's that mean anyway, true love?

LOUIE
Nothin'. It's all just chemicals. Endorphins or whatever. Fallin' in love's simple as one, two, three. Any idiot can do it. What's hard is gettin' ta know someone, and after all that, still likin' 'em.

TEX
No kidding.

LOUIE

But that's not even the hardest thing. Hardest thing is what makes all the difference.

TEX

What's that?

LOUIE

. . . Finding someone you can trust.

Tex thinks about it.

LOUIE (Cont'd)

Chelsee's givin' you a shot, Murph . . . but she's not gonna wait forever. There's a whole load of guys who'd give their right arm for one minute of Chelsee's attention. You know it.

CLOSER ON TEX . . .

. . . as he continues to reflect on what Louie has said.

The Walkthrough

After the script, Conners developed the walkthrough (part of which is included at the end of this chapter). This is a description of the story line and the key interactive elements. A walkthrough of a video game is similar to a linear film/TV treatment, which gives the basic story line without extensive dialogue or calling shots. The *Pandora* walkthrough primarily explains how to get through the B path, but it also refers to key interactions with the other paths.

Conners divided the walkthrough story into days. This device not only makes the transitions between the program's multiple discs easier, but the writer also feels that this structure makes good sense for an interactive movie. Because an interactive movie can include as much as sixty hours of game play, it should be thought of not as a feature film but rather as a miniseries with a number of small conflicts and cliffhangers at the end of each day that gradually lead to the major climax at the end.

Puzzles

After developing the basic walkthrough storyline, Conners came up with puzzles that the player must solve to advance in the game. Integrating puzzles into interactive narrative is one of the challenges that faces writers of interactive movies. Many of the users of a program, such as *The Pandora Directive,* are primarily interested in following the interactive story. For dedicated gamers, however, the challenge of solving difficult puzzles and racking up high point scores is a prime appeal.

Conners and his codesigner solved this problem by coming up with two levels of play: a game player level and an entertainment level. On the game player level, there is no access to hints, there are additional puzzles, and the solutions to the puzzles are more difficult. For their extra effort, the game players can earn twice as many points as the entertainment-level players, who in addition to having hints and easier puzzles can skip the puzzles altogether by simply typing, "I am a cheater," on their keyboard. Both categories of user earn points by solving puzzles and making the right choices to advance the story. A running tally of points scored is constantly on the screen.

Interactive Conversations

For Conners, the last phase of writing an interactive movie is coming up with the characters' interactive conversation. To do this, Conners makes a list of the characters and develops the interactive dialogue, flowcharts, and Ask Abouts (key information that the player/Tex can ask other characters about). Each of these elements is explained in detail later in this chapter.

Game Play Addendum

Another document the writer created during development of this project is the addendum, which consists of 500 pages explaining all the rules of interaction and game play. These clarifying inserts are sometimes referred to in the walkthrough or other production material to make it clear to the people putting the program together how the game is supposed to work.

There is no unified document that unites all of these written elements that the game is based on. That is the job of Conners and his codesigner, Chris Jones.

Creating Smooth and Realistic Interactivity

Interactive Dialogue

One of the more innovative elements of *Under a Killing Moon* and *The Pandora Directive* is the degree of interactivity that is allowed at the dialogue level. In an interactive dialogue scene, the viewer is given a list of three Response Attitudes for Tex's dialogue. Clicking one of these attitudes causes Tex to respond in a certain way. If the player does nothing, there is a default path, a middle ground between the bad Tex and the good Tex.

Under a Killing Moon **Interactive Dialogue Examples** In the following examples from *Under a Killing Moon*, the dialogue in parentheses is Tex's girl, Chelsee, speaking. The empty brackets indicate that Chelsee's dialogue at the top of the list can initiate each of Tex's responses. The Response Attitudes are in all capitals. Clicking on one of those Response Attitudes causes Tex to respond with that line of dialogue to Chelsee. This is the list of all the Response Attitudes for a scene. Of course, the player would see only one list of three Response Attitudes in the menu at a time, and would not see all the dialogue written out. Tex would speak it in response to the attitude choice (see Figure 17–3, page 278).

Conners decided to use this approach as opposed to having all the dialogue options written out because it would slow the story too much if players had to read three lines of dialogue before making a choice, and the Response Attitudes maintain the element of surprise. Players don't know what line they will get when they click an attitude. Surprise is essential for humor and shock.

(See the flowchart in Figure 17–1, page 274, for a sense of how the scene below would play out interactively.)

(Tex/Chelsee)

Chelsee: ("Well, hello, stranger.")
Tex: [ ] SUBTLE INNUENDO Hey sweetheart, know anyone who could use my services today?
[ ] LOVESICK PUPPY Chelsee, you're breaking my heart.
[ ] CHARMINGLY CURIOUS Tell me, gorgeous, has the new *True Detective* come in yet?

Chelsee: ("I guess that depends on which services we're talking about, big guy.")
Tex: [ ] BLATANT INNUENDO Join me for a drink and I'll go over all the great services I have to offer.
[ ] SLEAZEBAG OFFER You know, I'm a certified love mechanic . . .
[ ] PLAY STUPID Well, duh. I guess you forgot—I'm a P.I.

Chelsee: ("Why? Because I've got a steady job?")
Tex: [ ] MAKE A PASS No. You're just so beautiful it makes me ache.
[ ] SARCASTIC RETORT Ha ha. You're a riot, Chelsee. You ought to be doing standup.
[ ] DEEPLY INSULTED Sure, kick me when I'm down. You think it's fun being broke?

Chelsee: ("Yeah, but you've gotta pay for it this time. When you finish a magazine, it's in no condition to sell.")

Tex: [ ] SARCASTIC RETORT Ha ha. You're a riot, Chelsee. You ought to be doing standup.
[ ] DEEPLY INSULTED Sure, kick me when I'm down. You think it's fun being broke?
[ ] MACHO P.I. TALK Think of it this way, Chelsee. Reading *True Detective* . . .

Chelsee: ("Gee, Tex, that kind of talk could get you into trouble, but I don't drink with customers.")
Tex: [ ] STUD RESPONSE Not even the hottest P.I. in town?
[ ] BLUE COLLAR OFFER I'd be happy to throw in a chili dog with that drink.
[ ] PRICKED BY CUPID'S ARROW It's quite painful, the way you toy with my emotions, Chelsee.

Chelsee: ("Did you hear that Rook's place got robbed?")
Tex: [ ] ON THE CASE I . . .
[ ] NO, BUT EAGER FOR INFORMATION No, I didn't. What do you know about it?
[ ] YES, BUT UNCONCERNED Yup. Darn shame. I hope the cops find out who did it.

Chelsee: ("I hear you took care of Rook. Pretty impressive.")
Tex: [ ] MODEST AND UNEMPLOYED Thanks. Maybe word will get around . . .
[ ] MODEST, BUT MANLY Oh, it was nothing. Just another day at the office.
[ ] WINK WINK, NUDGE NUDGE Let me show you my investigative abilities . . .

Chelsee: ("Oh, I'm sure it will. Maybe then you'll have some money and quit mooching off me.")
Tex: [ ] TENDER HEARTED C'mon, Chelsee. Let me savor success for awhile.
[ ] RUGGED BANTER Admit it, doll, you love me just the way I am.
[ ] INDIGNANT Hey, I don't like being broke. Why don't you lay off the insults and help me.

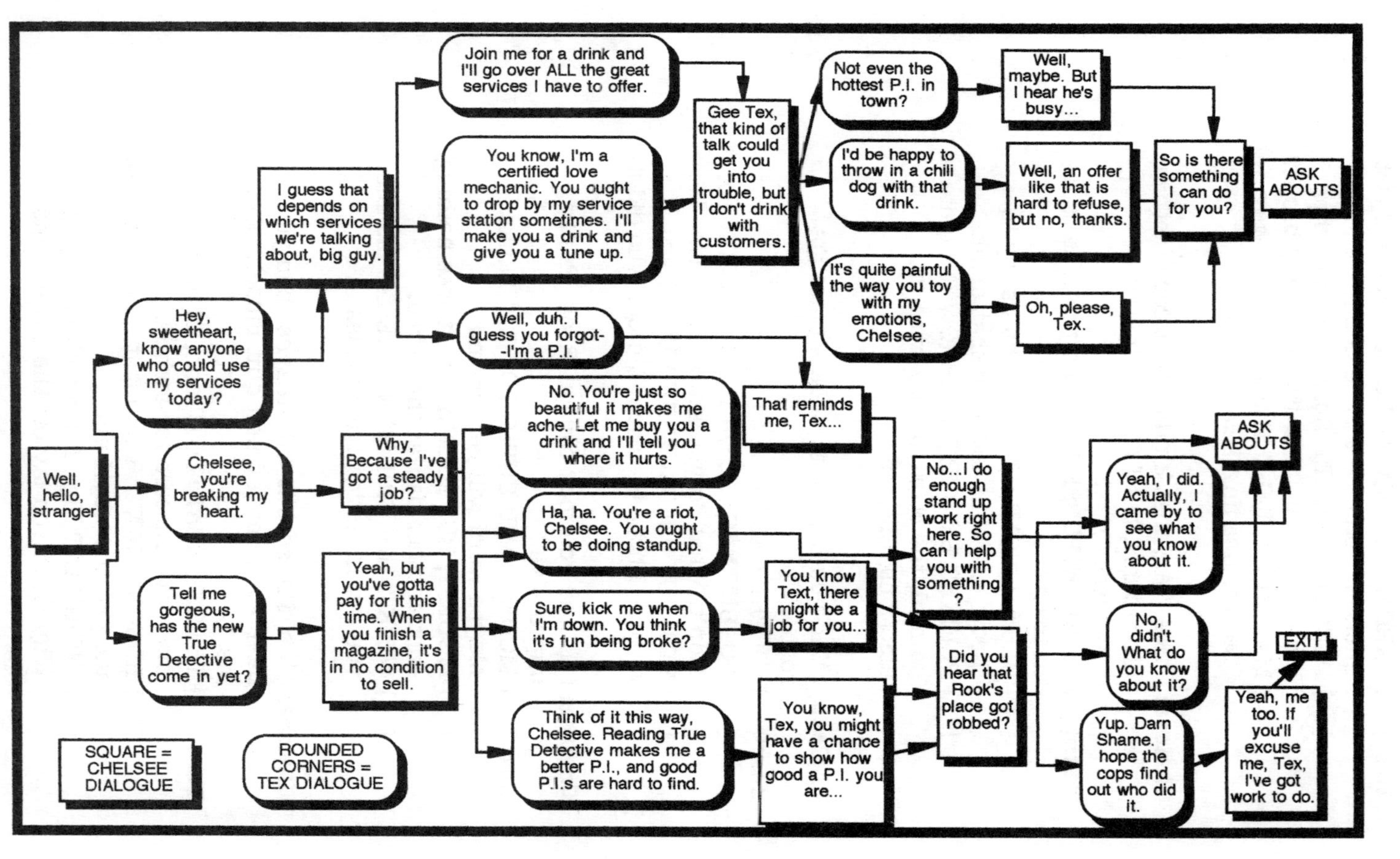

Figure 17–1 Dialogue flowchart for *Under a Killing Moon.*

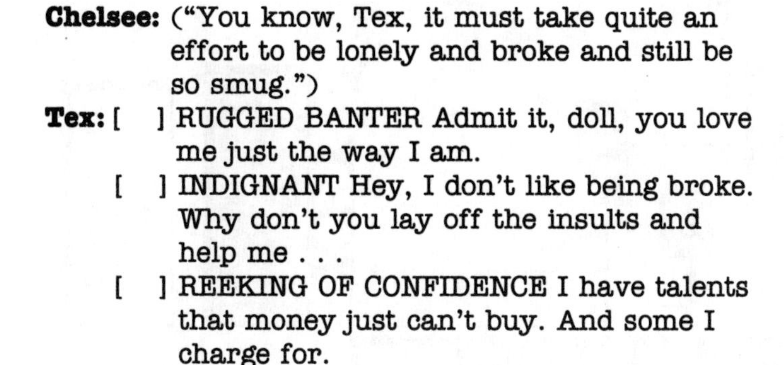

Chelsee: ("You know, Tex, it must take quite an effort to be lonely and broke and still be so smug.")

Tex: [ ] RUGGED BANTER Admit it, doll, you love me just the way I am.

[ ] INDIGNANT Hey, I don't like being broke. Why don't you lay off the insults and help me . . .

[ ] REEKING OF CONFIDENCE I have talents that money just can't buy. And some I charge for.

Chelsee: ("I'm sure I would, but I just don't date my customers. Especially ones with no money.")

Tex: [ ] INDIGNANT Hey, I don't like being broke. Why don't you lay off the insults and help me . . .

[ ] REEKING OF CONFIDENCE I have talents that money just can't buy. And some I charge for.

[ ] GOING FOR THE HARD SELL Did I ever tell you that I'm a gourmet chef . . .

***The Pandora Directive* Interactive Dialogue Example** The flowchart in Figure 17–2 and the dialogue examples are from a scene for the character Louie Lamintz, the owner of the greasy spoon, Brew & Stew. In order to make the example clearer, I combined the Response Attitudes and dialogue lists into one. Find a number on the flowchart and then look for the corresponding number in the dialogue table (page 277) to understand the flow of the conversation. Grey blocks on the chart are Louie's dialogue; white blocks are Tex's dialogue.

Interactive dialogue in *The Pandora Directive* follows the same general structure as that in *Under a Killing Moon*. The screen shot shown in Figure 17–3, page 278 from *The Pandora Directive* shows the dialogue on the bottom left and the response attitudes on the right.

The interactive dialogue in *The Pandora Directive* is, however, even more complex than that in *Under a Killing Moon*. It is broken down by character and written in three separate documents:

- A flowchart with the boxes numbered and shaded
- A numbered list of the other characters' and Tex's dialogue
- A numbered list of Tex's Response Attitudes

There are several possible responses to certain lines of dialogue depending on which story path (A, B or C) the player/Tex is on. On page 277, the Response Attitudes are in italics. The dialogue they elicit follows immedi-

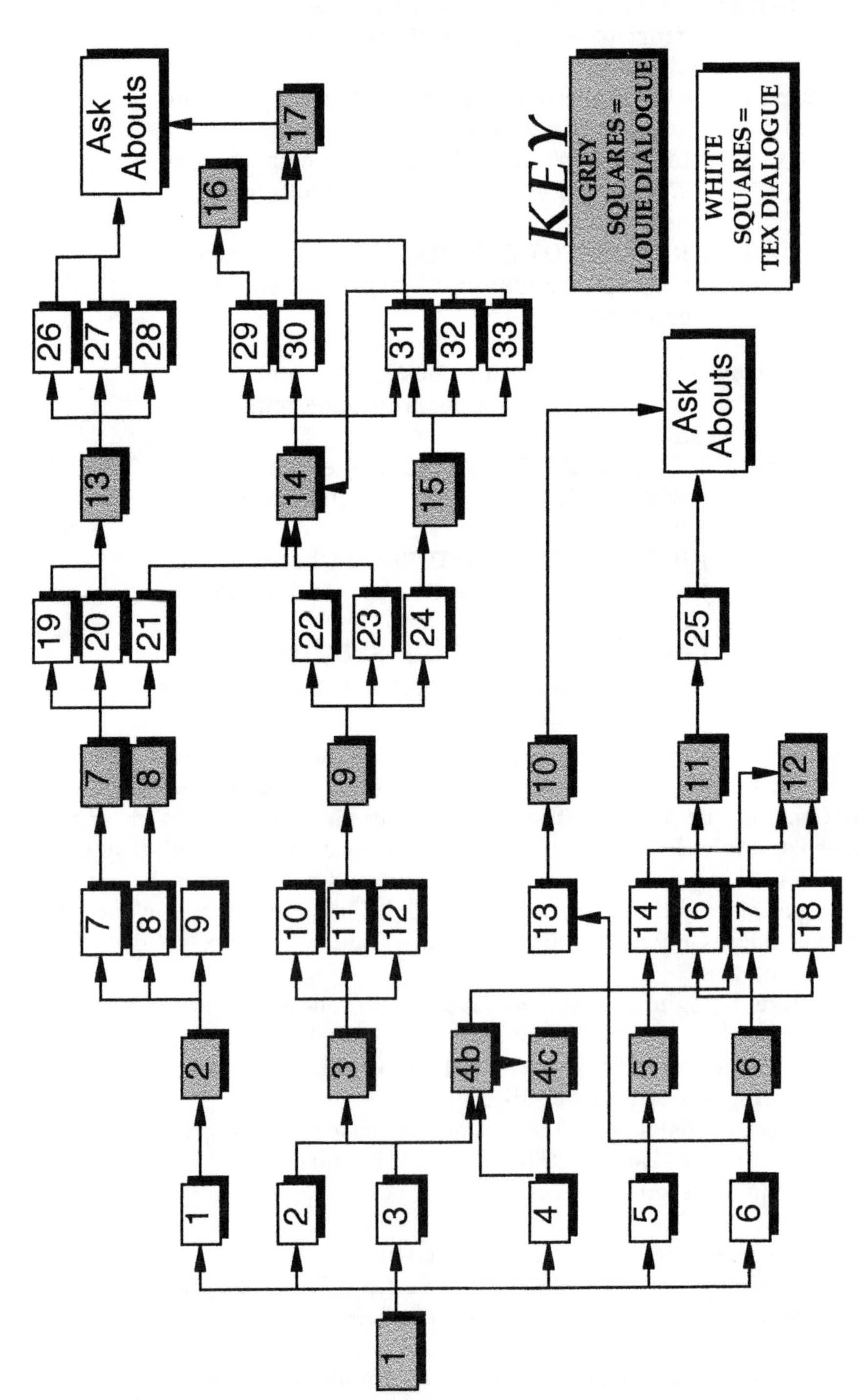

Figure 17–2 *The Pandora Directive*: Louie Scene 7, interactive dialogue flowchart.

Response Attitudes and Interactive Dialogue for *The Pandora Directive*

LOUIE
1. You just missed Chelsee. She stopped in to say good-bye. Apparently, she's off to Arizona. Everything OK with you two?

TEX
1. Definitely maybe
1. (A1) Let's see . . . Chelsee came by my office and redefined the word "frustration" and now she's headed off to Phoenix. I'd say things are going pretty darn well.

2. Dumb male response
2. (A2–B1) It's kind of hard to tell . . . Chelsee being a woman and all.

3. Look to Louie for illumination
3. (A3–B2) I have absolutely no idea. What did Chelsee have to say?

4. Nuptial worries
4. (C1–B3) We had a bit of a tiff at the Fuchsia Flamingo. Felt just like we were married.

5. Condensed explanation
5. (C2) No. We decided to go with the *Readers' Digest* relationship and break up on our first date.

6. Hard-boiled attitude
6. (C3)I don't want to talk about it. I'm so sick of dames I could puke.

LOUIE (Response to Tex #1)
2. That's kinda what I figured. She looked happier than I've seen her in quite awhile.

TEX
7. Pessimistic viewpoint
7. Well, she should. She's got a leash on most of my vital organs. That always makes women happy.

8. Play it down
8. Well then, my work is done. It's always been my mission in life to make anyone I can just a little happier.

9. Express total confusion
9. So, of course, she leaves town, just when things are picking up steam. I don't get it.

LOUIE (Response to Tex # 2 or 3)
3. Well, she and I talked for a bit. She's havin' a rough go of it.

TEX
10. Be moderately offended
10. Should take that personally? I think I'm going to.

11. Trivialize Chelsee's plight
11. Oh, you mean the unbearable trauma of turning thirty?

12. Manly incomprehension
12. Maybe I'm just not in touch with my feminine side. What exactly is so rough?

ately after. (The complete list of dialogue and response attitudes is available on the attached CD-ROM.)

Interactive Dialogue and Story Paths

The A1 before the first line of Tex's dialogue in the chart above refers to which story path Tex is on. Lines 1, 2, and 3 are the three possible lines of

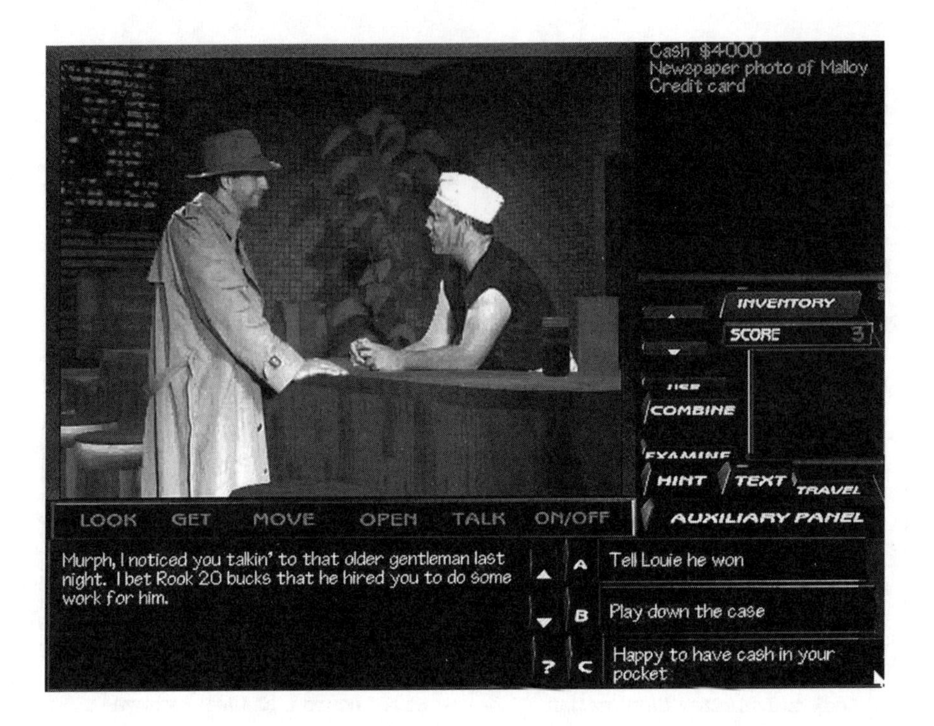

Figure 17–3 Interactive dialogue and response attitudes in *The Pandora Directive.*

dialogue for a player on the A path. Lines 2, 3, and 4 are the three possible lines for a player on the B path, and 4, 5, and 6 are for the C path. There is some reusing of lines in different paths. (The different paths will be explained later in this chapter.) This is only the interactive dialogue for one scene for one character. This has to be done for every scene that every character has.

Effect of Interactive Dialogue

The Response Attitude chosen and the resulting dialogue spoken mold Tex into the kind of character the player wants him to be. He can be a jerk or a hero, depending on which attitudes are clicked. These dialogue choices also have far-reaching effects on the story. These choices at the micro-level ultimately affect Tex's life (and the flow of the plot) at the macro-level. This is a more natural type of branching than that seen in many other interactive videos, where the user simply chooses major actions, such as shooting the sheriff or the outlaw.

In *Pandora,* such larger choices often become inevitable because of smaller choices made earlier in dialogue. This is one way that this game embraces the fatalistic viewpoint of its hard-boiled detective genre. In this genre, characters rarely make clear choices for their future. Instead they make a series of small choices that set off major consequences that shove them in one direction or another.

Emily's murder sequence is a good example of the effect of interactive dialogue. The steps that lead up to the death actually occur well before the actual event, and when the death does happen, it affects the rest of story.

Tex stumbles onto the dark path that leads to Emily's death long before he ever sets foot in her nightclub, the Fuchsia Flamingo. The trouble starts in the linear introduction to the program. Tex and Chelsee are sitting in Louie's diner. Chelsee, about to turn thirty years old, is feeling stuck and confused. She tries to get a response from Tex that would let her know that he really cares about her. But being an unsubtle male, Tex misses the point; she gets angry and leaves. Louie and Rook, who are also in the diner, however, understand her completely and lay into Tex after she has left: "Tex, you idiot, what she meant was . . ."

Once the game goes into the interactive mode, the player Tex can go back and talk to her at her newsstand. Tex knows that she is upset, and really wants to go out with her. He has wanted to go out with her for years. What the player/Tex chooses to say to Chelsee at this point can send Tex down the dark path to Emily's death or to the light path and Emily's rescue.

The response attitude choices are: ATTEMPT AN APOLOGY, PRETEND NOTHING IS WRONG, or LIGHTEN THE MOOD. If Tex pretends nothing is wrong and just asks, "Any new detective magazines?," he has stumbled onto the dark path because this will make Chelsee angry, and she'll respond with, "Sure, I've got Butthead Detective, you ought to like that one." Continuing this pattern of dialogue choices sets off an argument, which plants a seed of mistrust in Chelsee. Tex does, however, eventually calm her down enough to set a dinner date.

The player/Tex can take another step on the dark path when talking to Leach, Emily's boss. If Tex is rude to him, Leach gets mad and later will block Tex's entrance when he tries to rescue Emily.

After talking to Leach, Tex searches a room and gets knocked out, causing him to miss his dinner date with Chelsee. She, of course, is angry: "I can't believe you stood me up." At this point, Tex can try to explain and move up to the light path, or he can stay on the dark path by saying, "Look that's the way it is. I'm a PI," causing another argument between them.

When they finally do get to the nightclub, he tells Chelsee he wants to see if he can get backstage to see the singer, Emily. Chelsee snaps, "You're here with me, and you're watching another woman." She says this because she is still angry about the argument they had before they went to the club. They have a huge fight. She leaves. Tex stays and gets drunk.

When he finally does see Emily at the club, he is in a totally different frame of mind than he would have been if not for the fight with Chelsee and being drunk. Because of this and because Leach (mad from their earlier interaction) blocks him from Emily's room, he is unable to save her life.

After failing to save her, his whole perspective changes. He says, "I've got to get out this business; it's killing me." He's now in for the kill, trying to get money so he can quit the PI business. He also loses Chelsee and later hooks up with the dark woman, Regan. If he continues on this path, he is killed at the end of the story.

Dialogue Explosion and Reusability

Although interactive dialogue is an excellent way to give the viewer a high degree of control and create realistic interactivity, it is not without its drawbacks. This degree of interactivity demands that a vast amount of dialogue be scripted. *Pandora* has six to twelve totally unique paths of conversation, depending on the scene. This doesn't mean there are twelve different choices per line of dialogue; it means that there are a possible twelve dialogue sequences or paths that could be charted through a scene. (Take some colored highlighters and chart a few paths through the *Pandora* flowchart earlier in the chapter to see what I mean.)

A writer who isn't careful can be buried in a dialogue explosion of hundreds of lines for just one scene. The conversation grows vertically and requires massive amounts of dialogue writing. On the *Pandora* flowchart (see Figure 17–2), notice the towering vertical stack of the boxes 7–18, a total of eleven different lines of dialogue. *Pandora's* writer, Aaron Conners, said that the extra work of writing all these dialogue options doesn't pay off with viewer satisfaction. It is rare for the viewer to access all lines of dialogue, and because of the number of lines of dialogue in a scene, the lines had to be quite short.

Because of this limitation, Conners tried to make *Pandora* dialogue branching more horizontal by reusing the same lines in different situations. Notice on *The Pandora Directive* flowchart, the number of places where multiple arrows go into one box. This means that same line is being reused several times, such as Louie's shaded box #14, which is a possible response to four of Tex's dialogue lines.

The Mechanics of Flowcharting

Conners uses the software ABC Flowcharter to draw his charts. In *Moon*, he used flowcharts with dialogue typed in and indicated different characters by different-shaped boxes. Because the *Pandora* charts are more complex, he used numbers in the chart that refer to numbered lines of dialogue in a list. He indicated different characters by shading boxes. This technique makes it easier than the different-shaped boxes to distinguish the characters.

First-Person Point of View and Control of Character Movements

The *Pandora Directive* also gives the viewer a high degree of control over Tex's actions. Most of the interactive scenes are shot in first person. The player becomes Tex. He or she sees what Tex sees, and as Tex, the player can move all around the room and examine objects. The player can also click on items, such as a painting, to get Tex's sarcastic voice-over about art. Or the player can click on a picture of Tex's ex-wife, which might trigger a flashback video sequence. See the list of player options just above the dialogue in Figure 17–3.

Interactivity at the Scene and Sequence Level: Multiple Story Paths

These interactive choices at the dialogue and movement level launch the Tex character on one of three main story paths with seven possible endings. There are three main paths:

A—Light Path: This is the basic Hollywood ending where Tex saves the world and wins the good woman, Chelsee.
B—Middle Path: This is midground. He doesn't lose Chelsee, but he doesn't win her either.
C—Dark Path: This is film noir—a chance to explore the negative possibilities. Tex fails to save Emily. He loses the good woman, Chelsee, takes up with the bad woman, Regan, and dies at the end.

As Tex (the player) continues to make choices in dialogue and movement, he will hit key dialogue lines or flags that will shift him back and forth between paths. And redemption is hard won. Once entrenched in the dark C path, the best he can hope for is to move up to B. The saintly A path is out of reach.

The player molds Tex into what he wants him to be: good, middle, or bad. Sometimes one choice can mean the difference between life and death. For example, which of the seven endings the player gets depends to a large degree on whether Tex sleeps with the bad woman, Regan. If the player has been on the A or B path and says no to Regan, then Tex solves the final puzzle on the spaceship before escaping safely. If the player follows the C path throughout the game, but says no to Regan, the player gets the B ending: Tex is wounded and sent limping off the ship by Fitzpatrick. If the player follows the C path throughout the game and Tex says yes to Regan, depending on the player's choices in the last scene, Tex could end up dead.

Making a Complex Story and Interactivity Work Together in an Engaging and Coherent Fashion

A detective story is very information based. It requires readers or viewers to keep track of many characters, clues, and locations. This problem is exaggerated when the story has a high degree of interactivity as in *The Pandora Directive*. Aaron Conners does a number of things to keep the audience oriented. Several of the things he does can be seen in other games, such as voiceover for exposition and character background, a hints file, and a travel list and map.

Ask Abouts

Unique to this game is the use of Ask Abouts. As a detective, Tex is constantly asking people questions. If Tex/the player, chooses the right questions and goes to the right places, he gets key information. Where a real detective might scribble something in a notebook, Tex's key information automatically appears in his Ask Abouts list, which the player can access from the main interface at any time. See the top right in Figure 17–4, on page 282.

The following example from the *Pandora Directive* walkthrough explains how the Ask Abouts work. All the Ask Abouts are in bold. They appear on the on-screen Ask Abouts list (Figure 17–4), when someone tells Tex about them. He can then ask others about these Ask Abouts.

> When Tex finds a scarf, he takes it to the Brew & Stew and shows it to Louie, who tells him about a **young blonde woman. Young blonde woman** is automatically placed in your Ask About list. When Tex asks him more about the young blonde woman, he responds with "She was real pretty, though a little heavy on the makeup. I think she said her name was Emily." This puts **Emily**, in your Ask About list. You can now ask anyone about Emily including Louie, but all he has to say is, "I don't know anythin' else about her."
>
> However, when you ask another character, Clint, about Emily, he'll tell you she works for Gus Leach. **Gus Leach** is now placed in your Ask About list. Ask Clint about Gus Leach and he'll give you the **Leach's Key** Ask About. Ask Clint about Leach's key to get the key. You now know that the scarf belongs to the girl who sings at the Fuchsia Flamingo and that her name is Emily. You also know that the Flamingo is run by Gus Leach.

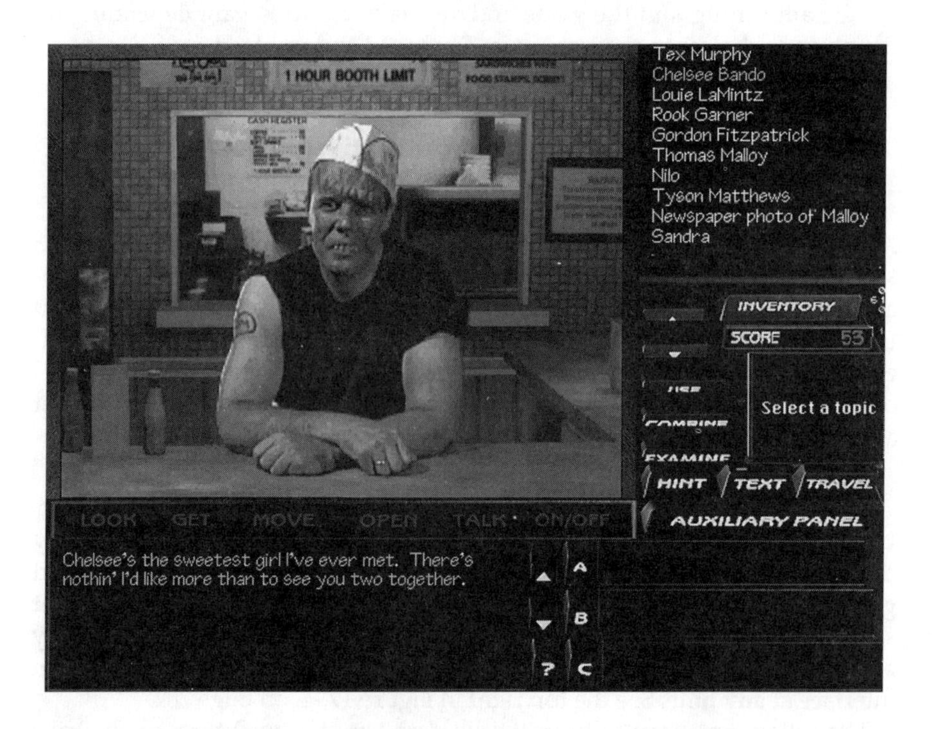

Figure 17–4 Ask Abouts in the *Pandora Directive.*

The Ask Abouts not only help the player keep track of key clues; they also limit the player to questions that the characters might have answers for. Otherwise, the viewer would be faced with the irritation of characters' constantly saying, "I don't know," or the writers would have to write Ask Abouts for everything mentioned in the game. The Ask Abouts also give a convenient way to ask questions. Simply click on the item on the list.

Louie's Ask Abouts Example Following are some of the responses that the Louie Lamintz character can make if questioned on various Ask Abouts. Note that in some cases, as in the Chelsee Ask About, his responses depend on what path Tex is on (A, B, or C). Refer back to the *Pandora* flowchart (Figure 17–2) and you'll see that all the interactive conversations eventually end up in Ask Abouts.

If Tex Murphy asks about:

1. Tex: (Louie answers) You're OK in my book, Murph . . . no matter what anyone else says.
2. Chelsee: (1) Chelsee's the sweetest girl I've ever met. There's nothin' I'd like more than to see you two together.
   (2a) Just between you and me, I get the feelin' she's sweet on ya.
   (2b) I don't know what to tell ya, Murph. The mind of a woman can be a great mystery.
   (2c) She called awhile ago. I guess she's gonna make her visit to Phoenix permanent. Sorry.
   (3a/b) Yeah, I've heard from her. She wanted me to say hi.
3. Louie: What are ya askin' 'bout me for? I ain't nothin' special.
4. Rook: Rook's just an ornery son-of-a-gun, but, believe it or not, he's pretty soft underneath.

(The complete Ask Abouts list: is on the CD-ROM.)

Sometimes Ask Abouts involve more than just asking about a name. They can involve showing things. What is shown and in what sequence affects Louie's response:

Offer photo of Malloy: Yeah. I've seen this guy. Lemme think . . . He came in here a week or two ago. Had a young blonde girl with him. Ordered liver and onions if I remember correctly.
Offer untranslated letter: Well Murph, if I had to guess, I'd say this is written in Yucatec. It's a Mayan language,

spoken in southern Mexico. I can't help ya with the translation, though. You know who might be able to help ya is Clint. I heard he's quite a world traveler. Might give it a try.
Offer scarf:
If Tex offers Photo of Malloy first: Yeah, I remember this guy. Came in here to eat a couple times. Probably a month ago.
Then Scarf: Oh, yeah. I remember this scarf . . . and the perfume on it. Young, blonde girl . . . In fact, she came in here with the guy in the photograph.
If offer Scarf first: Oh, yeah. I remember this scarf . . . and the perfume on it. Young, blonde girl. Came in here awhile ago.
Then Photo of Malloy: This guy was with that young blonde girl who wore the nice-smelling scarf.

Ask About Lead-Ins You as the player can't just walk up to and start quizzing a character about Ask Abouts. Like a real detective, it usually requires a bit of chatter to warm up the source and get to an Ask About. In the example that follows, the numbers refer to the *Pandora* flowchart (Figure 17–2):

Louie:
17. My point is, fallin' in love don't mean a lot. What's hard is knowin' someone real well and still likin' 'em. But that ain't even the hardest thing. The hardest thing is findin' someone you can trust. Remember that. [beat] Now I'll get off my soapbox . . . What can I do for you?
Tex:
25. Yeah, I'll keep that in mind. Not to be rude, but can I ask you a few questions before I go?

Sometimes, getting to the Ask Abouts requires quite a bit of smooth talking. Refer to *The Pandora Directive* flowchart to see the twisted path it takes to get to the Ask Abouts in that scene. Other times, Ask About lead-ins are fairly short, such as when Tex dials a telephone number and the person appears on the videophone ready for questions, but even these brief lead-ins can have relevance to the plot or character development.

THE PANDORA DIRECTIVE NARRATIVE WALKTHROUGH

To get a sense of how all of the elements discussed (complex story, interactivity, and Ask Abouts) work together, read the walkthrough sample that follows. The walkthrough is a rough description of the story and key interactive elements. It is an attempt to provide an overview of how the program is going to work. This is essential because much of the other written material for an interactive program can be simply lists of dialogue, flowcharts, and phrases.

The walkthrough is broken down by days as is *The Pandora Directive*. This makes it easier to use multiple CDs and to get the mini-series type of pacing that the writers and designers were looking for. Following is Day One of the walkthrough. (The complete walkthrough has ten days and is available on the book's CD-ROM.)

Options are frequently listed for the character in the walkthrough, such as, "Your options at the outset (in likely order of importance) are (1) find out about Malloy staying at the Ritz, (2) pay the rent to Nilo, (3) pay Rook and/or Louie, (4) go to the newsstand and talk to Chelsee, or (5) go to the Electronics Shop." In the actual game, these options are clear because of the situation or are explained through Tex's voice-overs (VO). There are different versions of voice-overs for the different paths. Voice-overs are enclosed by brackets.

The Pandora Directive Walkthrough

DAY ONE

After the Introduction is finished, we have met Louie, Rook, Glenda, Chelsee, and Fitzpatrick. You have also seen Sandra Collins (dead) and the Black Arrow Killer (Dag Horton).

In the introductory conversation with Chelsee, you learn that she is about to turn thirty years old and is in an emotional quandary about it. After she leaves, Louie and Rook lead us to believe that Chelsee is romantically susceptible.

In the introductory conversation with Gordon Fitzpatrick, you learn that he is looking for a Dr. Thomas Malloy, who recently stayed at the Ritz Hotel. Fitzpatrick and Malloy used to work together (where, unspecified). Fitzpatrick then says he saw a photograph of Malloy in the Bay City Mirror and found out that the photograph had been taken at a local university (San Francisco Tech). Fitzpatrick gives Tex a copy of the photo. The only person at SFT able or willing to recognize Malloy was a grad student named Sandra (Collins). She said she had worked with the man Fitzpatrick knew as Malloy, but that she knew him as Tyson Matthews. Fitzpatrick arranged to meet Sandra later to discuss what she knew, but she didn't keep the appointment and Fitzpatrick was unable to locate her again. Fitzpatrick then saw another reference to Malloy in the *Cosmic Connection*, an underground paranormal journal, which mentioned an upcoming interview with Dr. Thomas Malloy. The interview never appeared in the magazine and no explanation has been given. Finally,

Fitzpatrick says he was able to pay 500 dollars to get Malloy's address at the Ritz, but Malloy had already moved on.

Tex accepts the case and Fitzpatrick leaves. This initiates the first interactive portion of the game. [Play TEX VO—Tex owes $ to Rook, Louie, Nilo.] Your inventory consists of the newspaper photo of Malloy, $4000 cash, and Tex's Electronics Shop credit card (from UKM). Your options at the outset, in likely order of importance, are: (1) find out about Malloy staying at the Ritz, (2) pay the rent to Nilo, (3) pay Rook and/or Louie, (4) go to the newsstand and talk to Chelsee, or (5) go to the Electronics Shop.

Going to Rook, Louie, Chelsee, or the Electronics Shop can be done in any order at any time. In order to talk to Nilo, however, you must make a date with Chelsee (Path: A/A/A/A/C). Until this is done, Nilo isn't at the front desk of the Ritz.

Note: In order to initiate the A path, you must use Path C/B/B/ . . . In order to initiate the C path, you must use Path A/C/C/ . . . When returning to Chelsee (after initiating one of the alternate paths), you must use Path C/A/C to make the date.

Once the date with Chelsee has been set, she is still available at the newsstand for Ask Abouts until Tex gets jumped at the Ritz. After that, she's no longer at the newsstand at any point in the game. Also, once you've set the date, Nilo becomes available at the front desk in the Ritz lobby.

If you go to the Brew & Stew and talk to Louie, you can choose A, in which case, you lose $20 from inventory; otherwise, you don't lose any money. Once the Ask Abouts start, you can also offer $200 to pay your tab to Louie. This is totally optional, though it will earn you points. At the pawnshop, you must pay Rook $300 in order to get him to answer Ask Abouts. At the Electronics Shop, you must pay Zack $1230 in order to make a purchase.

Once you've made a date with Chelsee, you're free to talk to Nilo. You must pay Nilo $2100 for rent before doing anything else. After paying the rent, Nilo will ask for more money in order to get to the Ask Abouts. You must pay either $300 (choice A or B after "no comprende") or $100 (choice C after "no comprende"). Offering the photo of Malloy will get Nilo to tell you that Malloy stayed in Apartment A, but is no longer there. [TEX VO—Probably no one else has been there since Malloy left.]

When you go to Apartment A, you'll find the door locked. There is a security panel on the wall by the door, which requires a number code in order to enter. [TEX VO—Nilo keeps notebook on desk.] You now have two ways to get into the apartment: (1) Go back to Nilo and ask for the code, or (2) set off the fire alarm, getting Nilo to leave the front desk and allowing you to get his notebook. If you ask Nilo for the code, he'll ask for another $500. Using Path C/C will get you the code for free. Any other path will cost you $500. In order to find the fire alarm, locate the painting on the wall in the second floor hallway of the Ritz and move it. Get the screwdriver from Tex's office, and use it on the face of the fire alarm. This will initiate the fire alarm puzzle. Click the top left nodule, then the top right nodule. Next, click the second nodule from the top on the left; then click the bottom nodule on the right. Next, click the second nodule from the bottom on the left; then click the second nodule from the top on the right. Finally, click the bottom nodule on the left; then the second nodule from the bottom on the right. This will start the fire alarm. Go to the front desk in the lobby and get Nilo's notebook. Examine the notebook and find the code to Apartment A (4827). Go to the apartment and enter the code on the security panel . . . then enter the apartment.

A movie sequence is initiated. Tex is jumped and knocked unconscious.

CONCLUSION: RESPONSE TO THE PROJECT

As of this writing, *The Pandora Directive* has not been released. *Under a Killing Moon*, however, has been a major success. It was a best seller, on a number of critics top ten lists, and won a number of major awards, including the International Interactive Communications Society Award and the Software Publisher Associations Codie award for best Interactive Adventure Game. Considering the innovations in *The Pandora Directive*, it will likely be an even greater success than its predecessor.

REFERENCE

Conners, Aaron. Telephone interviews with the author, July 1994, August 1995, December 1995.

18

WORLDS NARRATIVE CASE STUDY: *DUST: A TALE OF THE WIRED WEST*

Summary

Name of production: *Dust: A Tale of the Wired West*
Writer: Andrew Nelson
Developers: CyberFlix Inc.
Audience: Rated for teenagers (13+ and up)
Medium: CD-ROM
Presentation location: Home
Subject: Western
Goal: Entertain
Structures: String of pearls, linear, hierarchical

Parts of this chapter originally appeared in *Creative Screenwriting*.

PROGRAM DESCRIPTION AND BACKGROUND

Program Description

Dust: A Tale of the Wired West is an interactive Western set in 1882 Diamondback, New Mexico. In the precredit linear video scene, the Stranger catches a gunslinger, the Kid, playing foul at cards and nails his cheating hand to the table with a knife. Before the Kid can recover, the Stranger flees.

In the next scene, the player becomes the Stranger as the rest of the game is played through first-person point of view. What the Stranger sees, the player sees. When people talk to the Stranger, they are talking to the player.

Running from the Kid, the Stranger stumbles into the town of Diamondback (see Figure 18–1) in the middle of the night with no gun, little money, and a hole in his size twelve boots. The goal is first to get cash, gun, and boots, and then to defend himself from the Kid, who is gunning for revenge. If the Stranger survives the high noon shootout, he may get appointed sheriff and lured into helping a Native American schoolteacher recover her tribe's lost treasure.

The town of Diamondback is a three-dimensional world populated with forty animated characters. *Dust*'s writer, Andrew Nelson, calls it "*Myst* with people in it." The Stranger can move through the town, exploring most of its buildings and talking to its citizens. They will sometimes help and sometimes mislead; a big part of the game is judging the character of the people the Stranger meets and deciding whose advice to follow.

In addition to the story, this program also has games to play, such as blackjack, poker, slot machines, checkers, and a shooting range. These games are well integrated into the story, and success at them helps the player advance the narrative. For example, on the Stranger's first night in town, he must win enough money gambling to stay at the hotel.

Figure 18–1 The main interface showing the town in *Dust: A Tale of the Wired West*.

Dust: A Tale of the Wired West and the Adventure Game

Dust's writer says that sophisticated navigability and interactivity sets this game off from other adventure games. The user in *Dust* enters a world populated by cyberpuppets who have lives and personalities of their own. They do their shopping, gambling, or drinking in real time, whether the player interacts with them or not. If the player does interact, they will address him or her directly, and they will remember how the player treats them. This can cause a chain of events that radically changes the progress of the narrative.

All the buildings in town can be entered whenever they are "open," and objects can be looked at and picked up. Sounds that are heard in the distance will get louder as the player approaches their source. This complex navigability and interactivity is made possible by CyberFlix's DreamFactory authoring program, described in detail later in this chapter. *Dust* is the first program to be completely developed in this process.

Production Background

Andrew Nelson wrote and produced *Dust: A Tale of the Wired West*. Michael Gilmore and Jamie Wicks were the art directors in charge of the design. The program was developed by CyberFlix Inc. of Knoxville, Tennessee. CyberFlix has had previous success with its arcade-type action games *Lunicus* and *Jump Raven*. Although the company will continue to produce action titles, company president Bill Appleton said, "*Dust* is really indicative of a larger direction for our company. What excited us most is the possibility of being able to create more character-driven, more story-driven, more cinematic titles." (Production Notes, 5) *Dust* is distributed in the United States by GTE Entertainment, in Japan by Bandai, and elsewhere by BMG Interactive.

GOALS AND CHALLENGES WRITING *DUST: A TALE OF THE WIRED WEST*

Goals

A primary goal for the developers of *Dust* was to create an inhabitable, believable world with its own constants and laws. They also wanted to give the user the maximum possible freedom to explore this world and interact with its citizens as part of a complex, interactive story. They hoped this program would have broad appeal and reach a wider audience than the typical video game.

Challenges

The key elements of these goals and the major challenges are the following:

- Creating an inhabitable, believable world.
- Giving the user the opportunity to explore this world and interact with its citizens.
- Developing a story within this highly interactive world through establishing plot points, characterization, and other story functions.

WRITING *DUST: A TALE OF THE WIRED WEST:* MEETING THE CHALLENGES

Creating an Inhabitable, Believable World

The key to *Dust*'s success in creating an inhabitable, believable world is CyberFlix's proprietary, multimedia, authoring tool, DreamFactory. This technology allowed writer Andrew Nelson to "write" *Dust* in a radically different way than most other multimedia programs are written today.

Preliminary Writing

The writing of *Dust* started off on paper, as do most other multimedia titles. First Nelson developed the back story on the town of Diamondback, giving the history of the town and the characters. When creating a world such as this town, the designers need to know background on every individual and building, so that they can create a consistent, realistic environment that has a life of its own.

The writer next wrote the walkthrough, outlining the basic story line and key interactions. Then came the game design, which is basically a blown-up storyboard showing the interactive puzzles. Finally came the table of events, which became the basis for the hint book. This book has suggestions which help the player solve key problems and move forward in the game. Up to this point, the writing process on *Dust* is similar to that of other world games. But from this point forward, the writer used DreamFactory, and the similarities quickly fade.

DreamFactory® Defined

DreamFactory is a set of multimedia authoring tools designed by CyberFlix's president, Bill Appleton, and used to create *Dust*. DreamFactory is designed so that nontechnical people, such as writers and designers, can develop an interactive multimedia piece without programming.

DreamFactory develops 3-D interactive environments that are peopled by "cyberactors" who interact with the user. The cyberactors are not videos of real people, nor are they traditional drawn animations. Instead they are created from photographs of real people that are developed into computer-generated animations. The final results are cyberactors who walk around town and talk to the user. (See Figure 18–2 later in this chapter.)

These synthetic actors allow for greater realism than cartoon-style animation, and they allow much higher levels of interactivity than video, because these computer-generated characters, like the letters on a word processor, are simply bits of code that can be instantly assembled and reassembled. This process allows the characters to respond smoothly to the user, remember interactions, and change future behavior based on these interactions. In *Dust*, most of the characters develop significantly during the four days of the story. The characters also move about on their own in real time, whether the user interacts with them or not.

DreamFactory has these specialized tools:

- SetConstruction: Builds 3-D digital sets that the player can move through in real time.
- PropDepartment: Creates accurately scaled props that increase or decrease in size as they get closer to or farther from the user.
- CentralCasting: Creates and animates the cyberactors who move through the 3-D sets, speak, and react to the user.
- HeadShot: Animates the close-ups of the talking characters based on photographs of actual actors.
- Movie Editor: Edits animation sequences and can add special effects, camera movement, and transitions.
- SoundTrack: Builds and controls the audio.
- FlatPainter: Creates backgrounds, interfaces, and interactive buttons.

DreamFactory and the Writer

After the writer develops the basic characters, story line, and some of the dialogue on paper, he or she stops writing a plan for a world and instead uses DreamFactory to build the world itself. Once the characters are defined, artists use the HeadShot and CentralCasting tools to create the characters. Other designers use the SetConstruction and PropDepartment tools to create the environment or world of the story (in the case of *Dust*, the town of Diamondback). The newly created cyberactors are placed in this world, and from this point forward, the writer doesn't put words on paper again.

The writer thus functions more like a writer-director. When the writer types lines for a certain character, the appropriate cyberactor on the computer screen will speak the lines. When the writer types in screen directions, the cyberactor will do what he or she is told to do. The writer thus gets to see the world being created come immediately to life.

Editing is just as easy. The writer can click on a cyberactor to get his or her dialogue and reaction to changes in the script. *Dust*'s writer, Andrew Nelson, said that there was no other effective way to test all the variables in a program as complex as *Dust*. DreamFactory allows the writer constantly to test game play and interaction all the way up to the alpha stage and beyond. (Alpha stage is the earliest full working version of a multimedia program.)

Nelson estimates that half of the original dialogue and most of the dialogue and story editing occurred in DreamFactory. Once he started working with DreamFactory, he did not work with paper again until the end of the project, when a hard copy of the script was printed out. The final script does not look like a screenplay. It is more like a treatment of the characters and character interactions off of which hangs huge amounts of dialogue. Nelson estimates that there are about 5,000 individual lines of dialogue in *Dust*.

Writing in DreamFactory requires using a special scripting language, but Nelson says that it was not much more difficult than learning to write in linear screenplay style, which has its own specific formatting and technical words. Like writing in linear screenplay format, writing in DreamFactory is cumbersome at first, but eventually it becomes second nature. What is difficult (and this is shared by any other highly interactive script) is the need to write mosaically. When a writer is using DreamFactory to develop a worlds program, such as *Dust*, there is no linear structure outside of the central story line. The linear progression is built by the user out of the snippets of dialogue and bits of interaction the writer creates.

Giving the User the Opportunity to Explore This World

Perhaps the best way to explain the extensive navigability the user has in *Dust* is to describe some of the options available the first night of the story. After the introductory material, *Dust* starts with the Stranger coming into town in the middle of the night. After a few preliminary interactions to orient the viewer to the game, the user/stranger is free to explore the town. He can wander the streets and talk to people he meets, or he can enter the buildings that are open. Because it is the middle of the night, the open buildings are limited to the saloon, the hotel, and the curiosities shop. The curiosities shop is owned by a character named Help, who is always there if the player gets stuck. The hotel has no rooms available when the Stranger arrives, but the saloon is hopping with gambling, music, and girls upstairs.

Players can visit each of these sites as often as they want and talk to anyone they meet. Because the characters all move in real time and have lives of their own, different characters appear as the evening progresses. However, in order to advance in the story and move on to the next day, the Stranger needs to find a place to sleep.

This can be done in a couple of ways. The Stranger needs money to stay at the hotel. He can get this by gambling or by searching the couch in the hotel, which has four dollars under the cushions. If he loses all his money gambling, he can ask Help for a loan. The other way to get a bed for the night is to be nice to the mayor's wife, who will then ask him home. But this works only if the Stranger sees her on the street and says just the right things. In *Dust*, there is usually an easy way and a hard way to achieve goals.

There are myriad story paths the user/stranger could travel the first night, depending on where he decides to go and whom he decides to talk to, but all the story paths will eventually lead to the Stranger's going to bed that night. Nelson describes this structure as a circular experience with several doors that will shoot the player out to the next level of the story. Depending on what the player does on one level of the story, he will be better or less prepared to meet the challenges in the next level. Eventually all of these story paths on all of the levels lead to a common destination, which is a branching of six different endings.

The overall structure can be compared to a string of pearls (Figure 13–6, page 184) with each pearl being a set time period and location that the character is free to explore. To leave the pearl and advance the story, the player must achieve certain things, such as get a place to sleep, get a gun, get bullets, and so on.

This type of structure means that the writer and other developers must prepare vast amounts of dialogue, interactions, and places for the user to explore. It also means that it is difficult to create many emotions common to linear video that require a tight sequencing of action, such as suspense. However, Nelson explains that *Dust* offers something different from the linear experience. He compares *Dust* to Disneyland. Whatever players would like to do, they can find it in *Dust*. They can play cards, shoot in an arcade, and if he is lonely, there are lots of folks willing to talk. The experience of *Dust* essentially revolves around getting things, doing things, and having fun. (See the *Dust* demo on the CD-ROM.)

Interactive Dialogue

Dust's Approach to Interactive Dialogue

A major way to get information and have fun in *Dust* is through talking to the characters. Like the creators of *The Pandora Directive*, the developers of *Dust* decided that interactive dialogue provided the best opportunity for detailed and fluid interaction. The two games, however, take different approaches to dialogue interactivity. In *The Pandora Directive*, the primary dialogue interaction is through the main character, Tex, who has a series of response attitudes that the user can click to elicit different lines of dialogue. The user cannot choose Tex's actual dialogue. The other characters do not have attitudes to click on; their responses are dictated by Tex's lines. They also have considerably less variation in their dialogue than Tex does.

Dust takes the opposite approach. The Stranger's lines are presented in a menu of written choices. We never hear him speak. The other characters speak in response to the Stranger's questions that the user picks from the menu. For example, when the player first encounters the character Marie Macintosh, she will be in the form of what CyberFlix calls an "actor," which is an animation of Marie going about her daily business in the streets of Diamondback (see Figure 18–2). When the player clicks on her, she will walk toward the player,

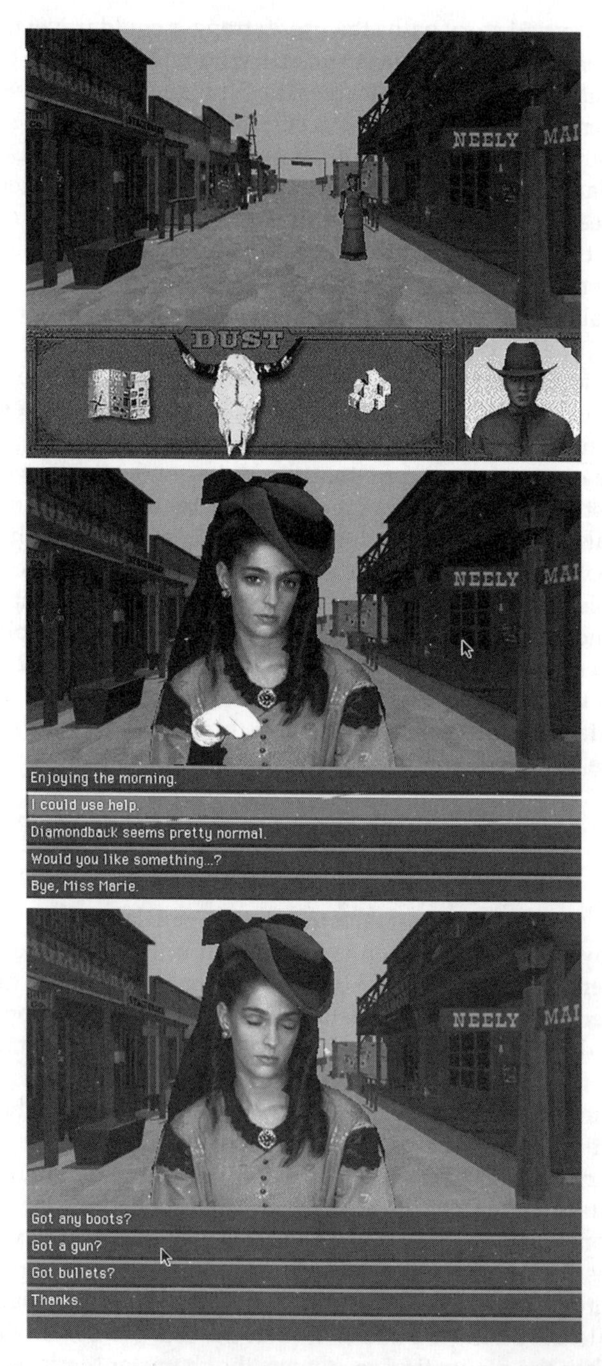

Figure 18–2 Top: Marie as "actor" before user clicks on her. Middle: Marie in interactive conversation after the user clicks on her (menu items are the user's questions/comments. In this example, the user clicks, "I could use help"). Bottom: Marie continues interactive conversation (the menu is narrowed to the things the user needs help with).

then dissolve to a more lifelike close-up. At this point she will speak her opening lines: "Why, if it isn't the stranger in our midst! I was out for a stroll."

Once she completes her opening lines, the player will have the option of responding by clicking text questions and comments from a menu at the bottom of the screen. If the player chooses "I could use help" from the menu, in Figure 18–2, Marie will say: "However can I be of assistance?" Now the menu will change to these options:

```
Got any boots?
Got a gun?
Got bullets?
Thanks.
```

The user can choose one of the above menu items, and Marie verbally responds. The conversation continues until the user cuts it off with a menu item such as "Thanks" or "Bye." But the user/Stranger never speaks.

Andrew Nelson chose this approach to interactive dialogue because he thought that the written lines were more neutral than choosing attitudes and hearing the main character speak. He said that with the written text, it is easier to infer that the dialogue would be delivered in the way the player imagines. He also said that he wanted to give the user more choices by: 1) giving the user the option of choosing the specific lines to speak and 2) by giving a number of possible user responses for each line of the other character, as opposed to a limited number of Response Attitudes. Nelson does not, however, rule out all use of Response Attitudes and may use them in his next program, *R.M.S. Titanic*. (See *The Pandora Directive* case study in Chapter 17 for a discussion of the Response Attitudes approach.)

Effect of the Interactive Dialogue in *Dust*

The characters in *Dust* remember and react to what the player/Stranger says to them. If the Stranger is rude, they may not give him the information he needs or help when he needs them. For example, when he first meets the mayor's wife, if he flatters her, she'll invite him home to spend the night. If he insults her, she'll run off in a huff.

How the Stranger treats one character may also affect how a character who is connected to that character will treat him. Marie Macintosh hates her father. If the Stranger is rude to her father, she'll like the Stranger. This type of complex reaction to the user's dialogue choices can change the progress of the story.

Possible Dialogue Scene: Marie Macintosh—Day One—Morning

Following is an example of a more complex dialogue scene, but it is only one possibility. (The sequence is from the morning of Day One.) The actual dialogue sequence depends on which questions the user chooses to ask. This conversation is not written out in order like this in the actual script. It was reconstructed here to explain how the interactive conversation works. The complete list of dialogue options as they appear in the actual script follows this example (the Stranger\user's questions and comments in boldface type are answered by Marie Macintosh's comments that have the same number as his questions):

MARIE MACINTOSH

MORNING—DAY ONE

MARIE: *A1. Cheerful greeting*
Why, if it isn't the stranger in our midst!

MARIE: *B. Question to user*
(She's suspicious) However do you do?

STRANGER: **C1. I'm doing fine.**

MARIE: *C1. Teasing you*
I'm delighted to hear that Diamondback provides all that you need, but aren't you curious about us?

STRANGER: **C1a. Should I be?**

MARIE: *C1a. Being mysterious*
(tinkling laugh) Diamondback is a town of secrets. Some are useful. Others aren't. But I don't mean to imply mystery. You have, no doubt, more pressing questions . . .

[This is an example of the writer nudging the user to ask more questions to advance the story.]

STRANGER: **C1b. Why is the school deserted?**

MARIE: *C1b. Explaining simple facts of life*
The mission school? Well, once the Yunni left, there really was no need for it. Diamondback's youngsters go to the Hildago school five miles from here. And there are no more Indians . . .

STRANGER: **C1b-1. Why was that?**

[Her answers to some of the questions depend on whether she likes the Stranger, which is based on the types of questions asked earlier. For example, for C1b-1, if she doesn't like the Stranger, she will answer:]

MARIE: *C1b-1. Impatient. Not answering him, but speaking from the heart*
Really. That's all in the past.

[If she does like the Stranger, however, she will say:]

C1b-1a. Confiding in you.
"You know, since you came here I have felt a (looks for word) kinship with you. I feel you have known great tragedy, and because of that you, you understand me.

Dialogue Transcript: Marie Macintosh—Day One—Morning

This is a list of the Morning Day One dialogue for Marie Macintosh and the Stranger as it appears in the actual script. This is a first draft; the final draft as seen on screen deals with the mission, not the school. Using DreamFactory, most of the editing and revisions are done on screen, and there is no working second draft on paper.

In the dialogue that follows, the Stranger's questions are in boldface type, Marie's attitudes are in italics, and her response matches his question of the same number. "Home base" refers to the location where the cyberactor is usually stationed. For Marie, it is outside Bolivar's store, but like the other characters, she can wander about on her day's activities.

MARIE MACINTOSH

(Marie is a petulant, spoiled girl who, at 17, is thoroughly bored with this backwater she finds herself in. She's very intelligent and wants to appear older than she is, which makes her very young indeed. With her alliance with Raddison, Marie can become suspicious of your motives, guessing you may know about their pyrite mine scheme. She can also shift her allegiance, if you choose the right questions to ask her. We meet her usually in the street where she whiles away the day fingering the fabrics at Bolivar's or teasing the cowboys who wander into the Hard Drive Saloon.)

MORNING—DAY ONE

A1. Cheerful greeting
"Why, if it isn't the stranger in our midst!"
A2. If unknown from previous night
(offering hand) "I'm the mayor's daughter, Marie."
A1a. if outside home base
"I was out for a stroll . . ."
A1b. if outside first destination
"I was out for a stroll . . ."
A1c. if inside first destination
"I often come here. To think . . ."
A1d. if outside second destination

"Picking up a few items at Watsons . . ."
A1e. if inside second destination
"I was fetching something . . ."
A1f. if outside third destination
"I'm returning home from shopping . . ."

B. Question to user
(She's suspicious) "However do you do?"

C1. I'm doing fine.
C2. I could use help.
C3. Play, if possible
C4. Thanks. Bye.

C1. Teasing you
"I'm delighted to hear that Diamondback provides all that you need, but aren't you curious about us?"
C2. Amused
"However can I be of assistance?"
C3. Giving you the hankie, speaking softly
"There's sweat on your brow. Here . . . Take my hankie. A token of a friendship?" (She ends this on a provocative note.)"
C4. End conversation comment
"Goodbye. I am so very glad you've come to stay in Diamondback. If we are lucky, perhaps you'll stay for a long, long time."

C1a. Should I be?
C1b. Why is the school deserted?
C1b-1. Why was that?
If Marie likes Stranger
C1b-1a.
C1c. Who was the school teacher?

C2a. You got boots, size 12?
C2b. You got a gun?

C1a. Being mysterious
(tinkling laugh) "Diamondback is a town of secrets. Some are useful. Others aren't. But I don't mean to imply mystery. You have, no doubt, more pressing questions . . ."
C1b. Explaining simple facts of life
"The mission school? Well, once the Yunni left, there really was no need for it. Diamondback's youngsters go

to the Hildago school five miles from here. And there are no more Indians . . ."

C1b-1. Impatient. Not answering him, but speaking from the heart

"Really. That's all in the past."

If Marie likes Stranger

C1b-1a. Confiding in you.

"You know, since you came here I have felt a (looks for word) *kinship* with you. I feel you have known great tragedy, and because of that you, you understand me."

C1c. A little irritated to be back on the subject of Indians

A Yunni called Sonoma, who lived with the Grangers until they died. Now I wouldn't know where she was. She is, after all, an *Indian.*"

C2a. She is amused

(tinkling laugh) "Oh, I do not mean to make light of your situation, but your feet [giggles], they are *simply* enormous. The only ones bigger belong to the Nevans boy, Jay, who has a terrible crush on me" [giggles]

C2b. Lying sweetly through her teeth

"Oh, no! I don't even know how to shoot a gun! Guns scare me!"

If Marie is suspicious

C2c. She responds

"Now, if I don't know a Colt from a Remington what would I know about bullets? [laughs] Maybe you could borrow a few from some cowpoke!"

Additional dialogue transcripts are available on the attached CD-ROM.

Developing a Story within This Highly Interactive World

This level of dialogue interactivity coupled with the nearly unlimited opportunity to explore Diamondback creates a highly interactive world in the control of the user. In order to create a story within such a world, the writer must develop a series of devices that nudge the user in the right direction, while still leaving the impression that the user is making the ultimate choice. These nudges establish key plot points, introduce characters, engineer confrontations, manipulate the user where the writer wants him or her to go, and generally keep the story moving forward.

Help

One of the ways this is done in this program is through the Help option. Unlike many other programs where help is a text-hints window that clearly disrupts the story, help in *Dust* is a Chinese gentleman named Help who runs a curiosities shop. He always knows where the player is in the game and gives just the assistance needed. For example, if the Stranger runs out of cash, he'll give him a five dollar loan but also chase him out of the store, calling him a "hopeless case."

Other Characters' Dialogue

It is not only Help who knows where the player is in the story. The other characters are also aware of the Stranger's situation and can prompt him in the right direction. For example, when the Stranger gets a note at the hotel to meet a character outside, the hotel clerk says, "So you going out again?" The Stranger can ignore the note and the prompt and go to bed, but if he does, he will miss the fun of a fist-fight with a local bully and some key information. Even if dialogue in this piece is not prompting the user in a certain direction, it is usually giving key plot points or setting up character. There is not much room for idle chatter in an interactive program. The same information must be included in a variety of ways in different pieces of dialogue, because there is no guarantee that any one piece of dialogue will be accessed by the user.

Written Material

The note mentioned above is only one example of written material used to prod the character. *Dust* also includes a book on Diamondback in the curiosities shop that gives key information about the town. The town's newspaper also provides updates. At one point, the user can read in the paper that Congress has passed anti-Asian legislation. A smart user realizes that the Chinese gentleman Help might be endangered and rushes to his store, saving it from being burned. This was also a way to bring in historical events as context for the story.

The Narrator

The narrator allows the writer to compress and deliver instructions. In *Dust*, the narrator is triggered automatically at key times, particularly at the beginning of each day, telling the user what he or she has to accomplish. This is one way to ensure that the user will get key plot points without intruding significantly on the interactive experience. The narrator will be used even more in CyberFlix's next program, *Titanic*, which is told in flashback.

Short Linear Movies

Short linear movies also occasionally appear to give important information, such as the opening card game that shows the Stranger's fight with the Kid.

Film Language and Genre

Film has spent a hundred years teaching the audience its visual language.

Smart interactive writers can take advantage of this language to communicate meaning. *Dust* makes particularly good use of the icons associated with the Western genre. For example, when the town of Diamondback rises up from the desert, it creates a whole range of associations that users bring from their experience of other Westerns.

CONCLUSION: RESPONSE TO THE PROGRAM

Dust: A Tale of the Wired West was named Best Multimedia Game of the year by *MacWorld*. It has also received critical acclaim in such publications as *Newsweek, People, Next Generation*, and *CD-ROM Today*, and it continues to be a best seller for CyberFlix.

REFERENCES

Nelson, Andrew. Telephone interview with the author, December 22, 1995.
Production Notes. *Dust: A Tale of the Wired West*. Knoxville, TN: CyberFlix Inc., 1995, p. 5.

19

KEY POINTS FROM PART III: HOW TO WRITE NARRATIVE MULTIMEDIA

A STORY WITH INTERACTIVE POTENTIAL

There are no hard and fast rules about what makes a good interactive narrative, but some things that have worked in the past include the following:

- A clearly defined goal to lead the player through the story. Examples: Finding a lost girl (*Patrol Theater*, Chapter 14), exposing a corrupt billionaire (*Voyeur*, Chapter 16), rescuing a lover from a haunted house (*The 11th Hour*, Chapter 15).
- An interesting role for the player that allows some control over the narrative flow. Example: In *Dust* (Chapter 18) the player becomes an Old West drifter named the Stranger. The player controls what this character says and does.
- Various plot possibilities and choice points. Scenes can be played out in a number of ways, and the player's choices in these scenes can lead to a number of possible endings. Example: In *The Pandora Directive* (Chapter 17,) the player/Tex Murphy can choose to have a fight with his girlfriend and can decide to sleep with the evil woman, but these choices lead to his death at the end.
- A story line into which puzzles and games can be easily integrated. Examples: *The 11th Hour* (Chapter 15) justifies its games narratively by making the antagonist an evil toy maker who likes to torture his victims with deadly games. Other programs, such as *The Pandora Directive* (Chapter 17), integrate the puzzles into the obstacles facing the player, such as deciphering a secret code to disarm an alarm.
- An intriguing, unusual world to explore. Examples: Part of the fun of immersing ourselves in the multimedia experience is a chance to explore unusual locations, such as a desert town in the Old West (*Dust*, Chapter 18), the mansion of a billionaire (*Voyeur*, Chapter 16), and the urban future (*The Pandora Directive*, Chapter 17).

STRONG LINEAR NARRATIVE (CHAPTER 13)

Most of the writers in the programs featured in the case studies first wrote a linear story, which they later developed into an interactive narrative. The main reason is to make sure that the idea can be developed into a strong story. All the interactivity in the world won't make a bad idea interesting. It is also sometimes hard to determine the full interactive potential of a story idea until it has been fully developed.

CLASSICAL STRUCTURE (CHAPTER 13)

Many successful interactive narrative programs are based on classical narrative structure. Classical narratives usually have a lead character who has a need or goal that he or she wants to accomplish. When the lead character tries to achieve that need, he or she meets obstacles that create conflict. Obstacles can be another person, the environment, or inner conflicts. The conflicts build until the climax, where the character achieves the goal or not.

CHARACTERS

The Player (Chapter 13)

At the same time as the writer lays out the basic story, he or she needs to define the role of the player(s) clearly. Who are they in the story? The lead character? A minor character? What will they get to do? How much control will they have over the characters' behavior? What is the player's goal? What are the key obstacles to achieving that goal? Will these obstacles be personalized in the form of an opponent?

Character Interactivity (Chapters 14, 17, 18)

It's necessary for the writer to devise a way for the lead character/player to interact with his or her environment. If it is limited interactivity, the writer might merely need a menu or map of options, as in *Patrol Theater*. However, if there is to be complex interactivity, the writer has to come up with a more sophisticated approach, such as interactive dialogue. One approach to interactive dialogue, as used in *The Pandora Directive*, is to allow the other characters to speak and give the player/main character a series of Response Attitudes to choose from. What Response Attitude the player chooses determines what line the character will speak.

Another approach, as used in *Dust: A Tale of the Wired West*, is to have dialogue menus for the main character that show the complete dialogue that the user can choose. In addition to dialogue, most programs also give the user other options such as moving, picking up objects, and clicking on objects and characters to get information or initiate interactions.

STRUCTURE (CHAPTER 13)

Once the writer has a clear idea of the plot, characters, goals, and conflicts, he or she can decide which interactive structure might work best. The types of structure available depend to a large degree on the authoring system-story engine that will be used to produce the program.

Linear with Scene Branching (Chapters 13, 14)

If the story will be primarily linear with occasional branching choices for the users that eventually loop back to the main plot, consider a scene branching structure. This approach is used in *Patrol Theater*. In this piece a Boy Scout patrol searches for a little girl. The player assumes the role of one of the scouts and can decide which locations to search, such as the school or a farm. Once launched on the search of a location, the scene is primarily linear until the next branching point. Although interactivity is limited in this approach, it does allow the writer more control over story elements. In this case, the writer thought that limited interactivity was the best way to maintain the suspense of the search for the girl.

Puzzle-Based Narrative (Chapter 15)

A writer whose major interest is presenting puzzles and games might want to use a puzzle-based narrative. This is the basic approach used in *The 11th Hour: The Sequel to the 7th Guest*. The lead character/player searches a haunted house for his girlfriend. To win clues to her whereabouts, he has to solve numerous puzzles in this house. The main interactivity is in the puzzles, not in the narrative itself. In this case, the reward for solving a puzzle is a video fragment of the girlfriend's story.

Hierarchical Branching (Chapter 13)

If a story has a number of major choices that take it in a completely different direction, then the writer is involved in hierarchical structure. The problem with this structure is branching explosion. Five options with five choices each equals 25 scenes; five choices for each of those scenes equals 125 scenes. This quickly becomes too much to write or produce. This is why hierarchical branching is primarily limited to the endings of stories as in *The 11th Hour: The Sequel to the 7th Guest*, *The Pandora Directive*, and *Dust: A Tale of the Wired West*.

Parallel Structure (Chapters 13, 17)

A way to have multiple story paths and avoid the branching explosion of hierarchical structure is to have parallel story paths. In this case, there are multiple story paths that the user can explore, but the paths are limited, usually to three or four. Choices the user makes send him or her back and forth between these paths instead of onto completely new story paths as in hierarchical structure.

Parallel structure is useful for showing multiple perspectives on a story or various ways a story could unfold based on user choices. *The Pandora Directive* uses this structure. Its "A" path is a basic Hollywood story where everything turns out all right and the hero gets the woman. The "C" path is bleak film noir, ending in death for the hero. The "B" path is a more realistic, midground compromise story. This approach allows a high degree of interactivity for the user but still allows the writer some control over the story.

String of Pearls Structure (Chapters 13, 18)

The string of pearls structure combines a worlds approach with a narrative. In this structure, the character is allowed to explore a certain world or portion of a world, but to move on in the story, he or she has to achieve certain plot points. In *Dust: A Tale of the Wired West*, the first pearl of the story allows the player/lead character to explore a desert town at night. But to advance in the story to the next pearl, the player must find a place to sleep. The next morning is the next pearl of the story. The player/Stranger can continue to explore the town, but now he must find guns, bullets, and boots. This type of structure allows maximum interactivity for the player and the least writer control over the narrative.

STORYTELLING DEVICES (CHAPTERS 13, 18)

Structure gives the overall approach to the story, but to develop narrative within that structure, the writer needs to use a number of storytelling devices. It helps the players to have some sort of map of the story and/or location so that they know where they are at any give time. Often this is an actual map, such as the map of the town in *Dust* or the map of the house in *The 11th Hour*.

Interactive devices help make the user aware of interactive possibilities. These devices can be as simple as text menus or icons that indicate what action is allowed in a certain situation. The Help feature, on-screen text, the narrator, and linear movies are other useful tools for telling an interactive tale.

MECHANICS OF SCRIPTWRITING (PART 1)

There are a number of organizational devices that help in the plotting of narrative, such as flowcharting (Chapter 3) and character charts (Chapter 16).

The writer has to keep in mind the basic techniques of the scriptwriter, such as showing the audience the story with dramatic action instead of telling them, as in a novel (Chapter 2). Finally, the writer must come up with a proposal and script format suitable to the project (Chapter 4).

PART IV

CONCLUSION

20

CONCLUSION: CHALLENGES FOR THE INTERACTIVE WRITER

THE CHALLENGES

As the case studies demonstrate, multimedia is an exciting and complex form of communication. A writer faces a number of challenges to succeed in this medium.

Artistic Challenges

The interactive writer has to be a master of most linear scriptwriting skills, as well as understanding the communication potential of interactivity and the demands of writing for many media. Using these skills to communicate information and tell stories in multimedia poses unique problems and opportunities.

Technological Challenges

In addition to meeting artistic challenges, the interactive writer needs a certain amount of technical knowledge. The writer does not have to be a programmer or have any formal technical training, but he or she does need to have a general understanding of interactive technology. Some writers become so technically proficient that they become designer-writers or writer-producers. This level of expertise is not essential, but a writer should at least understand some of the potential and limitations of the technology in order to communicate effectively. A hyphenate writer (writer-producer, writer-designer) is also far more employable.

Productivity Challenges

The sheer volume of work that must be produced for an interactive program—multiple stories, scenes, and characters—is a challenge. For example,

Zelda's Adventure has 100 speaking parts, 500 locations, and an 800-page script. An interactive writer has to write quickly to meet production deadlines. It also doesn't hurt to have strong word processing skills and knowledge of information management software, such as flowcharters and databases. Many writers find such tools make them more efficient and effective writers.

Legal Challenges

Multimedia writers need to have some understanding of the complex legal issues involved in multimedia. Multimedia is a young industry, and the legal principles governing it are still evolving. The key legal issue involves ownership of intellectual property. Because multimedia is often created by combining works from many media, the writer must understand what media from other sources can be used and what are protected. The writer also needs to understand what constitutes publishing a work, particularly in the area of World Wide Web publishing. The laws of major concern to the multimedia writer are those dealing with copyright, patent, trademark, defamation, libel, and publicity. (See the Background Section of the attached CD-ROM for additional information on this topic.)

THE FUTURE

As difficult as it is to master the required skills, it is perhaps even more challenging to predict exactly what will be required of an interactive writer in the future. Nevertheless, a few developments seem likely.

Online Networks

Online networking, such as the World Wide Web, will continue to grow. One industry survey predicts that the number one job in communication in the near future will be Web designer. As soon as the technology allows for a full multimedia experience online with a user base substantial enough to view the programs produced, then all sorts of options open up: online multimedia narratives that the user can join as a character; virtual worlds of information, such as ancient Rome, that students could explore; and virtual shopping malls that will make current efforts look primitive.

Interactive TV, Mergers, and CD-ROM

Other developments are hard to predict. Interactive television has been in tests sponsored by major companies for years. The broadband cable networks used in these tests are better delivery technology than today's CD-ROMs. It still remains to be seen if these systems will achieve their potential.

Where CD-ROM will be in ten years is also questionable. Some industry insiders see it as a transitional medium that will be replaced by online networks, interactive TV, and better disc technology, such as the Digital Versatile Disc (DVD). However, with CD-ROM technology constantly improving and a large installed user base, it may not disappear as fast as some predict.

Communication mergers will certainly continue in the future with many independent multimedia companies being bought up by corporate giants. Some of the best pieces analyzed in this book were produced by small independent companies. The question is whether the corporate "art by committee mentality" of mega-corporations will foster or stifle the growth of multimedia.

THE REWARD

The challenges for writers of multimedia are many, but the potential rewards are also great. As exciting as many of the programs discussed in this book are, multimedia is still in its youth. Writers involved in multimedia now have the opportunity to help shape a powerful new medium.

Many of the interactive writers and designers chronicled in this book have already posed intriguing solutions to some of the challenges facing multimedia. Their success and that of the new writers who join them will increase as technology improves, allowing interactivity to be more fluidly responsive to the player's commands. When this happens, the developers of interactive multimedia will be able to create a new screen language, just as the early pioneers of cinema developed the language of motion pictures. When audiences learn and eventually enjoy this new language, interactive multimedia will fully mature as a medium of communication and creative expression.

APPENDIX

WRITER AND DESIGNER BIOGRAPHIES AND COMPANY DESCRIPTIONS

The following individuals or companies either contributed script material or gave interviews for this book. They are listed alphabetically by company or individual name. The name of their multimedia program discussed in the book is next to their name. For detailed descriptions of the companies and biographies of the individuals, see the References Section of the CD-ROM.

Peter Adams (T. Rowe Price Web Site)

Peter Adams is Director of Interactive and Creative Services at poppe.com/New York, advertising agency Poppe Tyson's interactive division. Peter acts as both creative director and technical lead for all interactive clients. Adams is also one of the pioneers in the Internet arena, setting up one of the first Web sites on the Internet in 1993.

Access Software (*Under a Killing Moon, The Pandora Directive*)

Access Software Inc. of Salt Lake City, Utah, is a major developer of multimedia entertainment, including the Tex Murphy detective series and *Microsoft Golf Links 386 Pro* and *Links 486 CD*.

Fred Bauer (*Vital Signs*)

Fred Bauer has written over 200 scripts for linear video, interactive video disk, and interactive multimedia since opening his Marblehead, Massachusetts-based business, "Fred Bauer, the writer."

Butler, Raila & Company (Boy Scout Patrol Theater)

Butler, Raila & Company has specialized exclusively in the development of high quality custom interactive media presentations since 1985. Markets and application areas served include publishing, sales and marketing, public information, museum exhibition, and learning (medical, technical, consumer).

Aaron Conners (*Under a Killing Moon, The Pandora Directive*)

Aaron Conners joined Access Software in 1991 as its first full-time writer. In addition to writing the Tex Murphy CD-ROMs *Under a Killing Moon* and *The Pandora Directive,* he has recently signed with Prima Publishing to write three Tex Murphy science-fiction novels.

Chedd-Angier Production Company (*The Nauticus Shipbuilding Company)*

Chedd-Angier is a Boston-based media production company.

John Cosner (*Vital Signs*)

John Cosner is an instructional designer, multimedia producer, and president of PLAY 100, Inc., a training and consulting company that develops multimedia programs and training seminars.

Mathew J. Costello (*The 7th Guest, The 11th Hour*)

Mathew J. Costello is the author of 14 novels and numerous nonfiction books. He wrote the script for *The 7th Guest,* an interactive drama that has become a bestselling CD-ROM (nearly 2,000,000 copies). The sequel, *The 11th Hour,* was released in 1995 and also became an immediate best seller.

CyberFlix Incorporated (*Dust: A Tale of the Wired West*)

An interactive storytelling company and CD-ROM publisher, CyberFlix was founded in 1993 and is based in Knoxville, Tennessee. Current titles include *Titanic, SkullCracker,* and *Red Jack's Revenge.*

Shannon Gilligan (*Who Killed Sam Rupert?*)

Shannon Gilligan is an author of children's and mystery books, founder of the Santa Fe, N.M.–based Spark Interactive, and writer of numerous successful multimedia titles including: *Who Killed Sam Rupert? Who Killed Elspeth Haskard?* and *The Magic Death.*

D.C. Heath and Company (*Sky High*)

D.C. Heath and Company has as its basic mission the development, publication, and marketing of materials of instruction to schools and colleges. These include textbooks, computer software, videos, and CD-ROMs.

Interwrit Designs (*Re-Elect Dan Fenn Web Page*)

Interwrit Designs of Londonderry, New Hampshire, specializes in writing and authoring CD-ROMs, multimedia presentations, and Web pages.

Jane Jensen (*Gabriel Knight*)

Jensen is a writer-designer who has worked on *Police Quest 3, Ecoquest, King's Quest VI,* and *Pepper's Adventures* for Sierra On-Line. She is also the designer of the award winning *Gabriel Knight I—Sins of the Fathers* and *Gabriel Knight II—The Beast Within.*

Matt Lindley (ZD Net's *Personal View* Ad Campaign)

Matt Lindley is the creative director of advertising for Ziff-Davis Interactive Media and Development. He struggles daily with millions of different ways to say "click here."

Ron McAdow (*Sky High*)

Ron McAdow has written books, CD-ROMs, and the award-winning films *Hank the Cave Peanut* and *Captain Silas*. He is currently a multimedia developer for CAST Inc. of Peabody, Massachusetts.

National Scouting Museum (*Patrol Theater*)

The National Scouting Museum, Murray, Kentucky, is a place where history, theater, and technology combine to give visitors an engaging interactive experience with the history of the Boy Scouts of America.

Andrew Nelson (*Dust: A Tale of the Wired West*)

Andrew Nelson is producer and writer for *Dust* and writer for *Jump Raven* and *RMS Titanic* Nelson is one of CyberFlix's founding members and is the company's creative director.

Maria O'Meara (*Sky High, Patrol Theater*)

Maria O'Meara has been a scriptwriter for seventeen years. Her interactive clients include Harvard Community Health Plan, Videologic, Federal Express, Merck, IBM, GTE, Allstate, and Southwestern Bell. She also wrote Kidvidz's *Paws, Claws, Feathers and Fins,* TV Guide's "Best Children's Videos for 1993."

Philips Media (*Voyeur*)

During the 4th quarter of 1995 alone, Philips Media launched more than 15 new CD-ROM titles, including such hits as *Burn:Cycle,* among the first interactive discs to successfully combine a cinematic adventure with compelling game play. . . . This year, the company plans to develop and distribute more than 30 titles across virtually every major product caregory": games, children's entertainment, home reference, multimedia music and Video CD. [from their Web site] poppe.com (T. Rowe Price Web Site)

poppe.com is Poppe Tyson's online development unit dedicated to strategic Web planning, content design, and data capture systems. Web sites poppe.com has created include The White House, AT&T, Chrysler, IBM, Jeep, LensCrafters, Merrill Lynch, Netscape, T. Rowe Price, and Valvoline.

Lena Marie Pousette (*Voyeur*)

Lena Marie Pousette is a writer, producer, and designer. Some of the multimedia titles she has been involved with include *Caesar's World of Boxing, Droid Wackers, and Endorfun.*

David Riordan (*Voyeur*)

David Riordan is the creative director for the Internet Entertainment Studio for Disney Interactive. Prior to joining Disney Interactive, Riordan was vice-president of production for Time Warner Interactive. He is also the designer of *Voyeur*, Phillip POV's adult political thriller, and *Thunder in Paradise*, an action adventure interactive television show for CD-ROM.

Anthony Sherman (*Dracula Unleashed, Club Dead*)

Anthony Sherman is the game designer for Viacom New Media's *Dracula Unleashed* and *Club Dead*. Anthony currently works for Kinesoft Development, where he is finishing a strategy game and starting up another project.

Tarragon Interactive (*The Nauticus Shipbuilding Company*)

Tarragon is a custom developer of multimedia titles for marketing and sales, training, and infotainment (museum and CD-ROM titles).

Tello Media Associates (*Accessible Media*)

Tello Media Associates of Pelham, New Hampshire, specializes in the design and development of multimedia projects, training, and World Wide Web pages accessible to individuals of all abilities and learning styles.

Trilobyte Inc. (*The 7th Guest* and *The 11th Hour: The Sequel to The 7th Guest*)

Trilobyte Inc., located in Medford, Oregon, is a major developer of video games and other software including the best sellers *The 7th Guest* and *The 11th Hour: The Sequel to the 7th Guest.*

T. Rowe Price Associates (T. Rowe Price Web Site)

T. Rowe Price Associates is a Baltimore-based investment management firm that serves as investment adviser to the T. Rowe Price family of no-load mutual funds and to individual and institutional clients, including pension, profit sharing, and other employee benefit plans, endowments, and foundations.

Ziff-Davis Interactive Media and Development (*Personal View* Ad Campaign

Ziff-Davis Interactive Media and Development repurposes print material from Ziff Davis Publishing's computer magazines and creates original content about buying and using computers. The content is distributed via the online service ZD Net and through most of the other major commercial online services and the World Wide Web.

See the References Section of the attached CD-ROM for additional appendixes and other information. The CD-ROM table of contents is at the beginning of the book.

INDEX

Writing for Multimedia — The CD-ROM

To Start The CD-ROM

This CD-ROM works on both Macintosh and Windows. For the launch instruction for your computer, open the readme.txt file on the CD-ROM.

Partial CD-ROM Contents

Genre & Title	Scripts	Images	Demos/Video	WWW Links
Advertising *Personal View*		√		√
Cinematic Narrative *Voyeur*	√	√		√
Museum Kiosks *Nauticus*	√	√		√
Multiplayer Narrative *Patrol Theater*	√	√		√
Parallel Stories Narrative *The Pandora Directive*	√	√	√	√
Puzzle Based Games *The 11th Hour*	√	√	√	√
Training *Vital Signs*	√	√		√
Web Sites *T. Rowe Price*		√		√
Worlds Narrative *Dust*	√	√	√	√

Software Demos

Scriptwriting	Flowcharting	HTML	Story Development
√	√	√	√

Background and Reference

Searchable Glossary of Multimedia Terms	√
Production & Playback Issues Important to the Writer	√
Legal Issues Affecting the Writer	√
Resources for Teaching and Learning Multimedia	√

System Requirements:

Windows MPC Level II: Windows 3.1 or Windows 95; 486 25Mhz or higher processor; double speed CD-ROM drive; 5 megabytes RAM; 256 color video; 8-bit sound; mouse and standard keyboard

Macintosh: System 6.5 or higher; LC II or higher processor; double speed CD-ROM drive; 5 megabytes RAM; 256 color video; 8-bit sound; mouse and standard keyboard